Lone-Actor Terrorists

This book provides the first empirical analysis of lone-actor terrorist behaviour.

Based upon a unique dataset of 111 lone actors that catalogues the life span of the individual's development, the book contains important insights into what an analysis of their behaviours might imply for practical interventions aimed at disrupting or even preventing attacks. It adopts insights and methodologies from criminology and forensic psychology to provide a holistic analysis of the behavioural underpinnings of lone-actor terrorism.

By focusing upon the behavioural aspects of each offender and by analysing a variety of case studies, including Anders Breivik, Ted Kaczynski, Timothy McVeigh, and David Copeland, this work marks a pointed departure from previous research in the field. It seeks to answer the following key questions:

- Is there a lone-actor terrorist profile and how do they differ?
- What behaviours did the lone-actor terrorist engage in prior to his/her attack and is there a common behavioural trajectory into lone-actor terrorism?
- How 'lone' do lone-actor terrorists tend to be?
- What role, if any, does the internet play?
- What role, if any, does mental illness play?

This book will be of much interest to students of terrorism/counter-terrorism studies, political violence, criminology, forensic psychology, and security studies in general.

Paul Gill is Lecturer in the Department of Security and Crime Science, University College London, and has a PhD in Political Science from University College Dublin.

Political violence
Series Editors: David Rapoport

This book series contains sober, thoughtful and authoritative academic accounts of terrorism and political violence. Its aim is to produce a useful taxonomy of terror and violence through comparative and historical analysis in both national and international spheres. Each book discusses origins, organisational dynamics and outcomes of particular forms and expressions of political violence.

Aviation Terrorism and Security
Edited by Paul Wilkinson and Brian M. Jenkins

Counter-Terrorist Law and Emergency Powers in the United Kingdom, 1922–2000
Laura K. Donohue

The Democratic Experience and Political Violence
Edited by David C. Rapoport and Leonard Weinberg

Inside Terrorist Organizations
Edited by David C. Rapoport

The Future of Terrorism
Edited Max Taylor and John Horgan

The IRA, 1968–2000
Analysis of a secret army
J. Bowyer Bell

Millennial Violence
Past, present and future
Edited by Jeffrey Kaplan

Right-Wing Extremism in the Twenty-First Century
Edited by Peter H. Merkl and Leonard Weinberg

Terrorism Today
Christopher C. Harmon

The Psychology of Terrorism
John Horgan

Research on Terrorism
Trends, achievements and failures
Edited by Andrew Silke

A War of Words
Political violence and public debate in Israel
Gerald Cromer

Root Causes of Suicide Terrorism
The globalization of martyrdom
Edited by Ami Pedahzur

Terrorism versus Democracy
The liberal state response, second edition
Paul Wilkinson

Countering Terrorism and WMD
Creating a global counter-terrorism network
Edited by Peter Katona, Michael D. Intriligator and John P. Sullivan

Mapping Terrorism Research
State of the art, gaps and future direction
Edited by Magnus Ranstorp

The Ideological War on Terror
Worldwide strategies for counter-terrorism
Edited by Anne Aldis and Graeme P. Herd

The IRA and Armed Struggle
Rogelio Alonso

Homeland Security in the UK
Future preparedness for terrorist attack since 9/11
Edited by Paul Wilkinson

Terrorism Today, Second Edition
Christopher C. Harmon

Understanding Terrorism and Political Violence
The life cycle of birth, growth, transformation, and demise
Dipak K. Gupta

Global Jihadism
Theory and practice
Jarret M. Brachman

Combating Terrorism in Northern Ireland
Edited by James Dingley

Leaving Terrorism Behind
Individual and collective disengagement
Edited by Tore Bjørgo and John Horgan

Unconventional Weapons and International Terrorism
Challenges and new approaches
Edited by Magnus Ranstorp and Magnus Normark

International Aviation and Terrorism
Evolving threats, evolving security
John Harrison

Walking Away from Terrorism
Accounts of disengagement from radical and extremist movements
John Horgan

Understanding Violent Radicalisation
Terrorist and jihadist movements in Europe
Edited by Magnus Ranstorp

Terrorist Groups and the New Tribalism
Terrorism's fifth wave
Jeffrey Kaplan

Negotiating with Terrorists
Strategy, tactics, and politics
Edited by Guy Olivier Faure and I. William Zartman

Explaining Terrorism
Causes, processes and consequences
Martha Crenshaw

The Psychology of Counter-Terrorism
Edited by Andrew Silke

Terrorism and the Olympics
Major event security and lessons for the future
Edited by Anthony Richards, Peter Fussey and Andrew Silke

Irish Republican Terrorism and Politics
A comparative study of the official and the provisional IRA
Kacper Rekawek

Fault Lines in Global Jihad
Organizational, strategic and ideological fissures
Edited by Assaf Moghadam and Brian Fishman

Militancy and Political Violence in Shiism
Trends and patterns
Edited by Assaf Moghadam

Islamist Radicalisation in Europe
An occupational change process
Daniela Pisoiu

An International History of Terrorism
Western and non-Western experiences
Edited by Jussi Hanhimäki and Bernhard Blumenau

Democracy and Terrorism
Friend or foe?
Leonard Weinberg

State Terrorism and Human Rights
International responses since the end of the Cold War
Edited by Gillian Duncan, Orla Lynch, Gilbert Ramsay and Alison Watson

Prisons, Terrorism and Extremism
Critical issues in management, radicalisation and reform
Edited by Andrew Silke

The Psychology of Terrorism 2nd Edition
John Horgan

Victims of Terrorism
A comparative and interdisciplinary study
Edited by Orla Lynch and Javier Argomaniz

Lone-Actor Terrorists
A behavioural analysis
Paul Gill

Lone-Actor Terrorists
A behavioural analysis

Paul Gill

LONDON AND NEW YORK

First published 2015
by Routledge
2 Park Square, Milton Park, Abingdon, Oxfordshire OX14 4RN

and by Routledge
711 Third Avenue, New York, NY 10017

First issued in paperback 2016

Routledge is an imprint of the Taylor & Francis Group, an informa business

© 2015 Paul Gill

The right of Paul Gill to be identified as author of this work has been asserted by him in accordance with sections 77 and 78 of the Copyright, Designs and Patents Act 1988.

All rights reserved. No part of this book may be reprinted or reproduced or utilized in any form or by any electronic, mechanical, or other means, now known or hereafter invented, including photocopying and recording, or in any information storage or retrieval system, without permission in writing from the publishers.

Trademark notice: Product or corporate names may be trademarks or registered trademarks, and are used only for identification and explanation without intent to infringe.

British Library Cataloguing-in-Publication Data
A catalogue record for this book is available from the British Library

Library of Congress Cataloging-in-Publication Data
Gill, Paul (Lecturer)
Lone-actor terrorists : a behavioural analysis / Paul Gill.
  pages cm. – (Political violence)
  Includes bibliographical references and index.
  ISBN 978-1-138-78756-8 (hardback : alk. paper) –
  ISBN 978-1-315-76634-8 (ebook : alk. paper)
  1. Terrorists. 2. Terrorists–Psychology. 3. Terrorism.
  4. Internet and terrorism. I. Title.
  HV6431.G5463 2015
  363.32501'9–dc23   2014032634

ISBN 13: 978-1-138-22179-6 (pbk)
ISBN 13: 978-1-138-78756-8 (hbk)

Typeset in Times New Roman
by Wearset Ltd, Boldon, Tyne and Wear

For Laura, Noah, Charlie & 'Bump'

Contents

List of figures x
List of tables xi
About the author xii
Acknowledgements xiii

1 Introduction 1

2 Who are the lone-actor terrorists? 26

3 The behavioural underpinnings of lone-actor terrorism 47

4 Why go it alone? 76

5 The role of the internet 86

6 Mental illness and lone-actor terrorism 103

7 Comparing lone-actor terrorists 120

8 A situational crime prevention approach 131

9 Lone-actor terrorist dilemmas 169

Select bibliography 183
Index 188

Figures

2.1	Age crime curve of 1,240 PIRA members	29
2.2	Age crime curve of 111 lone-actor terrorists	30
2.3	Age crime curve of first criminal offence of 111 lone-actor terrorists	31
2.4	Employment status	33
2.5	Word cloud of Anders Breivik's compendium	37
2.6	Word cloud of Paul Hill's 83-page justification for his actions	37
5.1	Lone-actor terrorists per year	87
5.2	Has the individual learnt through virtual sources?	88
5.3	Has the individual communicated with others virtually?	88
5.4	Behaviour covariates	99
7.1	Smallest space analysis of 45 lone-actor terrorist characteristics and behaviours	126
8.1	Problem triangle	166

Tables

3.1	Prevalence of distal factors	51
3.2	Prevalence of proximal behaviours	51
3.3	Network related behaviours	53
7.1	Comparing lone-actors across ideological domains	123
8.1	Lone-actor terrorist event script and intervention points	162

About the author

Dr. Paul Gill is a lecturer at UCL's Department of Security and Crime Science. His research applies behavioural science approaches to the study of criminals, crime patterns, and criminal behaviour. His research has been funded by the U.S. Department of Homeland Security, the U.S. Office of Naval Research, the U.S. National Institute of Justice, the U.K. Home Office, the Defence Science and Technology Laboratory, the European Union and the U.K. North-West Counter Terrorism Unit. He has published in several leading criminology, psychology, and political science journals. The European Consortium for Political Research awarded his PhD the best political science dissertation in Europe in 2010.

Acknowledgements

Just like every successfully completed book, this one would not have come into fruition without the help, guidance, and support of a very wide network of people. Hopefully I manage to namecheck all of you over the proceeding paragraphs. If I don't, my apologies, you generally were a great help just not one I could remember at this moment in time after a sleepless night with my twin boys who are teething.

First, thank you to everyone at Routledge for your help over the past few months. My editor, Andrew Humphrys encouraged me to develop my research on the topic into a book. His editorial assistant Hannah Ferguson was an excellent source of help throughout the writing process. My constant emails asking for 'one more week' were always taken in good spirits. The series editor, David Rapoport, and the original anonymous reviewers provided some excellent ideas for the book's contents also.

My research on lone-actor terrorism originally started off as a one-year project sponsored by the U.S. Department of Homeland Security's Science and Technology Directorate and coordinated through the U.K. Home Office. The work was undertaken at the International Center for the Study of Terrorism (ICST) at Penn State. I wouldn't have found myself there (and managing that project) without John Horgan's massive influence on my career. I owe him big time. Over the past few years, Mia Bloom has acted as supporter, PhD examiner, colleague, co-author and most importantly, feeder. Machelle Seiner kept me sane when deadlines and deliverables were mounting up. Bryan Carter and Alex Novak played key roles within the project also while Paige Deckert acted as a research assistant and helped manage the data collection process. Both Paige Deckert and John Horgan co-authored Chapter 8.

Speaking of which, there wouldn't be such an extensive dataset without the PSU and UCL undergraduate data collection teams. Major thanks are therefore due to Patrick Boynton, James Byers, Jordana Clark, Brittney Contacos, Jordan DeMatto, Sarika Dewan, Jonathan Duffy, Valerie Falkow, Bryan Gelles, Drew Grossman, Evan Jarusewski, Emily King, Amy Lafferty, Linh Le, Zachary McCornac, Brian 'Lee' Naylor, Danna O'Rourke, Matteo Pezzella, Sophie Preisendoerfer, Joe Ranollo, Matthew Rhodes, Kyle Rice, Nicholas Rodriguez, Matthew Roy, Adriana Santamaria, Emma Schoedel, Benjamin Snyder-Kamen,

Robert Wieczorek and Dana Yanocha. Both Matteo Pezzella, and Sophie Preisendoerfer also provided key language skills for a couple of texts.

Each of the following I've been very fortunate to work with in some capacity over the past few years and who provided some valuable input into this research: John Morrison, Kurt Braddock, Jim Silver, Mary Beth Altier, Cale Horne, Lily D. Cushenbery, Sam Hunter, Jim Piazza, Noemie Bouhana, Jyoti Belur, Emily Corner, Aiden Sidebottom, Richard Wortley, Shane Johnson, Paul Taylor, Victor Asal, Karl Rethemeyer, Neil Johnson, Joe Young, Allison Smith, Danielle Hawkins, Michelle Keeney, Scott Stanley, Joel Rodriguez, Randy Borum, Robert Fein, Bryan Vossekuil, Paul Betley, Paul Hitchen, and Amy McKee. Thanks also to Karen, Charles, and Emma for their valuable input. Emily Corner co-authored Chapters 5 and 6 and expertly got the data into a workable position.

Massive thanks for everything else to my parents, Mark, John, Tanya, Ciara, Martina, Stu, and the Kehoes appreciation team (Mick, Haines, Niall, Killian). Kennedy's ... sorely missed.

Finally, thanks to my wife Laura and our twin boys for their patience, support, and encouragement over the past few months. I really couldn't have done it without you and the thanks I owe are a book in and of itself. Charlie and Noah's best efforts to distract me from writing by banging on the locked conservatory door that I was on the other side of were very welcome. Once this book becomes a Harry Potter-esque sensation, I'll be able to afford the psychological treatment you may need after seeing your father pretend he couldn't see or hear you during his writing time.

1 Introduction

2.45 p.m. Anders Breivik uploads a self-produced film to YouTube and writes the last message in his 1,500-page compendium. At 3:05 p.m., Breivik emails the compendium to over 8,000 people. He leaves his mother's apartment and walks to a rented Volkswagen Crafter parked nearby. He drives to Grubbegaten Street, central Oslo, and arrives at 3.13 p.m. He stops the car 200 metres from the 'H-Block', a government building housing the Office of the Prime Minister, the Ministry of Justice and the Police. He waits for two minutes and puts on a bulletproof vest and a visored helmet. At 3:15 p.m. he drives the remaining 200 metres and parks again. He lights the fuse of the bomb he developed in the month's prior, leaves the car, and whilst carrying a Glock pistol in his hand, walks away quickly. By 3:20 p.m., he reaches Hammersborg Square where he had previously parked another rental car. He drives toward the ferry MS Thorbjørn at Utøkaia in Tyrifjorden, 25 miles north-west of Oslo. At 3:25 p.m., the bomb explodes, killing eight and injuring 209. At 4:55 p.m., Breivik arrives at the ferry and boards. He travels to Utøya Island, a venue hosting a Workers' Youth League summer camp. He arrives at 5:18 p.m. and begins shooting at 5:22 p.m. In total, 67 were shot and killed at Utøya, two more died in their attempted getaway and a further 110 were injured, 33 by gunfire. 50 of those killed at Utøya were 18 years of age or younger.

Outrage, condemnation, and shock at Breivik's actions quickly followed. The Norwegian Prime Minister, Jens Stoltenberg, called it Norway's 'worst atrocity since the Second World War', a 'national tragedy', 'unfair', 'incomprehensible', and an 'evil act [of] horror'. The European Union, NATO, the United Nations and over 75 states expressed similar sentiments. Condemnation of Breivik was not universal however. Three far-right elected members of parliament (one in Italy, one in the European Parliament and one in Austria) expressed sympathy for Breivik's anti-Islamic stance. Within a month of the attacks Norwegian far-right groups, Norwegian Defence League and the Stop Islamization of Norway movement, reported membership growths of over 300 and 100 respectively. Within a couple of years, authorities disrupted two apparent copycat plots in Poland and the Czech Republic while a third disrupted plot's perpetrator labelled Breivik his 'hero' in a series of Facebook posts.

The independent parliamentary report on the attacks acknowledged that the threat from lone-actor terrorism was underestimated in terms of the devastation it can cause. Under interrogation, Breivik distinguishes between the combat and media success of the attacks. In the early interviews, Breivik doubts his media success. He concedes that few of his co-ideologues would defend his 'bestial actions' (Husby & Sorheim, 2011: 16), and that the day of the actions was 'the worst day of his life' (Husby & Sorheim, 2011: 17). He acknowledges further that the events were 'completely awful' and that he was 'not proud' of what he 'was forced to do' in response to Labour Party policies (Husby & Sorheim, 2011: 20). Much of this early antipathy towards his own actions was due to the fact that he defined these victims as relatively low value compared to the political elites of the country. On the other hand, however, he saw the attacks as a combat success, and stated that the fight will continue via 'the pen from jail' (Husby & Sorheim, 2011: 23). On the whole, Breivik states that the success of the violent actions could only be 'measured by the spreading of the compendium' (Husby & Sorheim, 2011: 131) that he wrote in the years prior which elaborated upon his ideological motivations.

This short illustration provides a number of questions including:

- Is there a lone-actor terrorist profile?
- Is there a common behavioural trajectory into lone-actor terrorism?
- How 'lone' do lone-actor terrorists tend to be?
- What role, if any, does the internet play?
- What role, if any, does mental illness play?
- How rational are they?
- What risk do they pose?
- How do lone-actors learn and prepare for a violent attack absent of group membership?
- How do lone-actor terrorists differ?
- How can we minimize the threat of lone-actor terrorism?
- Can lone-actor terrorists be detected, prevented, or disrupted prior to engaging in a violent attack?

Until recently, existing research on the topic of lone-actor terrorists was incapable of answering such questions. The literature remained methodologically, conceptually, and theoretically weak. At best, it was certainly underdeveloped, and there was relatively little that the counter-terrorism community could usefully glean from what analysis had been conducted on what most still refer to as 'lone wolf' terrorism (a description avoided here). This book provides the first empirical analysis of lone-actor terrorism that focuses upon a range of factors including who lone-actor terrorists are, how they differ from each other (and from other kinds of terrorists), their developmental pathways into terrorism, their pre-attack behaviours and aspects concerning their offence-commission. It therefore marks a departure from previous research on lone-actor terrorism because it largely focuses upon behavioural aspects of each offender. The book adopts insights and methodologies from crime science, criminology and forensic psychology to provide a holistic analysis of the behavioural underpinnings of lone-actor terrorism. Based on an extensive analysis of open-source material, this book contains important insights into what an analysis of their behaviours might imply for practical interventions aimed at disrupting or even preventing attacks. The analyses in this book are based on a unique dataset of 111 lone actors. The dataset includes over 180 variables spanning socio-demographic characteristics to ancillary and antecedent behaviours to terrorist event-related behaviours. The variables cover the life span of the individual's development, later radicalization and right through to the execution of the terrorist event. As such, this book encompasses what LaFree (2013: 60) refers to as the third major development in the empirical study of terrorism; the expansion of our knowledge of terrorism based on 'specialized data sets on specific subsets of terrorism cases'.[1] Rather than treating all terrorists homogenously, recent improvement in our understanding of terrorist behaviour has come through disaggregated analyses that focus upon types of terrorist behaviours, roles, and functions (more on this later). This book seeks to build upon this strand of research and bring the field closer towards a scientific approach to terrorist behaviour.

As you'll see from the chapter outline further on, each chapter focuses upon a different aspect of lone-actor terrorist behaviour (and how to potentially counter the threat). First, however, we should take stock of a few factors including the strategy of lone-actor terrorism (and how it differs across ideologies), the drivers behind its diffusion across ideologies, the dynamics that make lone-actor terrorism a threat, definitional issues (it would not be a terrorism book without such an endeavour) and what the existing literature has to say on the topic.

An adaptive idea

High profile examples such as Anders Breivik pushed the threat of lone-actor terrorism to the forefront of national security across the world. The nature and threat from lone-actor terrorism is not new however. For example, Jensen (2014: 86) likens the period from 1878 to 1934 as the 'classic age' of lone-actor terrorism dominated by the actions of lone anarchists. The tradition of anarchists acting alone did not end during this phase however. An understudied example is that of Stuart Christie, who at 18 years of age left his native Scotland with the intention of assassinating the fascist leader General Franco in Madrid. This historical acknowledgement of lone actors is also not confined to academic research. Al-Qaeda in the Arabian Peninsula's *Inspire* magazine issue number two provides a detailed outline of lone actors dating back to the time of Muhammad.

Like most terrorist tactics or strategies, lone-actor terrorism diffused easily across ideological domains with many different ideological movements espousing the strategic need for operatives to act alone. According to Kaplan, Lööw, and Malkki (2014: 1), the 'lone avenger motif has appeared in every era and virtually every culture in the world'.

This book focuses upon lone-actor terrorism from 1990 to mid-2014. This is largely a practical decision based on data availability but it is also because during this period movement leaders of different ideological shades explicitly called for an uptake in lone-actor operations.

Within the extreme right-wing movement for example, the white supremacist Louis Beam championed the 'leaderless resistance' idea (Kaplan, 1997). Beam published the original 'leaderless resistance' essay in the February 1992 issue of his newsletter, *The Seditionist* (Beam, 1992). The essay's introduction credits Colonel Ulius Amoss with the idea. Amoss proposed a 'phantom cell' strategy in the event of a communist takeover in the United States. Beam acknowledges that he took Amoss' 'theories and built upon them'. The purpose of Beam's 3,388 word essay is to inspire innovation within resistance movements. Without tactical and organizational innovation, 'the government's efforts at suppression [remain] uncomplicated'. For Beam, hierarchical organizations are 'not only useless, but extremely dangerous for the participants when it is utilized in a resistance movement' because they are 'easy prey for government infiltration, entrapment, and destruction of the personnel involved'. Beam's essay considers and rejects the use of a cell system. Beam concludes the patriot movement lacks the necessary level of central direction, funding and outside support to make a cell system viable. Instead Beam calls for a broad movement in which 'all individuals and groups operate independently of each other, and never report to a central headquarters or single leader for directions or instruction' because they 'would be extremely difficult to identify'. Beam's essay is often depicted as one that considers whether to act alone or within a cell or group setting. This is not the case. It is really a consideration of whether to act within a movement that is centrally directed or not. Acting within a cell without central authority is given as much, if not more, prominence in the essay as acting completely alone. Beam strongly concludes:

> Patriots are <u>required</u> therefore, to make a conscious decision to either aid the government in its illegal spying, by continuing with old methods of organization and resistance, or to make the enemie's [*sic*] job more difficult by implementing effective countermeasures.
>
> (Original emphasis)

Interestingly, Beam regards 'leaderless resistance' a 'child of necessity' because of pervasive state powers and electronic surveillance that made the actions of groups easier to track than those of lone actors. Over 20 years later, many argue the same dynamics drove al-Qaeda's championing of lone-actor attacks. The Danish Centre for Terror Analysis, for example, contends al-Qaeda's focus on lone actors is a result of having 'limited possibilities for central planning as a result of the international efforts against terrorism' (cited in Spaaij, 2012: 26).

Beam published his essay in February 1992. Later that year, the fatal siege at Ruby Ridge occurred in Idaho. This event centred on an investigation into Randy Weaver. Weaver previously attempted to sell firearms to a Bureau of Alcohol,

Tobacco and Firearms (ATF) informant at an Aryan Nations event. ATF officers attempted to recruit Weaver as an informant in return for dropping the pending charges. Weaver refused and police charged him for the attempted firearms sale. Weaver then missed his court date due to a clerical error. The case passed from the ATF to the U.S. Marshals who were tasked with arresting Weaver. From March to October 1991 a series of negotiations attempting to encourage Weaver to surrender peacefully proved fruitless. The Marshals began plotting to capture Weaver and surveilled his 20-acre plot of land at Ruby Ridge. On one such surveillance sortie, an exchange of gunfire killed Weaver's 14-year-old son and a U.S. Marshal. A day later an FBI sniper shot Randy Weaver, injuring him in the back. Soon after, the same sniper fatally shot Weaver's wife while she held her 10-month-old son. An associate of Weaver's (who had killed the U.S. Marshal) was also injured in a shooting that day.

A couple of months after these events, a 160-strong delegation of far-right adherents and leaders attended a meeting convened by Pete Peters. According to the anti-Defamation League, Peters is a leading 'anti-Jewish, anti-minority and anti-gay propagandist'. Attendees formed a Sacred Warfare Action Tactics committee to 'evaluate what our people would be forced to consider should tyranny and despotism become the order of the day'. The committee recommended Beam's 'leaderless resistance' essay to supporters. Between the events at Ruby Ridge and Waco a year later, the concept of leaderless resistance moved from being an 'isolated theory' to being 'seen as a matter of survival in the face of a government now determined to eradicate the righteous remnant of the patriot community once and for all' (Kaplan, 1997: 85). Beam's mantle was later taken up by other white supremacists such as Tom Metzger and Alex Curtis in the early 1990s. While Beam's essay allowed for small autonomous cells as well as lone actors, both Metzger and Curtis pushed the lone actor to the forefront.

Metzger authored essays entitled *Begin with the Lone Wolves* and *Laws for the Lone Wolf*. The latter[2] starts with the words 'Anyone is capable of being a Lone Wolf'. Both make the case that the lone wolf strategy is necessary at the beginning of a movement's mobilization. Metzger's *Laws of the Lone Wolf* stems from the same worries as Beam's essay e.g. the ability of pervasive state powers to monitor communications and disrupt plots. Metzger therefore also frames this strategy as a child of necessity. In a 2013 interview with a white nationalist podcast, Metzger states that he was involved with membership organizations since 1963 'and they all failed' because such organizations were too difficult to manage internally ('short of using brute force') and externally (against the FBI) (HerrNordkamp, 2013). In one of his essays, Metzger outlines that

> the less any outsider knows, the safer and more successful you will be. Keep your mouth shut and your ears open. Never truly admit to anything.... Communication is a good thing, but keep your covert activities a secret. This will protect you as well as others like you.

Metzger also lauded a series of lone-actor attacks. In 2000, Richard Baumhammers killed five people in a racially motivated spree shooting in Pennsylvania. Metzger commented on the incident:

> Since we never get an apology for the thousands of hate crimes inflicted on whites each year from the nonwhite community, I no longer make any judgments on the acts of white men or women against nonwhites or other racial integrationists. Every individual in society is either a lone wolf or a lone sheep.

Two days after the shooting, Metzger's website wrote: 'Mr. Richard Baumhammers, a white man from Mt. Lebanon in Pennsylvania, recently decided to deliver Aryan justice in a down home way'. Metzger's group was also linked to Dennis Mahon's bombing of city officials in Phoenix in 2004.

Whereas the extreme right-wing essays cited previously solely focus upon strategic calls for lone actors, the writings of Alex Curtis went a step further and provided some instruction on target selection. Curtis developed a 'Lone Wolf Point System' (adapted from a previous Louis Beam essay) that would help potential lone actors 'intelligently judge the effectiveness of proposed acts against the enemy' (Anti-Defamation League, 2012).

The anti-abortion group the Army of God likewise provided (albeit more) detailed instructions on how to carry lone-terrorist attacks (something later copied by al-Qaeda in the Arabian Peninsula's *Inspire* magazine). Through the 1990s, the Army of God explicitly championed the activities of lone actors (often referred to as termites or covert activists in their propaganda). Their manual states that they are not

> a real army, humanly speaking. It is a real Army, and God is the General and Commander-in-Chief. The soldiers, however, do not usually communicate with one another. Very few have ever met each other, and when they do, each is usually unaware of the other soldiers status.

The manual is an interesting and often contradictory read. The vast majority of the manual's space is spent providing 99 non-violent methods of covert activity for lone actors to pursue. These methods are largely aimed at disrupting the activities of abortion clinics. Method number one, for example, lauds the benefits of gluing the locks of abortion clinics. In these sections, prominence is given to the quantity of actions conducted rather than conducting a single high-profile event. Violent and highly destructive techniques are relegated to the manual's appendix. The manual states this

> is not because they are wrong or ineffective. On the contrary those methods are powerful, appropriate and discriminate. The difficulty is cost i.e. charges, jail time, etc. Some tactics cost about half a lifetime in prison. Also, some ring in federal investigation crews and they have almost unlimited

money and manpower. So ... other tactics can be very effective when used over and over, and carry minimal risk.

On one occasion, the manual relinquishes the prominence of low profile and regular attacks if the individual has very little time to live. 'Whatever activities are undertaken (torching, bombing, thumb removal, other) carry on with prodigal, reckless, abandon! If, perchance, you are apprehended, it will be over soon anyway!'

On another occasion, the manual argues that since the cost of some non-violent disruption activities may warrant a felony charge, an escalation in activities may be necessary. In other words, the manual states that punitive legislation ensures 'the bombs and fires are not going to be just here and there every now and again, but here, there, and everywhere, now and again and again and again'. But it is in the appendix where most of the preceding text on passive resistance is minimized. 'Passive resistance is woefully inadequate against mass murder. The use of force is also woefully inadequate against mass murder, unless that force is directed against the perpetrator of the crime'. So while passive resistance may stunt, delay, or disrupt an abortion clinic, only the death of the doctor can really solve the problem according to the manual. The Army of God website provides a number of in-depth profiles of lone-actors who violently opposed abortion clinics and the people who work in them. One such profile is that of Stephen Jordi. Alongside an FBI source, Jordi plotted to attack an abortion clinic. They bought gasoline cans, flares, starter fluid, and propane tanks. The informant provided Jordi a .45-caliber pistol, silencer and empty magazines in exchange for $200. Jordi's profile warns he is,

> another example not [to] tell ANYONE; <u>before, during or after</u>, if you are planning on taking action. Your family, pro-lifers and your church 'friends' will rat you out in a heartbeat, thinking they are doing God's will. Stephen Jordi's own brother and his church turned him in to the authorities.
> (Army of God website, original emphasis)

Within the al-Qaeda inspired movement, the 2003 document *Sada al Jihad* (Echoes of Jihad) encouraged sympathizers to act without waiting for instructions (Bakker & de Graaf, 2011: 45). A year later, the influential Abu Musab al-Suri released a 1,600-page strategy document titled a 'The Global Islamic Resistance Call'. He evokes strikingly similar sentiments to Louis Beam's essay mentioned previously. Al-Suri paints the image of traditional hierarchical organizations as being out-dated and lacking security. He 'proffers an individual, secret jihad that takes place globally, which lets any Muslim take part in the battle against the United States and contribute to jihad' (Michael, 2012: 145). In 2006 another document circulated online renewing the call to 'fight alone' written by Abu Jihad al-Masri. In 2010, al-Qaeda's media wing produced a video titled 'A Call to Arms' that encouraged people to 'undertake lone-wolf operations in the West' and praised the actions of Nidal Malik Hasan (the Fort

Hood shooter). Al-Qaeda in the Arabian Peninsula's English language magazine, *Inspire*, also regularly lauds the efforts of lone actors. The calls for individual jihad within this magazine are largely inspired by al-Suri's previous writings (Spaaij, 2012: 26–27). Issue one praises Umar Farouk Abdulmutallab who attempted to bomb a civilian aircraft whilst on board in December 2009. The same issue offers detailed bomb-making instructions to the 'lone mujahid'. Issue two offers a number of attacks types for individual jihad including vehicular assaults (involving cars supplemented with blades), public mass shooting attacks like those of lone actors Nidal Malik Hassan and Abdul Hakim Mujahid Muhammad and IEDs constructed from pressure cookers (like those used in Boston in 2013). This theme of 'open-source' jihad continues throughout these issues. The types of attacks highlighted range from very violent attacks like those just mentioned to non-violent actions similar to the Army of God manual. The leaders of AQAP, the Army of God and the extreme right-wing share a sentiment that low profile and regular attacks may be strategically more useful than one-off single events. Later in this book, we return to this issue and highlight that this strategic call may clash with the types of factors (increasing social status, fame, retaliation) that motivate some (possibly most) lone actors alongside their ideological affinity.

Inspire issue four praised the actions of Roshonara Choudhry (who stabbed a British MP) and Taimour Abdulwahab al-Abdaly (who committed a suicide bombing in Stockholm in December 2010). Issue five contains a condensed essay by Abu Musab al-Suri on 'individual terrorism jihad'. In June 2011, another al-Qaeda video was published, this one titled 'You are Responsible Only for Yourself'. Adam Gadahn calls for more lone-actor operations and praises the Fort Hood shooter Nidal Malik Hasan. Using his native U.S. as an example, Gadahn urges his audience to 'go down to a gun show at the local convention center and come away with a fully automatic assault rifle, without a background check, and most likely without having to show an identification card. So what are you waiting for?' AQAP published issue nine of *Inspire* magazine in 2012. It rank orders the most important targets for those engaging in individual jihad. Issue 10 evokes similar sentiments to Tom Metzger's *Laws for the Lone Wolf*. The first question answered in the Q and A section deals with lone actors and whether small operations can affect powerful states. The answer states:

> First the idea of lone jihad is simple and easy. Every Muslim in the *kafir* enemy's land can carry it out. Its impact is big and great and its means and ways are possible, plentiful and easy to access.... The targets are many.... It's difficult for the enemy to provide security for its wide range of targets. It's difficult to identify the executor. Hit and run. Numerous operations could be done in one day by the very same individual.

In essence the main adherents of lone-actor actions within the right-wing and anti-abortion movements actively acknowledged that group-based operations were doomed to failure because of pervasive state powers. This was during the

1990s remember. Since then, we have witnessed an exponential growth in the ability of states to track, monitor and store communications (evidenced by the Edward Snowden leaks). Facing a far greater asymmetric situation, the al-Qaeda movement has not admitted that their turn toward promoting lone actors is due, in large part, because of the constraints they face. If lone-actor terrorism is an adaptation to adversity, what are the traits that make it such a threat? It is this question that we turn to in the next section.

The nature of the problem

Bakker and de Graaf (2011: 46) highlight numerous supposed features of lone-actor terrorists that make them difficult to prevent. First, lone actors are idiosyncratic and their history 'hardly gives away anything in the sense of patterns or recurring methods'. Second, it is difficult to discern lone actors with violent intent from lone actors with radical beliefs. Third, lone actors inspire copycats. Fourth, some lone actors such as Breivik and McVeigh caused a lot of fatalities. Finally, and perhaps the biggest factor that makes them such a problem is that they act alone. The usual tools of tracing communications and contacts are therefore supposedly not applicable here. Barnes (2012: 1653) highlights the fact that

> the evolution of homegrown terrorism to the individual level, therefore, renders obsolete much of the post-9/11 law enforcement architecture. Lone wolf terrorists will not be caught in stings, make inculpatory statements to confidential informants, or divulge their plans in intercepted calls or emails.

Anders Breivik was well aware of this issue. In his compendium, Breivik estimates the risk to reward ratio of gaining help in manufacturing IEDs. He calculates that a single individual can complete the work in 30 days with 30% risk of apprehension. The incorporation of one co-offender reduces the time by 33% but doubles the risk of apprehension. A team of five can complete the work in 12 days but with a 90–95% risk of apprehension.

Public discourse largely reflects the concerns listed by Bakker and de Graaf (2011). The former CIA Director Leon Panetta testified before Congress that the 'lone wolf strategy' is one that the United States needed 'to pay attention to as the main threat to this country'. In 2011, President Obama agreed, outlining that

> the risk that we're especially concerned over right now is the lone wolf terrorist, somebody with a single weapon being able to carry out wide-scale massacres of the sort we saw in Norway.... When you've got one person who is deranged or driven by a hateful ideology, they can do a lot of damage, and it's a lot harder to trace those lone wolves.

Obama outlined that this scenario is more likely than a 'large, well-coordinated terrorist attack'. The U.S. Homeland Security Secretary Janet Napolitano noted that lone actor plots are the 'most challenging' to stop because 'by definition they're not conspiring. They're not using the phones, the computer networks, ... they're not talking with others any other way that we might get some inkling about what is being planned'. In 2012, the director of the U.S. National Counterterrorism Center, at a hearing before the House Committee, stated that:

> lone actors or insular groups pose the most serious homegrown violent extremist (HVE) threat to the homeland. HVEs could view lone offender attacks as a model for future plots in the United States and overseas. The perceived success of previous lone offender attacks combined with al-Qa'ida and AQAP's propaganda promoting individual acts of terrorism is raising the profile of this tactic ... [Previous examples] underscore the threat from lone offenders who are able to adapt their plans quickly by rapidly changing timelines, methods, and targets to meet existing circumstances – all without consulting others.
>
> (Olsen, 2012)

The calls for lone actors by Tom Metzger and *Inspire* magazine share something in common with these statements by public figures. They both paint the picture of the lone-actor terrorist as being free from constraints. However, the reality is often quite different. Take this example from the abortion clinic bomber Paul Ross Evans:

> At the time, I possessed very little knowledge concerning the improvised construction of explosives, improvised incendiary powder mixes, and various triggering mechanisms (especially for mail bomb devices). I did, however, have a basic knowledge of chemistry, and had even created some small explosive devices in my mischievous late teen years. I also had little or no money, and lacked the resources necessary to obtain high-explosive materials.

Some empirically rigorous research also downplays some of the doomsday scenarios proffered on lone-actor terrorists. For example, Ackerman and Pinson's (2014) analysis of CBRN plots shows that lone actors need to calibrate their ambitions to their capabilities particularly in relation to how they are deployed.

We return to the case of constraints and hurdles throughout the book. If we can learn lessons on how successfully executed lone-actor attacks overcame the inherent hurdles associated with acting in the absence of a group and its pooling of human, financial, and social capital, we may gain some understanding of how to prevent and disrupt future plots.

Over the course of this book, we will also re-examine some of these supposed features of lone-actor terrorism. How lone are they really? Can we identify clusters of behaviours in their radicalization and attack planning? Are lone actors inspired by the actions of others? Are lone actors a greater risk than group-based plots? Next we turn to the minefield that covers all things related to defining lone-actor terrorism.

Definitional issues

As you would expect, terminological differences abound within the literature. Perhaps the most popularly used term is that of the 'lone wolf' (Baaker & de Graaf, 2011, Berntzen & Sandberg, 2014). On the other hand, a small number of studies specifically warn against using the term 'lone wolf' because 'it carries the potential to glorify or to imbue an image of power to attackers who are otherwise powerless and often ineffectual' (Borum, Fein, & Vossekuil, 2012: 390). Jenkins (2011) similarly argues that it is a 'romanticizing term that suggests a cunning and deadly predator'. This book agrees with these sentiments and avoids the term unless specifically mentioned by another academic or someone who promotes the actions themselves.

Some terms relate to the actors themselves. For example, frequently utilized terms include 'freelancers' (Hewitt, 2003), 'lone operator terrorist' (van der Heide, 2011), 'solo terrorists' (PET, 2011), 'solo actor terrorists' (Spaaij, 2012), 'loners' (Gruenewald, Chermak, & Freilich, 2013), 'stray dogs' (Jenkins, 2011), 'lone offenders' (Borum et al., 2012) and 'menacing loners' (van Buuren & der Graaf, 2014). Other terms relate to it as a strategy and tactic and utilize phrases such as 'leaderless resistance' (Kaplan, 1997), 'leaderless terrorism' (Jensen, 2014), 'individual terrorism' (Iviansky, 1977), 'single actor terrorism' (Nesser, 2012), and 'self activated terrorism' (Feldman, 2013). Other studies fluidly interchange between terms (Ackerman & Pinson, 2014). For once, terminological confusion is not the sole confine of academics. In December 2013, a new jihadist group (that either lacks a grasp of the English language or is excellent at irony) called The Brigade of Lone Wolves emerged.

Regardless of the terminology, a debate persists on what constitutes this type of actor. Some insist on excluding individuals with any connections to a broader network (Burton & Stewart, 2008) while others argue the exact opposite (Bakker & de Graaf, 2011). Berntzen and Sandberg (2014) make the distinction that while lone actors can be defined by the fact they act out their violence alone, their ideological beliefs can often emerge from larger, sometimes radical, social movements. Some definitions argue that only one person can be involved in the plot (Spaaij, 2012). Other studies allow for isolated dyads (Meloy & Yakeley, 2014, Gill, Horgan, & Deckert, 2014) or even more accomplices to be part of the plot (van der Heide, 2011, Hewitt, 2003). Pantucci (2011: 24) goes as far to include the 'lone wolf pack' defined as 'a group of individuals who self-radicalize' into his typology. One of Pantucci's ideal types for the 'lone wolf pack' is that of the Fort Dix plotters, a group of six like-minded individuals! In a similar vein, MI5's website dedicates a page to lone actors and includes a plot to bomb an English Defence League event that involved six conspirators. Some definitions restrict the observation pool to those inspired by specific ideologies (Bakker & de Graaf, 2011) while others allow for personal or criminal motivations

(Simon, 2013). Some interpretations include offenders whose political motives are not immediately obvious (Michael, 2012, in the case of the D.C. snipers and James Holmes). Other definitions highlight the importance of who is targeted. For Feldman (2013), non-military targets must be attacked. Kaplan's definition (1997), on the other hand, allows for government agents or buildings to be targeted. Some allow for lone actors to be directed in some way by a wider group or movement (ITAC, 2007; Feldman, 2013), others explicitly reject this component (Spaaij, 2012). Finally, some definitions exclude individuals with a history of mental illness (Burton & Stewart, 2008).

This particular problem is largely a result of the fact that interpretations of what a 'group' is differ widely within the literature. Taylor (2010) asserts there is a need for researchers to be clear about their understanding of group phenomena, and, in turn, what it entails for understanding commitment to engage in violence, terrorist behaviour and group membership. Gill (2012) offers four different interpretations. Group membership can be conceived broadly as membership in a social movement, membership in an ideological support network, membership in an operational support network, and/or more strictly defined as membership in an operational cell.

Within the social movement interpretation, epistemic authority figures provide the broad call to arms and legitimating ideology and narratives without which there would be no violence. At this level, the would-be actor has no direct interaction with such individuals and group membership is akin to membership of a social movement. Such authority figures frame the necessity of violence and seek to increase the social allure of violence to both the constituency they claim to represent and, at a more micro level, potential future lone actors (Gill, 2007). Within the ideological support network interpretations are individuals that provide and inhabit the space for face-to-face and virtual interaction that further normalizes ideological narratives, increases a sense of in-group identity, and provides a location to physically and mentally prepare to engage in violence. The operational support network interpretation can include those who were intrinsic to the actual attempted violent act. Here, the network can provide the hands-on expertise needed to actually carry out violence, as well as other roles including disseminating last will and testament videos and propaganda that typically occur in the days following a terrorist attack. The individuals that take part in the violence are the sole occupants of the operational cell interpretation. Each level differs dramatically in terms of how many people are members of that level, the proximity to which they are engaged in violent acts, and finally the contextual, facilitative and causal qualities that group membership contributes towards violent acts. This book considers lone actors to be individuals who belonged to the fourth level by themselves.

There are a number of other factors that add confusion to the terminological debate. Contemporary media accounts usually have a low threshold in deeming offenders as lone wolves. For example, the FBI regularly utilizes undercover agents posing as al-Qaeda or terrorist organization operatives to ensnare individuals (who may have indicated some degree of radicalization) within a wider plot. Media accounts regularly refer to these cases as a 'lone wolf' plots. This is despite the charged individual thinking he was part of an al-Qaeda cell along.

Identifying motivation can also be difficult at times (see Chapter 2 for a longer elaboration). This is because the ideological motivation espoused by the individual could be a mask for what was actually an act driven by personal grievance. In May 2014, Elliot Rodger killed six in a stabbing and shooting spree around the Isla Vista campus of the University of California at Santa Barbara before killing himself. Prior to the killings Rodger posted a series of videos online outlining his misogynistic views as well as a 141-page manifesto. Sections of the manifesto refer to his 'ideology' and 'desire to destroy all of the injustices of the world, and to exact revenge on everyone I hate and envy'. This last sentence, with its mixture of personal and (albeit idiosyncratic) political narratives makes distinguishing the case as an act of terrorism or of mass casualty violence very difficult. Even if personal motivations were glaringly obvious, researchers would probably not face the same difficulties in assigning Rodger's actions as terrorism if (a) his manifesto espoused jihadist or extreme right-wing beliefs or (b) if he targeted individuals or groups that these types of movements typically target. In a similar vein, Malkki (2014) outlines an interesting account of the presence (or lack) of political drivers amongst a sample of 28 school rampage shooters; a type of offender often overlooked within the terrorism literature. Four of the identified cases rationalized their deed using clear political content with 'references to political thinkers, movements or actors, using a political terminology and/or a political goal for the act'. A further 13 cases made specific reference to Columbine, perhaps indicating the perpetrators 'wanted [their] deed to be seen as part of a larger phenomenon' (2014: 191). Unpicking motivation is therefore very difficult and there is a tendency to cede toward master narratives that place individuals in very neat 'motivational boxes' (e.g. school shooter, terrorist, mentally ill, politically inspired, acting on a personal grievance). In reality, offenders may traverse a number of these.

Another factor that may add to confusion is the type of weapon utilized within a plot (or threatened to use). Some weapons fall more readily into the terrorism category despite the motivations being ambiguous. For example, the FBI interrupted a plot involving the development of ricin in order to attack the judicial system that the offender had a grievance against. An FBI spokesman referred to the plot as a 'pretty routine case. It's just a different choice of weapon. Usually they threaten to blow up or strangle. This is just a modern twist' (cited in Atkins, 1999). However, the case was regulrly referred to as terrorism because of the ricin-component.

A further factor that may add some confusion is that many state policies make categorical distinctions between types of lone actors. For example, the Danish Security and Intelligence Service distinguish 'solo terrorists' from 'lone wolf terrorists' because the latter 'has no contact to terror groups (not even historically) or any other radicalized individuals and consequently the individual acts completely isolated and without instruction from any other militant individual' (PET, 2011). The Dutch National Counterterrorism Strategy 2011–2015 stratifies 'menacing loners' across two types; 'radicalized individuals', and 'fixated persons'. Radicalized individuals are defined as 'individuals who are inspired, motivated, and sometimes directed by (virtual) networks of a more or less known ideology or religion'. This definition therefore incorporates both individuals lacking guidance and control and those directed by others – a distinction that the Danish Security and Intelligence Service is also keen to stress. Finally, the Dutch define fixated persons as those individuals 'who have no ideological motivation for their deeds'. Fixated persons, according to the strategy document, can be further delineated between those who are 'confused' and those who possess a 'hatred of the system' (van Buuren & de Graaf, 2014: 174).

Academic research has also differentiated lone-actor terrorist types based on a number of factors including the numbers of terrorist attacks they engaged upon (Bates, 2012), the levels of risk seeking they exhibited in the preparation and commission of their attack (Phillips & Pohl, 2011), and their level of loneness (Pantucci, 2011). As briefly mentioned previously, Pantucci (2011) offers a typology of lone Islamist terrorists. The first category is that of the 'loner' who has had no real contact with other extremists beyond consuming literature over the internet. The 'Lone Wolf', on the other hand, had some level of contact with members of a terrorist organization either in person or online. 'The Lone Wolf Pack' constitutes a small group of self-radicalized individuals devoid of formal command and control within a wider terrorist organization. 'Lone Attackers' on the other hand are formal members of terrorist groups but engage in their attacks alone (i.e. a 'one man terror cell').

Even for a field as disunited in its discussion of definitions as terrorism studies is, I doubt there is a subject that has so little written about it as lone-actor terrorism that maintains such a wide repertoire of potential terms and definitions. Borum (2013) makes the case that instead of debating definitions, it may be more useful to view each key feature along a continuum.

> Analyzing cases by their features, rather than by their types, might better aid the investigative process, particularly if each dimension is linked to a key facet of the attack and tracked across the spectrum of attack-related activity from idea to action.
>
> (2013: 104)

Borum et al. (2012) forward three such features; loneness, direction, and motivation. Loneness measures independence of activity. The loneness continuum plots the degree to which offenders received assistance in initiating planning, preparing for, and executing the attack. Direction measures the level of autonomy the lone actor displayed in decision-making. The direction continuum plots the degree to which the offender received instruction or guidance on issues concerning whether to attack, what to target and the attack type to deploy. The motivation continuum plots the degree to which the action is ideologically or personally driven. This book largely takes the same position as Borum. Included within the sample are individuals who span both the loneness and direction continuums. The key distinguishing features for inclusion in the study sample was that (a) the violence was carried out alone and (b) the violence was motivated (at least in part) or framed by the offender as ideologically driven. This is not to suggest that the motivation continuum is unimportant but rather the data is not currently available. However, a research project funded by the National Institute of Justice and conducted by researchers at University College London and the University of Massachusetts-Lowell is currently collecting similar behavioural data on mass casualty offenders who carried out their actions absent of an ideological cause.

Review of existing research

In 2010, Spaaij notes, 'there exists a major discrepancy between the recent political, judicial and media attention for lone wolf terrorism on the one hand, and scientific investigation of this phenomenon on the other. Research into lone wolf terrorism remains extremely scare' (2010: 855). There are a couple reasons for this general lack of research. First, terrorism is often purely viewed through a group-lens. Second, terrorism research can often be event driven and few high-profile lone-actor events occurred in the decade that followed 9/11 which itself helped create a surge of research interest in terrorism. Since 2010 however, at least 32 articles on lone-actor terrorism have appeared in peer-reviewed journals, almost half of which appeared in the first six months of 2014 (albeit with the help of a special issue of the journal *Terrorism and Political Violence*). A further three books (not including this one) are also available. Just like the terrorism literature in general however, much of this research is either empirically or methodologically lacking with an emphasis on theory, strategy, or anecdote. Notable exceptions include Spaaij (2010), Ackerman & Pinson (2014), and especially Gruenewald et al. (2013a, 2013b).

Existing research on lone-actor terrorism clusters around a number of factors including motivation, antecedent event behaviour and offence-commission. In terms of motivation, Berntzen and Sandberg (2014) focus upon the ideological belief-system of various lone-actors. Ackerman and Pinson's (2014) analysis of the difference between lone-actor and group-based CBRN plots outlines that 'lone actors … tend to be motivated less by collective religious or ethno-nationalist concerns … focusing more on narrow or solipsistic drivers'. These narrow drivers include issues concerning abortion, animal rights, the environment, personal grievances, and a number of other single-issue causes.

Moskalenko and McCauley (2011: 125) examined the psychology of lone-actor terrorism. They concluded that this form of terrorism 'requires the combination of strong capacity for sympathy with an experience that moves sympathy to personal moral obligation to act'. In a later study largely based on the same case studies, McCauley and Moskalenko (2014) suggest two types of lone-actor terrorists. They label the first as 'disconnected-disordered' who are 'individuals with a grievance and weapons experience who are social loners and often show signs of psychological disorder'. The other type is 'caring-compelling' whom 'strongly feel the suffering of others and feel a personal responsibility to reduce or avenge this suffering' (2014: 69).

Many other analyses focus upon the behaviour that helps underpin the lone actor's radicalization. Bakker and de Graaf (2011: 43) correctly argue 'not the profile of the perpetrator, but the modus operandi offer clues for a better response to this particular threat'. Utilizing three case studies (Timothy McVeigh, Eric Rudolph, & Ted Kaczynski), Springer (2009) attempted to identify common markers in their radicalization pathways. Springer found that each experienced problems across their childhood, family life, and home environments. This later led to being isolated, incapable of forming relationships with women, failing to bond within wider social groups, and failing to develop their own activist group. From there, their idiosyncratic ideologies developed over a long period of time.

Other aspects of research focus upon the plots and attacks conducted by lone actors. Some of these studies are speculative. Fifteen years ago, Laqueur (1999: 269) saw lone actors and small groups as the 'most likely candidates to use weapons of superviolence'. Many speculate along the same lines today. For example, Simon (2013) hypothesizes that future lone-actor terrorist events will likely utilize some form of chemical, biological, radiological, or nuclear materials. Ellis (2014) warns of the dangers of the proliferation of new biotechnologies and the 'amateur do-it-yourself' capabilities and its impact upon the future of lone-actor terrorism. Other studies are more empirically grounded. Ackerman and Pinson (2014) analysed the 'Profiles of Incidents Involving CBRN by Non-State Actors Dataset' and the 'Radiological and Nuclear Non-State Actors Database'. They found that 'historically, lone actors have engaged in cruder, smaller scale, and less frequent CBRN plots and attacks than their formal terrorist organization counterparts' (2014: 226). The study also found no evidence of prior plots involving lone actors rigorously pursuing nuclear materials. However, Ackerman and Pinson do find evidence to suggest that lone actors have been more successful in deploying biological agents compared to group-based actors. They conclude with a word of caution however:

> While historical patterns can often be valuable indicators, the future is an undiscovered country variously populated by Black Swans and Wild Cards. This is especially true in the current technological environment.... The probability that the wrong individual will come into contact with the wrong technology at the wrong time might thus be trending inexorably upwards.... We need to at least remain cognizant of the possibility, to our disquiet, that it might be only a matter of time before a misanthropic individual or small, nebulous group becomes superempowered and attains a WMD capability.
>
> (2014: 241)

Spaaij (2012) identified 88 cases of lone-actor terrorism between 1968 and 2010. He catalogued the ideological motivation for over 30% of these cases as either 'unknown' or 'other'. The extreme right wing inspired 17%, 15% were jihadists, 8% were anti-abortion activists, and 7% were national-separatists. They typically targeted softer targets like civilians (58%) rather than government officials and politicians (13%). He also compares the nature and level of lone-actor terrorism to group-based terrorism. According to data from the Global Terrorism Database, lone-actor terrorism remains a marginal phenomenon registering just 1.8% of the total number of terrorist attacks. Although marginal, Spaaij does note that the numbers of lone-actor attacks is increasing over time and that this increase is particularly evident in the United States. Smith (2004) links this increase to the proliferation of Louis Beam's 'Leaderless Resistance' narrative in the early 1990s. Spaaij also illustrates that lone actors more frequently utilize firearms (43%) whereas group-based attacks more frequently utilize explosives (65–75%). On the other hand, lone actors only use explosives 28% of the time. Spaaij also notes that U.S.-based lone actors more likely use firearms than non-U.S. lone actors and links this to the opportunity afforded by U.S. gun laws. In terms of the offenders themselves, Spaaij notes that they often experience a mix of personal problems and ideological drivers. Ideological affinity often comes through varying levels of interaction with wider movements. Spaaij highlights that many lone actors experience mental health issues, social isolation and the inability to fit into groups. Finally Spaaij notes that lone actors tend to be well educated and teach themselves the art of bomb making.

Nesser (2012) critiques the Spaaij study on the grounds that the dataset only includes successfully committed attacks. Nesser stresses that unsuccessful plots should also be included and offers an alternative analysis of 15 lone-actor jihadist plots in Western Europe between 1995 and 2012. Nesser finds that lone-actor plots accounted for 14% of the total number of European plots in this period. Nesser also claims that lone-actor plots were potentially more deadly. Given the relatively small numbers under consideration here it is difficult to assess how different the results truly are from the Spaaij study.

This brief review of the existing research (which is returned to in more detail in many of the chapters) highlights many gaps. The next section outlines which particular gaps this book seeks to fill.

Chapter outline

Chapter 2 analyses the socio-demographic characteristics of the lone-actor terrorist sample. It begins with an outline of existing research that compares lone-offenders to group-offenders across a broad range of crimes and elaborates upon key variables (e.g. mental health) that commonly occur in lone-offender samples but are relatively rare in group-offender samples. The results of the proceeding sections illustrate that there is no clear lone-actor terrorist profile. The chapter concludes with a discussion surrounding how even if such a profile were evident, an over-reliance on the use of such a profile would be unwarranted for a number of reasons.

Chapter 3 describes the network characteristics and antecedent behaviours and experiences of lone-actor terrorists leading up to their planning or conducting of a terrorist event. Using a mixture of descriptive statistics and illustrative case studies the intention is to demonstrate how lone-actor terrorism is usually the product of a crystallization of different factors that span issues concerning motivation, opportunity, and capability. The rhythm and tempo of a lone-actor terrorist's radicalization are also addressed here. The fundamental principle of this chapter is that it is more important to focus on what lone-actor terrorists do than who they are. This chapter also acts as a basic introduction to some of the core concepts that are elaborated upon in Chapters 4–7.

A popular perception exists that lone-actor terrorists are isolated from the rest of society while their grievance grows and plot develops. Chapter 4 elaborates upon some of the more surprising results based in this book. In the time leading up to most lone-actor terrorist events, evidence suggests that other people generally knew about the offender's grievance, extremist ideology, views, and/or intent to engage in violence. This chapter explores the nature of how others knew this information, what they did with this information and how it can be harnessed for counter-terrorism efforts. The analysis highlights that most 'lone actors' don't originally set out to be 'lone actors' but instead either aim to recruit others (and fail) or try to be a part of a wider group but disengage, sometimes voluntarily, sometimes not.

Over the past few years, a number of concerns have been raised about both the nature of the internet's relationship with terrorism and the threat posed by lone-actor terrorists. The relatively large timeframe under consideration here (1990–2014) allows for a longitudinal study of whether the growth of the internet has led to a different behavioural manifestation of lone-actor terrorism. One of the key findings here is that those who typically tend to interact with co-ideologues online are also significantly more likely to do so face-to-face. The idea that radicalization is either an online or face-to-face experience is therefore a false dichotomy in terms of lone-actor terrorism. Chapter 5 investigates whether the nature of these interactions differ (for example is attack planning conducted virtually while ideological discussions carried out face-to-face).

Chapter 6 briefly outlines the literature concerning mental illness and terrorism and illustrates that much of the current consensus is based on group actors. This chapter empirically outlines the other antecedent event behaviours and experiences that are correlated with mental illness. It also investigates whether differing or multiple diagnoses affect the actions of the lone-actor terrorist sample. It concludes with a discussion toward utilizing partner services (e.g. health or social services) in the attempt to counter certain manifestations of lone-actor terrorism.

Lone-actor terrorists tend to be depicted in a binary fashion; subjects either 'are' or 'are not' lone-actor terrorists. However, there is a distinguishable difference in lone-actor behaviour. The analysis in Chapter 2 also suggests there is no uniform profile of lone-actor terrorists. As a response to this diversity, Chapter 7 considers how the lone-actor terrorists studied in this research differ and assesses a number of grounds upon which a lone-actor terrorist typology can be developed. We conclude with a quantitatively derived typology based on a combination of antecedent behavioural, operational, and network qualities. These distinctions are important because they highlight the need to consider tailored response strategies.

Introduction 19

To facilitate the development of intervention strategies, Chapter 8 incorporates Crime Scripting approaches to provide case studies of select lone-actor terrorist operations. Current analyses of terrorist events rarely pay attention to the development of a single attack. Consequently, we have a poor understanding of how lone-actor terrorist activity unfolds. A striking feature of analysing single attacks as sequences of events and behaviours is that we can derive important findings in the absence of sophisticated analyses. Often, simply deconstructing events into sequences of behaviours can illuminate what has previously been overlooked. Mapping the evolution of a number of lone-actor terrorist events may help identify regularities in the histories of those who engage in this form of terrorism, and not least, detectable behaviours that may form the basis of intervention planning for future similar cases. Finally, the chapter outlines potential situational crime prevention approaches.

The book concludes with a discussion surrounding the lone-actor terrorist dilemma, countering the threat and avenues for future research.

Data

Students and scholars of terrorism studies alike are well versed in the problems the field has faced with regards to data. Put simply, the field has lacked data in large parts. Indeed reviews of the literature consistently highlight the scarcity of data (Schmid & Jongman, 1988; Silke, 2001, 2004, 2013). Although the past decade has witnessed a sharp uptake in inferential statistical methods, these tend to be analyses of terrorist events (thanks largely to the efforts of the team behind the Global Terrorism Database at the University of Maryland) rather than on individual offenders. However, a small number of studies are beginning to emerge that focus upon terrorist group members within Irish Republican groups (Horgan & Morrison, 2011; Gill & Horgan, 2013), ETA (Reinares, 2004), right-wing groups (Gruenewald et al., 2013) and al-Qaeda (Sageman, 2004). Collectively, studies like these provide us with a finer grained understanding of who becomes a terrorist group member, what patterns tend to be generalizable or are case specific and importantly tend to disaggregate their sample and compare across roles, eras, and group compositions.

The data utilized in this book builds upon these types of data collection processes and analyses. Importantly, given the fact that lone-actor terrorism is still a black-swan type event, the level of available granular behavioural data is far higher than that of offenders who operate on behalf of a prolific group. Speaking from experience of previous data endeavours, it is very difficult to obtain much more than the very basic socio-demographic information of such group offenders from open sources. This is for a very simple reason. Once it is the fifth or fourth or even third Paddy Murphy who has been convicted of planting a bomb on a Belfast street on behalf of the Provisional IRA, the story is no longer front page news. Instead it is buried away in the final paragraph of a somewhat unrelated story on page 10. But, when we have rare events, these are a different story altogether.

This book's dataset encompasses a sample of 111 individuals who engaged in or planned to engage in lone-actor terrorism[3] within, or by citizens of, the United States and Europe and were convicted for their actions or died in the commission of their offence. We therefore do not include in the statistical analyses cases from Israel and the Middle East such as Yigal Amir (who assassinated Israeli Prime Minister Yitzhak Rabin) or Baruch Goldstein (who carried out the Cave of the Patriarchs massacre) or the recent lone-actor attacks in China. The defining criterion for inclusion is whether they carried out or planned to carry out the terrorist attack alone. Lone-actor terrorists can operate with or without command and control links therefore. Some operate autonomously and independently of a group (in terms of training, preparation, and target selection etc.). Within this group, some may have radicalized towards violence within a wider group but left and engaged in illicit behaviours outside of a formal command and control structure. Those with command and control links on the other hand are trained and equipped by a group – which may also choose their targets – but attempt to carry out their attacks autonomously. Unlike the Gill et al. (2014) study, this book's analysis does not include isolated dyads (pairs of individuals who operate independently of a group) who may become radicalized to violence on their own (or one may have radicalized the other), and who conceive, develop, and carry out activities without direct input from a wider network. In other words, fatal terrorist attacks like those carried out in Boston and Woolwich, London are not included in the analysis. Also unlike the Gill et al. study, it does not include those individuals who acted alone but in facilitative roles. A violent plot carried out (or planned to be carried out) by the individual alone on behalf of some form of ideology is the second key inclusion criterion.

Prior to data collection, academic literature on lone-actor terrorism was examined and from there an actor dictionary was built. This actor dictionary encompassed a list of offenders fitting the above criteria. Further names were also sourced through tailored search strings developed and applied to the LexisNexis 'All English News' option. More individuals were also identified through the Global Terrorism Database developed by the National Consortium for the Study of Terrorism and Responses to Terrorism (START) and lists of those convicted of terrorism-related offences in the United Kingdom and the United States. It was then decided to limit the population to post-1990 events because a large component of our data is coded from the LexisNexis[4] archive whose archives remain relatively limited for the pre-1990 years. Even the more basic task of identifying not-so-famous lone actors pre-1990 is a difficult challenge. Some are easier to identify and remain important in terms of the history of lone-actor terrorism however they are omitted from the proceeding statistical analysis. These include Joseph Paul Franklin, Marx Essex, Neil Long, Richard Barnes, and Joseph Christopher. Where possible, illustrative examples from these cases are included in various chapters. In total, 111 offenders fit the specified geographical, temporal, and operational criteria.

The codebook used in this project was developed based on a review of literature on individuals who commit a wide range of violent and non-violent crimes, are victimized, and/or engage in high-risk behaviours as well as a review of other existing codebooks used in the construction of terrorism-related databases. The variables included in the codebook span socio-demographic information (age, gender, occupation, family characteristics, relationship status, occupation, employment, etc.), antecedent event behaviours (aspects of the individual's behaviours towards others and within their day-to-day routines), event specific behaviours (attack methods, who was targeted) and post-event behaviours and experiences (claims of responsibility, arrest/conviction details, etc.). Data were collected on demographic and background characteristics and antecedent event behaviours by examining and coding information contained in open-source news reports, sworn affidavits and when possible, openly available first-hand accounts. The vast majority of sources came from tailored LexisNexis searches. Information was gleaned from relevant documents across online public record depositories such as DocumentCloud.org, biographies of a number of lone-actors and all available scholarly articles.

Three independent coders coded each observation separately. After an observation was coded, the results were reconciled in two stages (coder A with coder B, and then coders A+B with C). In cases when three coders could not agree on particular variables, differences were resolved based on an examination of the original sources that the coders relied upon to make their assessments. Such decisions factored in the comparative reliability and quality of the sources (e.g. reports that cover trial proceedings vs. reports issued in the immediate aftermath of the event) and the sources cited in the report.

It is important to emphasize some limitations inherent in the sources used in this study. First, the sample only includes information on individuals who planned or conducted incidents reported in the media. It is possible incidents could be missed altogether because they either (a) led to convictions but did not register any national media interest but may have been reported in local level sources not covered in the LexisNexis archives or (b) were intercepted or disrupted by security forces without a conviction being made. Second, as the level of detail reported varied significantly across incidents, data collection was limited to what could reasonably be collected for each case. Finally, it is often difficult to distinguish between missing data and variables that should be coded as a 'no'. Given the nature of newspaper and open-source reporting, it is unrealistic to expect each biographically-oriented story to contain lengthy passages that list each variable or behaviour the offender did not conduct (e.g. the offender was not a substance abuser, a former convict, recently exposed to new media, etc.). For the statistical analyses that follow, where possible, I do report or distinguish between missing data and 'no' answers but it should be kept in mind that the likely result is that 'no' answers are substantially undercounted in the analysis. For the typology chapter later in this book, each variable in the analysis is treated dichotomously (e.g. the response is either a 'yes', or not enough information to suggest a yes). Unless otherwise stated, each of the figures reported below are of the whole sample ($n=111$). There is precedent for this in previous research on attempted assassinations of public figures, fatal school shootings and targeted violence affecting institutions of higher education (Fein & Vossekuil, 1999; Vossekuil et al., 2002; Drysdale, Modzeleski, & Simons, 2010).

Despite these limitations, open source accounts can provide rich data. This has been demonstrated in other studies focusing upon the socio-demographic characteristics, operational behaviours and developmental pathways of members of formal terrorist organizations. Given the particularly low base rate of lone-actor terrorism, the volume of reporting tends to be much higher compared with campaigns of violence where trials and convictions are a weekly occurrence. For example, we have educational data for 65% of the lone-actor sample. This is compared to less than 10% of Gill and Horgan's (2012) sample of Provisional Irish Republican Army (PIRA) members, for whom level of education could generally only be inferred from the individual's occupational status. The next chapter outlines some the basic descriptive findings from this unique dataset.

Notes

1 The first being the development of international databases of terrorist attacks. The second being the collection of domestic international attacks.
2 Available at: www.resist.com/Articles/literature/LawsForTheLoneWolfByTomMetzger.htm.
3 For the purposes of this book, I define terrorism as the use or threat of action where the use or threat is designed to influence the government or to intimidate the public or a section of the public and/or the use or threat is made for the purpose of advancing a political, religious, or ideological cause. Terrorism can involve violence against a person, damage to property, endangering a person's life other than that of the person committing the action, creating a serious risk to the health or safety of the public or a section of the public.
4 LexisNexis currently provides an electronic online archive from more than 20,000 global news sources.

References

Ackerman, G. A., & Pinson, L. E. (2014). An Army of One: Assessing CBRN Pursuit and Use by Lone Wolves and Autonomous Cells. *Terrorism and Political Violence*, 26(1), 226–245.
Anti-Defamation League (2012). Alex Curtis: 'Lone Wolf' of Hate Prowls the Internet. Retrieved from: www.adl.org/assets/pdf/combating-hate/Alex-Curtis-Report.pdf. Accessed 6 October 2014.
Army of God website (Unspecified Year). Profile of Stephen Jordi. Retrieved from: www.armyofgod.com/StephenJordi.html. Accessed 6 October 2014.
Atkins, A. (1999, 8 November). Man denies threatening with poison. *The Tampa Tribune*. Retrieved from: www.mail-archive.com/ctrl@listserv.aol.com/msg28357.html. Accessed 1 June 2014.
Bakker, E., & de Graaf, B. (2011). Preventing lone wolf terrorism: some CT approaches addressed. *Perspectives on Terrorism*, 5(5–6).
Barnes, B. D. (2012). Confronting the one-man wolf pack: Adapting law enforcement and prosecution responses to the threat of lone wolf terrorism. *BUL Rev.*, 92, 1613.

Bates, R. A. (2012). Dancing with wolves: Today's lone wolf terrorists. *The Journal of Public and Professional Sociology*, *4*(1), 1.
Beam, L. (1992). Leaderless Resistance. *The Seditionist* Issue 12. Retrieved from: www.louisbeam.com/leaderless.htm. Accessed 6 October 2014.
Berntzen, L. E., & Sandberg, S. (2014). The Collective Nature of Lone Wolf Terrorism: Anders Behring Breivik and the Anti-Islamic Social Movement. *Terrorism and Political Violence*, (ahead-of-print), 1–21.
Borum, R. (2013). Informing Lone – Offender Investigations. *Criminology & Public Policy*, *12*(1), 103–112.
Borum, R., Fein, R., & Vossekuil, B. (2012). A dimensional approach to analyzing lone offender terrorism. *Aggression and Violent Behavior*, *17*(5), 389–396. Bureau of Alcohol, Tobacco and Firearms ATF.
Burton, F., & Stewart, S. (2008). The 'Lone Wolf' Disconnect. *Terrorism Intelligence Report-STRATFOR*. Retrieved from: www.stratfor.com/weekly/lone_wolf_disconnect. Accessed 1 June 2014.
Drysdale, D., Modzeleski, W., & Simons, A. (2010). *Campus Attacks: Targeted Violence Affecting Institutions of Higher Education*. Washington D.C.: United States Secret Service, United States Department of Education and Federal Bureau of Investigation.
Ellis, P. D. (2014). Lone Wolf Terrorism and Weapons of Mass Destruction: An Examination of Capabilities and Countermeasures. *Terrorism and Political Violence*, 26: 1, 211–225.
Evans, P. R. (Unspecified Year). Methodical Terrorism: How and Why. Retrieved from: www.armyofgod.com/POCPaulRossEvansMethodicalTerrorism.html. Accessed 6 October 2014.
Fein, R. A., & Vossekuil, B. (1999). Assassination in the United States: an operational study of recent assassins, attackers, and near-lethal approachers. *Journal of Forensic Sciences*, *44*(2), 321–333.
Feldman, M. (2013). Comparative Lone Wolf Terrorism: Toward a Heuristic Definition. *Democracy and Security*, 9:3, 270–286.
Gill, P., & Horgan, J. (2013). Who Were the Volunteers? 1 The Shifting Sociological and Operational Profile of 1240 Provisional Irish Republican Army Members. *Terrorism and Political Violence*, *25*(3), 435–456.
Gill, P., Horgan, J., & Deckert, P. (2014). Bombing Alone: Tracing the Motivations and Antecedent Behaviors of Lone – Actor Terrorists. *Journal of forensic sciences*, *59*(2), 425–435.
Gruenewald, J., Chermak, S., & Freilich, J. D. (2013a). Distinguishing 'loner' attacks from other domestic extremist violence. *Criminology & Public Policy*, *12*(1), 65–91.
Gruenewald, J., Chermak, S., & Freilich, J. D. (2013b). Far-Right Lone Wolf Homicides in the United States. *Studies in Conflict & Terrorism*, *36*(12), 1005–1024.
HerrNordkamp (2013, 5 October). Bill Rhyes Interview Tom Metzger (part 3) [video file]. Retrieved from: www.youtube.com/watch?v=sottRwubNQg. Accessed 6 October 2014.
Hewitt, C. (2003). *Understanding terrorism in America: from the Klan to al Qaeda*. Hove: Psychology Press.
Horgan, J., & Morrison, J. F. (2011). Here to stay? The rising threat of violent dissident republicanism in Northern Ireland. *Terrorism and Political Violence*, *23*(4), 642–669.
Integrated Threat Assessment Center (Canada) (2007). Lone-Wolf Attacks: A Developing Islamist Extremist Strategy?, 29 June, retrieved from: www.nefafoundation.org/miscellaneous/FeaturedDocs/ITAC_lonewolves_062007.pdf. Accessed 1 June 2014

Iviansky, Z. (1977). Individual terror: concept and typology. *Journal of Contemporary History*, 43–63.

Jenkins, B. M. (2011). Stray dogs and virtual armies. Santa Monica: RAND Corporation.

Jensen, R. B. (2014). The Pre-1914 Anarchist 'Lone Wolf' Terrorist and Governmental Responses. *Terrorism and Political Violence*, 26(1), 86–94.

Kaplan, J. (1997). Leaderless resistance. *Terrorism and Political Violence*, 9(3), 80–95.

Kaplan, J., Lööw, H., & Malkki, L. (2014). Introduction to the Special Issue on Lone Wolf and Autonomous Cell Terrorism. *Terrorism and Political Violence*, 26(1), 1–12.

LaFree, G. (2013). Lone-Offender Terrorists. *Criminology and Public Policy* 12(1): 59–62.

Laqueur, W. (1999). *The new terrorism*. New York: Oxford University Press.

Malkki, L. (2014). Political elements in post-Columbine school shootings in Europe and North America. *Terrorism and political violence*, 26(1), 185–210.

McCauley, C., & Moskalenko, S. (2014). Toward a Profile of Lone Wolf Terrorists: What Moves an Individual From Radical Opinion to Radical Action. *Terrorism and Political Violence*, 26(1), 69–85.

Meloy, J. R., & Yakeley, J. (2014). The Violent True Believer as a 'Lone Wolf'–Psychoanalytic Perspectives on Terrorism. *Behavioral sciences & the law*, 32(3), 347–365.

Metzger, T. (Unspecified Year). Laws for the Lone Wolf. Retrieved from: www.resist.com/Articles/literature/LawsForTheLoneWolfByTomMetzger.htm. Accessed 6 October 2014.

Michael, G. (2012). Lone Wolf Terror and the Rise of Leaderless Resistance. Nashville: Vanderbilt University Press.

Moskalenko, S., & McCauley, C. (2011). The psychology of lone-wolf terrorism. *Counselling Psychology Quarterly*, 24(2), 115–126.

Nesser, P. (2012). Research Note: Single Actor Terrorism: Scope, Characteristics and Explanations. *Perspectives on Terrorism*, 6(6).

Olsen, M. G. (2012, 25 July). Hearing before the House Committee on Homeland Security Understanding the Homeland Threat Landscape. National Counterterrorism Center. Retrieved from: www.nctc.gov/docs/2012_07_25_HHS_Understanding_Homeland_Threat_Landscape.pdf. Accessed 1 June 2014.

Pantucci, R. (2011). *A typology of lone wolves: preliminary analysis of lone Islamist terrorists*. London: International Centre for the Study of Radicalisation and Political Violence.

PET – Centre for Terror Analysis (CTA) (2011, April 5). The threat from solo terrorism and lone wolf terrorism. Copenhagen: Denmark. Retrieved from: www.pet.dk/upload/the_threat_from_solo_terrorism_and_lone_wolf_terrorism_-_engelsk_version.pdf. Accessed 1 June 2014.

Phillips, P. J., & Pohl, G. (2012). Economic profiling of the lone wolf terrorist: can economics provide behavioral investigative advice? *Journal of Applied Security Research*, 7(2), 151–177.

Reinares, F. (2004). Who are the terrorists? Analyzing changes in sociological profile among members of ETA. *Studies in Conflict and Terrorism*, 27(6), 465–488.

Spaaij, R. (2010). The enigma of lone wolf terrorism: an assessment. *Studies in Conflict & Terrorism*, 33(9), 854–870.

Sageman, M. (2004). Understanding terror networks. Pennsylvania: University of Pennsylvania Press.

Schmidt, A. P., & Jongman, A. I. (1988). *Political terrorism. A Research Guide to Concepts, Theories, Databases and Literature*. Amsterdam and New Brunswick: Transaction.

Silke, A. (2001). The devil you know: Continuing problems with research on terrorism. *Terrorism and Political Violence*, *13*(4), 1–14.

Silke, A. (2004). The road less travelled: recent trends in terrorism research. *Research on terrorism: trends, achievements and failures*, 186–213.

Silke, Andrew. (2013). Research on terrorism: A review of the impact of 9/11 and the global war on terrorism. In Adam Dolnik (ed.), *Conducting Terrorism Field Research: A Guide*. London: Routledge.

Simon, J. D. (2013). *Lone Wolf Terrorism: Understanding the Growing Threat*. New York, NY: Prometheus Books.

Smith, B. L. (2004). Terrorism and empirical testing: Using indictment data to assess changes in terrorist conduct. *Sociology of Crime Law and Deviance*, *5*, 75–90.

Spaaij, R. (2012). *Understanding Lone Wolf Terrorism*. London: Springer, *98*, 80–95.

Springer, N. R. (2009). *Patterns of radicalization: Identifying the markers and warning signs of domestic lone wolf terrorists in our midst*. Naval Postgraduate School Monterey CA: Dept of National Security Affairs.

van Buuren, J., & de Graaf, B. (2014). Hatred of the System: Menacing Loners and Autonomous Cells in the Netherlands. *Terrorism and Political Violence*, *26*(1), 156–184.

van der Heide, E. J. (2011). Individual terrorism: Indicators of lone operators. Masters Thesis, Utrecht University.

Vossekuil, B. (2002). The final report and findings of the Safe School Initiative: Implications for the prevention of school attacks in the United States. Washington D.C.: United States Secret Service and United States Department of Education.

2 Who are the lone-actor terrorists?

Since I began studying terrorism I have lost count at the number of family members, half-acquaintances, undergraduate essays, and taxi drivers that have offered their opinion to me on the 'terrorist profile' and terrorist 'motivation'. There is clearly a disjuncture between the general public's belief and fascination with 'profiling' on the one hand and the seeming consensus amongst prolific terrorism researchers that profiling is not possible or even of value on the other hand. This argument is not a new one (for example see Horgan, 2008). However, this is not to say that looking at the socio-demographic characteristics of terrorists is not of inherent research interest. We just need to be careful about what utility such endeavours possess. Looking at composite pictures of terrorist datasets will not provide predictive powers of who will become a terrorist later down the line, for example. They do however provide some insight into selection effects (e.g. who terrorist group recruiters tend to recruit, see De Mesquita, 2005), strategic shifts within a group (e.g. how a group's membership profile changes over time to reflect strategic priorities, see Gill & Horgan, 2013), and an understanding of recruitment hotspots (e.g. identifying particular towns/villages/estates that many members live, see Horgan & Morrison, 2011).

There is also a largely untapped benefit of examining aggregate datasets of terrorist offenders in terms of their socio-demographic characteristics – the ability to conduct comparative studies. In a field of research long devoid of useful data, it is unsurprising that comparative statistical approaches are few and far between. Data availability is not the only reason why the comparison of terrorist group members with criminal offenders does not exist. This is largely due to the selection effects brought on by organizational recruiters who may choose particular types of recruits (De Mesquita, 2005) for particular types of roles, tasks and functions (Gill & Young, 2011). Similarly, particular types of individuals may never be recruited because their psychological conditions may not make them a useful and discreet member of an underground terrorist organization (Horgan, 2005). Comparisons of criminals with terrorist group members need to take this selection effect into account. However, this is not the case for lone-actor terrorists.

This chapter outlines the basic socio-demographic features of the lone-actor terrorist cohort. Where possible, these results are compared with findings from case-study analyses of terrorist group members. The lone-actor demographics are also compared with studies of wider non-politically inspired criminal offenders. Selection effects and pre-recruitment screening do not play a direct role when we analyse the universe of lone-actor terrorists. To repeat, the aim here is not to create an offender 'profile'. Given the broad spectrum of motivations and ideologies across a low base rate of lone-actor terrorists such an endeavour is conceptually and empirically problematic and also questionable for investigative purposes. Instead, the purpose is to provide better insight into what variables we see universally across all crimes and terrorist types, and what offender characteristics appear to be particularly prominent within the lone-actor terrorist sample.

Do group and lone offenders differ?

In the study of crime, the literature on offender characteristics is vast. A very small subset of this literature specifically compares lone and group offenders as the principal research endeavour. Instead, many noted differences tend to be relegated to footnotes in studies that otherwise concentrate on more general aspects. This relative lack of attention is surprising given the significance of the findings (particularly the almost universal finding that lone offenders are significantly older). For example, Alarid, Buron, and Hochstetler's (2009) study of robberies showed that group offenders were more likely to be younger, unmarried, and less educated. Group offenders were also less likely to engage in spontaneous robberies and instead more regularly employed careful consideration of target selection. In terms of target selection there was little difference between the difficulty levels of robberies chosen by group and solo offenders, which runs counter to much theorizing concerning 'strength in numbers' and offending (see Felson, Baumer, & Messner, 2000 for example).[1] Using vastly different samples, studies comparing lone and group rapists found that the former tended to be significantly older (Wright & West, 1981; Ullman, 1999; Bijleveld & Hendriks, 2003; Hauffe & Porter, 2009; da Silva et al., 2013), significantly more likely to be married and have children, significantly less likely to have a history of substance abuse (Hauffe & Porter, 2009) and significantly more likely to be employed (Ullman, 1999).

Rather than comparing demographic characteristics, Bijleveld and Hendriks (2003) compared the personality traits of lone and group juvenile sex offenders. Using a set of standardized and validated instruments such as self-report questionnaires, Bijleveld and Hendriks (2003) found that lone offenders were significantly more likely to have problematic personality structures than group offenders (particularly on measures of neuroticism, impulsivity, and sociability) and were more likely to have had previous convictions. Lone offenders were also significantly more likely to have previously been an abuse victim (a finding the researchers corroborated with case files from the Council for Child Protection). Hickle and Roe-Sepowitz's (2010) study of female juvenile arsonists arrived at similar conclusions regarding developmental and personality factors. Solo offenders more often came from unstable homes, and more often experienced school difficulties, behavioural problems, negative emotions, and expressed suicidal thoughts more regularly.

Homicide research comparing solo and group offenders has also reached similar conclusions. Block's (1985) study of Chicago-based homicides illustrated that group offenders were significantly younger than lone offenders. Cheatwood and Block's (1990) study on homicides in Baltimore also found a disproportionate number of juvenile offenders engaging in homicides as members of groups rather than as individuals. In the most comprehensive of such analyses, Clark (1995) analysed data across nine U.S. cities in the United States. Again, group offenders were significantly younger. Similar to Hauffe and Porter's (2009) results, lone offenders were less likely to have a history of substance abuse than group offenders. Unlike research on robberies, group homicide offenders were more likely to have previous criminal convictions.

Aggregating a large number of crimes, Van Mastrigt and Farrington (2011) analysed U.K. police data. Group offenders were significantly younger than lone offenders and also tended to have more criminal convictions; a common finding when the offender sample is aggregated across crime types (Hindelang, 1976; Reiss & Farrington, 1991). In a similarly scoped study, Stolzenburg and D'Alessio (2008) illustrated that much of this difference is accounted for by the precipitous fall in co-offender crimes committed by those between the ages of 18 to 23 (a fall of 55% from juvenile crime) compared to the relatively milder fall of 14% for lone-offender crimes.

Finally, the criminal careers literature has addressed the transition from group to lone offending. Both Hood and Sparks (1970) and Reiss and Farrington (1991) illustrated that individuals increasingly engaged in solo offences as they became older. Building on approaches that view criminal careers longitudinally, Piquero et al. (2007) focused on the changing relationship of an offender's crimes and links to co-offenders. They found that the typical process begins with some individuals offending with others before increasingly engaging in solo offences. Rarely do offenders become purely solo but rather the proportion of their solo offences grow vis-à-vis group offences.

Turning to terrorism, Gruenewald, Chermak, and Freilich (2013a) examined the characteristic and behavioural differences between a sample of lone and group offenders inspired by the far right who participated in homicide. 'Loners' were significantly more likely to have a history of mental illness. Whereas 40% of their 'loners' had some mental health issues, this figure was 8% for group-based actors. 'Loners' were also significantly more likely to live alone or away from their family. They were also significantly more likely to use a gun, cause multiple fatalities, be older, have a military background, select government targets, experienced either the death, divorce or separation from a spouse and be involved in a possible suicide mission. In a follow-up study, Gruenewald, Chermak, and Freilich (2013b), disaggregated the loner category into those offenders who had formal connection to existing groups or not. They found that those loners without prior group experience more likely attacked abortion providers or government officials. This is largely reflective of their far-right inspirations as they were also more likely to be White Supremacists and/or single-issue inspired.

Throughout this broad range of crimes, we find significant differences between group and lone offenders. Some factors, such as age differences, are almost universally apparent. It might be safe to assume therefore (and the Gruenewald et al. studies cited above back up) that there may be a difference between lone- and group-actor terrorists in terms of their demographic make-up. We turn next to an examination of key demographic features (age, gender, family characteristics, education, and employment) before turning to the tricky problem of identifying what motivates these individuals.

Age

Let's start with age at time offence since it was found to be consistently different in the variety of group vs. lone offender studies cited above. Within criminology, there is a long held belief that the relationship between age and crime is curvilinear. In fact, many consider the relationship 'one of the brute facts of criminology' (Hirschi & Gottfredson, 1983: 552). When plotting age against crime rates, the relationship's slope typically 'ascends rapidly during adolescence, peaks in early adulthood and falls thereafter' (Stolzenberg & D'Alessio, 2008: 66). In other words, as individuals age they become less likely to become first time offenders. This has been demonstrated across a wide range of crimes including burglary (Vaughn et al., 2008) and hate crimes (McDevitt, Levin, & Bennett, 2002). Data from Gill and Horgan's (2013) study of 1,240 Provisional Irish Republican Army members demonstrates a similar relationship (see Figure 2.1). Here, the peak first-time offending years were between 17 and 21, followed by a

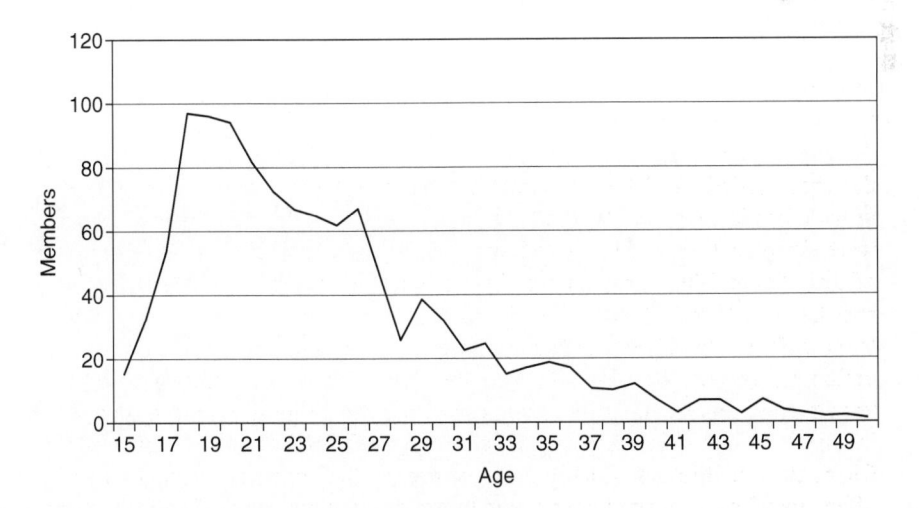

Figure 2.1 Age crime curve of 1,240 PIRA members.

slow decline until the age of 27 where there is a precipitous fall followed by a long slow decline.

The mechanisms that explain the interaction between age and offending onset are disputed and can be classified in three broad positions. One postulates single individual personality characteristics as causal. For example, some studies argued that anger tends to reduce with age, leaving young adults as a population particularly prone to experience anger and hence involvement in crime (Schieman, 1999; Simon & Nath, 2004). It has also been reasoned that individuals without 'self control' are more likely to commit crime as they engage in risky, impulsive behaviour regardless of the long-term effects. The second position argues that 'conceptually distinct causal factors underlie different measures of offending over an individual's life course' (Stolzenberg & D'Alessio, 2008: 66). For example, some studies explain that economic factors and lack of parental safeguards interact to make younger individuals particularly at risk of engaging in crime and illicit activities. Later in life, gainful employment and marriage may mitigate these effects, and the risk of the individual engaging in crime decreases. The final school of thought typically argues that the relationship between age and crime is driven by the social nature of youth-related crime and peer-relations.

The lone-actor terrorist sample does not reflect 'one of the brute facts of criminology' (Hirschi & Gottfredson, 1983: 552). Figure 2.2 illustrates no curvilinear relationship with peak offending occurring in the early 20s, late 20s and mid-30s. Indeed, the average age of the sample was 33 years of age, a figure that appears much higher than terrorist group-based studies previously highlighted. Florez-Morris' (2007) sample of Colombian terrorists averaged 20 years of age. Both Gill and Horgan's (2013) sample of Provisional IRA members and Sageman's (2004) global jihadist sample averaged 25 years of age.

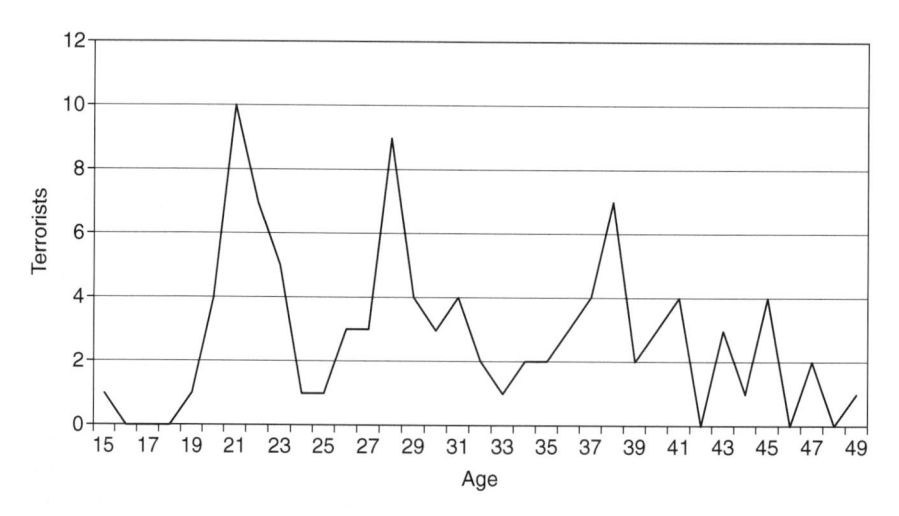

Figure 2.2 Age crime curve of 111 lone-actor terrorists.

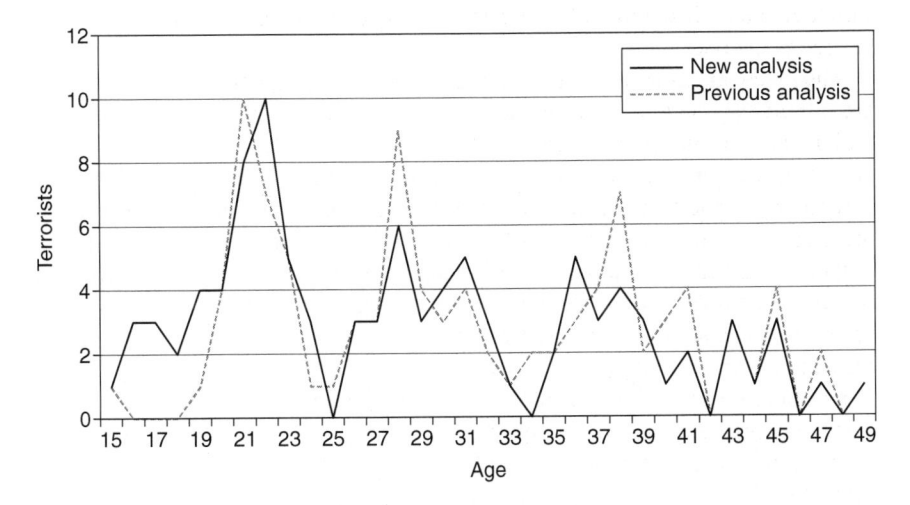

Figure 2.3 Age crime curve of first criminal offence of 111 lone-actor terrorists.

A problem with Figure 2.2's output is that it may be too specific. As we will see later in this chapter, a sizeable number of the lone-actor terrorist sample possessed prior criminal convictions. It begs the question therefore, what does the curve look like if we plot a more general indicator such as age of first criminal offence (see Figure 2.3). Again, no immediately obvious pattern emerges in the new analysis and certainly not one that looks distinctively different from the previous analysis.

The sum of these results suggest that in terms of age, lone-actor terrorists in general buck the trend apparent across a range of crimes including group-based terrorism. At different times in this book, we return to this finding in order to investigate in more detail whether age is just one of a number of explanations as to why the offender is acting alone and not in concert with others.

Gender

The study of the female terrorist is on the rise (Jacques and Taylor, 2009; Bloom, 2011). This is said to be a response to the growth in female involvement in terrorism 'regionally, logistically and ideologically' (Cunningham, 2003). Various analyses have focused upon aspects concerning the demographics of who becomes involved (Jacques & Taylor, 2013; Bloom, Gill, & Horgan, 2012; Pedahzur, Perliger, & Weinberg, 2003), the female terrorist's motivational structure and life experience (Alison, 2003; Ness, 2005; De Cataldo Neuburger, & Valentini, 1992; Lester, 2010), the strategic use of females in combat (Bloom, 2005; Zedalis, 2004; O'Rourke, 2009), the typical roles females undertake in terrorist organizations (McKay, 2005; Nacos, 2005; Nordstrom, 2005; Speckhard, 2008; Gonzalez-Perez, 2008) and case-study based accounts of specific terrorists or terrorist organizations (Knight, 1979; Reif, 1986; Alison, 2003; McKay, 2005;

Nivat, 2005; Schweitzer, 2006). These analyses however are purely focused upon group-based actors. In terms of lone-actor terrorism, the numbers of females remain marginal with only two females being captured in the sample. First, Rachelle 'Shelley' Shannon shot Dr. George Tiller (who himself was later assassinated by lone actor Scott Roeder) outside his abortion clinic in Kansas in 1993. Second, Roshonara Choudhry stabbed a Labour Party MP, Stephen Timms, in May 2010 in revenge for supporting the Iraqi War and the subsequent deaths of innocent people within Iraq.

This relatively low figure appears broadly similar to analyses of some terrorist groups like the Provisional Irish Republican Army (4.9%) and ETA (6.4%) (Gill & Horgan, 2013; Reinares, 2004). The wider crime literature also shows that males are also far more likely to engage in a wide range of violent and illegal behaviours such as workplace bullying, interpersonal aggression, intimate partner violence, arson, organizational aggression, child abductions, substance abuse, and burglary (Friedman, 1998; Hauge, Skogstad, & Einarsen, 2009; Hershcovis, Turner, Barling, Arnold, Dupre, Inness et al., 2007; Beasley, Hayne, Beyer, Kramer, Bersen, Muirhead & Warren, 2009; Arteaga, Chen & Reynolds, 2010; Vaughn, Fu, DeLisi, Wright, Beaver, Perron & Howard, 2010; Ellison, Trinitapoli, Anderson, & Johnson, 2007; Vaughn, Lisi, Beaver, & Howard, 2008). Indeed, males account for 93.2% of all sentenced prisoners in state or federal prisons according to a 2010 U.S. Department of Justice report (Guerine, Harrison, & Sabol, 2011). In effect, the relatively low preponderance of females in the sample is nothing extraordinary.

Education and employment

Using a mixture of sources such as prison statistics, arrest figures, and offender self reports, Lochner and Moretti (2004) illustrated that graduation from high school significantly reduces the probability of an individual being arrested and/or jailed (especially with offences related to murder, assault, and vehicle theft). Findings such as these make some intuitive sense. Greater education should lead to greater opportunities in the workplace and thereby (a) reduce the need for individuals to commit crimes and (b) reduce the individual's time in which he/she can actually do the offending. The lone-actor terrorist sample does not fit this general trend within the study of volume crime. Of those with available data ($n=74$), just over 60% took part in some form of university education with 26% possessing an undergraduate degree as their highest form of educational attainment, an additional 11% holding a masters and 7% holding an accredited doctoral degree. Only 12% dropped out of secondary education. Generally speaking, the mean education for this offender sample is actually quite impressive in terms of their success.

However, this educational success did not translate into direct success in the jobs market. Of the full sample, 44% were unemployed. Of those with some form of university education, over half were unemployed. Those working in the service or administrative sectors accounted for 23%. Only 10% were active

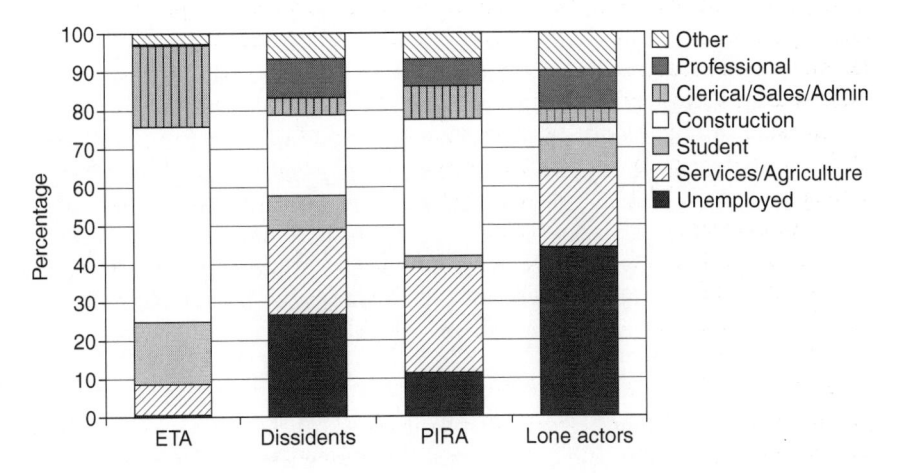

Figure 2.4 Employment status.

professionals. These figures are largely different from the studies cited earlier on PIRA and ETA as well as Horgan and Morrison's (2011) study of dissident Republicans particularly in terms of those unemployed and in the construction industry. The general aggregate picture from the cohort is that of a well-educated sample but one who largely failed to translate this to real-world success.

Family factors and relationship status

Unsurprisingly the study of crime shows that family and childhood experiences appear to have a large impact upon behaviour later in life. Indeed, the provision of multi-generational family histories is commonly recognized as an essential component of providing a competent case for the defence in trials concerning aggravated murder held in the United States (Freedman & Hemenway, 2000: 1757). Measurements of such experiences are wide-ranging across a number of studies. The lack of parental involvement has been linked to fire-setting behaviours in juveniles and violence in adolescence (Del Bove & Mackay, 2011), parental rejection to future intimate partner violence (Roberts, McLaughlin, Conron, & Koenen, 2011), and parental separation to intimate partner violence, male youth violence, female fire-setting, and homicide (Roberts et al., 2011; Farrington, 1998; Freedman & Hemenway, 2000; Hickle & Roe-Sepowitz, 2010; Beautrais, Joyce, & Mulder, 1998). Parental illicit drug use, substance abuse, alcohol problems, criminal offences, and intra-parental violence are predictive of a child's later engagement in a number of serious violent crimes (Freedman & Hemenway, 2000; Lim & Howard, 1998; Gover, Kaukinen, & Fox, 2008; Ehrensaft, Cohen, Brown, Smailes, Chen, & Johnson, 2003; Delsol & Margolin, 2004; von der Pahlen, Ost, Lindfors, & Lindman, 1997; Hill & Nathan, 2008; Fergusson et al., 2008). Unfortunately, due to the nature of open-source data collection, this data is difficult to find. What we can say for certain is that at least 30% of the sample's parents were still married at the time of the offence. At least a further 19% of the sample's parents were divorced or separated. There is a lot of missing data on this particular variable (44%).

However, the case of the French shooter Mohamed Merah may offer some insight into how family dynamics may play a role. Over the course of 10 days, Merah shot and killed three French paratroopers of North African descent, a rabbi, the rabbi's two sons, and an eight-year old girl. Merah's brother published a book on their family life soon after the events. Andre and Harris Hogan's (2013: 308) analysis of this book points to Merah's 'social familial milieu of delinquency, violence, racism and hatred'. The brother's account describes how the family are

> all infamously known by the social services and the police. My father, a former drug dealer, did five years of imprisonment; my brothers ... are thugs, recycled in the most radical Salafism, my sister ... is a notorious fundamentalist, my mother is a scandalous woman, most of our relatives are delinquents.
>
> (2013: 20)

The book outlines how the father was physically abusive toward his sons (but not Mohamed). After his father's imprisonment, one of Mohamed's brothers assumed the leader of the household position and became physically violent towards his mother, sisters, and also Mohamed. The book also traces how Mohamed was temporarily placed in care due to his mother's neglect. His mother also later celebrated Merah's mischief and petty crime despite Mohamed also being physically abusive towards her.

We did, however, get much better traction on the offender's relationship status. Single individuals who had never married accounted for 59%. Just over 20% were married and a further 15% had either divorced or separated from their spouse. This married figure finds itself halfway between comparatively high numbers associated with global jihadists (73%; Sageman, 2004), PIRA (41.6%; Gill & Horgan, 2012) and contemporary dissident republicans (just over 50%; Horgan & Gill, 2011) and significantly lower numbers associated with studies of ETA (11.6%; Reinares, 2004), and Pakistani militants (14%; Fair, 2008). Given the relatively older age of this sample, the marriage rates are actually smaller than what we might expect. When we consider the oft-cited inverted-U relationship between offender age and criminal offending decaying over time due to biographical constraints such as marriage, it is also unsurprising to find such a comparatively older sample to have a high proportion of unattached individuals.

Finally, at least 23% of the sample had children. This figure is comparatively much lower to Gill and Horgan's (2013) study of PIRA militants (41.4%) and significantly so when we take into consideration that the lone-actor sample is a much older cohort of individuals.

Motivation

Trying to understand motivation in the absence of first-hand interviews is very difficult. On a very shallow level, we may aggregate motivation to some form of political ideology. For example, we could just take at face value the ideology the individual espouses as being the true motivation. If we do this, the ideological motivation of these individuals can be clustered into two main groups – al-Qaeda inspired (34%) and right-wing inspired (39%). The rest constitute an aggregation of single-issues (27%) some of which inspired many individuals (anti-abortionists, environmentalists) and some of which were quite idiosyncratic (black nationalists, luddites etc.). For example, Ted Kaczynski's rhetoric mixed the ideals of anarchism, radical environmentalism, and ludditism (Spaaij, 2010). A less famous example is that of Luke Helder, who committed a series of pipe bombings placed in mailboxes. He wrote a six-page manifesto that denounces government control over its citizenry, promotes the legalization of marijuana and the use of astral projection in order to reach a higher state of consciousness. Individuals who act violently and possess a somewhat idiosyncratic belief system often justify the resort to violence as a means to spread the ideology further. For example, Anders Breivik refers to the actions at Oslo and Utøya as the 'marketing operation' for his compendium (Breivik, 2011: 8). Ted Kaczynski's manifesto includes a similar passage: 'In order to get our message before the public with some chance of making a lasting impression, we've had to kill people'.

The sort of aggregate measures depicted above hide a lot of intricacies however and only really provide a sense of what ideologies have inspired the turn towards lone action rather than getting to the heart of what really motivates the individual. For example, within the right-wing movement we have individuals who acted against all minority groups indiscriminately whereas others targeted members/institutions of the Jewish or Muslim faiths while others acted against government targets they believed to either be secretly controlled by minority factions or to be encroaching upon their personal rights too vigorously. Within the right wing cohort we have a wide range of individuals who do not necessarily share too much in common.

So rather than trying to understand motivation in such a crude fashion, it may be more illustrative to look in detail at a number of individuals. Fortunately, a part of the beauty of researching lone-actor terrorists is that their lack of group support, necessitates them to publish a lot of their own justifications (something I refer to as the lone-actor terrorist dilemma in the concluding chapter). This body of work provides a lot of excellent first hand material to try get a better understanding of what motivates them. Prominent examples include, Anders Breivik's 1,500+ page compendium, and Paul Hill's 83-page account of his justification for murdering an abortion clinic doctor. Eric Rudolph's freely available online autobiography runs to 240 pages. Paul Ross Evans' semi-written book *The Militant Christian* is also available online. James von Brunn, who committed the shooting attack at the United States Holocaust Memorial Museum, authored a 403-page book called *The Racialist Guide to the Preservation and*

Nature of the White Gene Pool. Various chapters are entitled 'The Conspiracy', 'The Illuminati', 'Spirochetes of Jew Syphilis', 'The Holocaust Hoax', 'Mendelism', 'The Negro', and 'The Aryan Force'. John Patrick Bedell maintained a blog espousing his libertarian views, although it must be acknowledged that there is no indication of violent intent within these posts that occurred three years prior to his shooting at the Pentagon in 2010 (Bedell, 2014a, 2014b). Luke Helder and Andew Joseph Stack both wrote six-page manifestos. Richard Baumhammers published his manifesto through his website. Others provide much shorter illustrations. Ali Hassan Abu Kamal wrote a two-page 'Charter of Honour' that was found on his body after he committed suicide directly after his mass shooting on top of the Empire State Building. James Lee posted a 1,149 word essay prior to his attack at the Discovery Channel referring to humans as 'filth' and demanding the Discovery Channel 'stop encouraging the birth of any more parasitic human infants'. Finally, others leave videos behind. Sean Gillespie filmed his firebomb attack of a Jewish temple in April 2004 announcing: 'I'm going to firebomb (the temple) with a Molotov cocktail ... for maximum damage. I will film it for your viewing enjoyment, my kindred. White power'. Yonathan Melaku also filmed his shooting attack at the Marine Corps Memorial in Virginia.

A very quick way of analysing these accounts is to produce a Word Cloud of their content. Word Clouds provide greater prominence to the most regularly used words within a text. Figure 2.5 represents a Word Cloud for Anders Breivik's compendium. It clearly depicts the key themes that Breivik is concerned with: 'Muslims', 'Islam', 'Christian', and 'European'. Breivik drew inspiration from a mixture of sources that evoke diverse principles such as Islamophobia, cultural conservative nationalism, anti-feminism, elements of White Power rhetoric, and far-right evangelical theology (Gardell, 2014). Berntzen and Sandberg (2014: 14) illustrate that 'using familiar narratives, he partly reproduced and partly constructed a new ideology for anti-Islamic terrorism'. Indeed, Breivik copied and rewrote the texts of influential anti-Islamic movement actors. He agrees with the anti-Islamic movement that 'Islam and Islamism are an existential threat, immigration and multiculturalism undermine Western values, and the Islamization for Western society is enforced by a multicultural political elite out of touch with the concerns of ordinary people' (Berntzen & Sandberg, 2014: 9). Where Breivik departs from the anti-Islamic movement in their diagnosis of the problem is his more radical framing of this creeping Islamization later causing a 'genocide' of Western cultures and values. Breivik also supports a more violent action-oriented approach to countering Islamism. Indeed, Berntzen and Sandberg's analysis of Breivik's compendium is suggestive of the fact that he began

> by supporting non-violent means and then came to reject these in favour of violent means, as part of a gradual process of radicalization. Assuming it was written consecutively during the last couple of years, it illustrates how he went from supporting democracy to advocating and preparing for violence and political terrorism.
>
> (2014: 11)

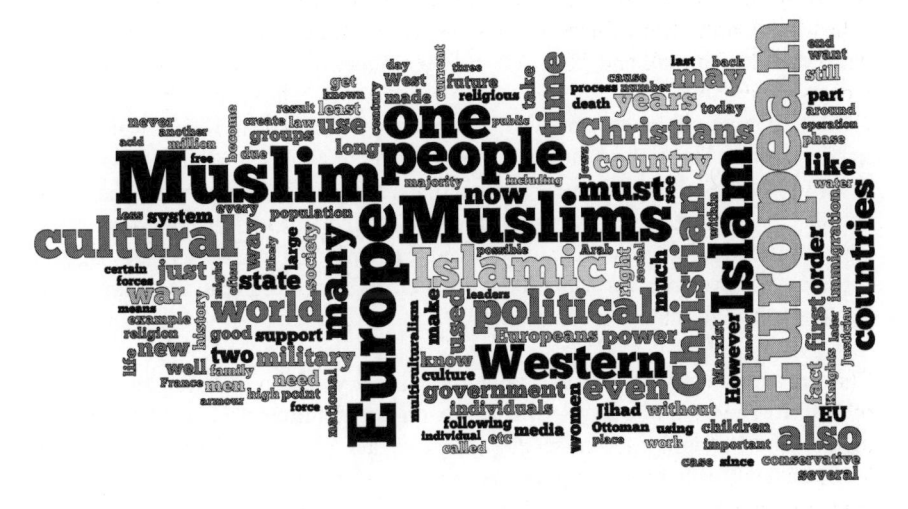

Figure 2.5 Word cloud of Anders Breivik's compendium.

Similarly, a word cloud of Paul Hill's justification for his killing of an abortion clinic doctor provides great insight into his thinking. Hill regularly invokes 'God' and 'defense' of the 'unborn' as reasons for the use of 'necessary force' against 'abortion' and the 'government' that allows it.

Stern (2003) however cautions against solely using these resources to get a sense of motivation. She argues that lone actors 'often come up with their own ideologies that combine personal vendettas with religious or political grievances'. This conclusion largely derives from Stern's interview with Mir Aimal

Figure 2.6 Word cloud of Paul Hill's 83-page justification for his actions.

Kasi who shot dead two CIA employees and injured another three outside of their headquarters at Langley, Virginia. Stern concludes her analysis of the Kasi interview with the following:

> He seems to have been moved, at least in part, by the anti-American fervor he was exposed to in his youth. However, terrorists often use slogans of various kinds to mask their true motives. It is, therefore, not inconceivable that Kasi's primary motivation was to exact personal revenge against an organization he believed had betrayed his father.... When Kasi says he was seeking revenge, was it for some perceived slight – either to his father or to himself? We may never know.

Indeed similar examples are numerous across the ideological span of lone-actor terrorists. In 2008, Jim David Adkisson opened fire on a church congregation, killing two and injuring seven. Adkisson had a history of drug and alcohol problems and repeatedly lost jobs. The opening and concluding page of his four-page suicide note/claim of justification[2] outlines:

> I guess you're wondering why I did this. Well let me explain in detail. Over the years I've had some good jobs, but I always got layed [sic] off. Now I'm 58 years old and I can't get a decent job. I'm told I'm 'overqualified', which is a codeword for 'too damned old'. Like I'm expected to age gracefully into poverty. No thanks! I'm done.... No one gets out of this world alive so I've chosen to skip the bad years of poverty. I know my life is going downhill fast from here. The future looks bleak. I'm sick and tired of being sick and tired. I'm absolutely fed up.

In his initial police interrogation, Adkisson admits to anger and depression stemming from his unemployed status and lack of future prospects. His food stamps were also at risk of being revoked, which Adkisson had only just learnt about prior to the shooting. Adkisson further admits he channelled this anger out on the church and its congregation. With these details, Adkisson appears to be like your typical mass casualty offender, acting without a political cause and acting out of personal grievances and life circumstances.

However, the contents of Adkisson's suicide note/claim of justification go into great detail on the political reasons for his actions. There, he calls the Democrat party an ally of the terrorists in the war on terror and labels liberalism 'the worst problem America faces today'. He accuses major news outlets as being the 'propaganda arm' of the Democrats. The note also blames liberalism for ruining the country and it's institutions 'from the boy scouts up to the military, from education to religion'. The church he targeted is framed as a 'cult', 'ultra-liberal', 'a den of un-American vipers', 'a collection of sicko's, weirdo's, and homo's', that 'embrace every pervert'. He refers to his actions variously as a 'hate crime', 'political protest', and a 'symbolic killing'. He concludes the note:

So I thought I'd do something good for the country and kill Democrats 'til the cops kill me.... Tell the cop that killed me that I said, 'Thanks, I needed that.' I have no next of kin, no living relative. If you would take my sorry carcass to the body farm, or donate it to science, or just throw me in the Tennessee River.

With this information, we can now depict Adkisson as an example of an individual whose personal life circumstances led to a series of problems that he largely blamed upon wider political processes, which after a period of time built up to the extent that he decided to act violently. He chose to attack a church that he felt was a mirror image of the decay he saw emanating from Washington D.C.

However, this was not just a random church. Adkisson had previous contact with this church. His ex-wife previously attended there. His marriage had not ended well by any measure. According to court documents, Adkisson had threatened to 'blow' both of their 'brains out'. With that information, the landscape of Adkisson's motivation changes again. We now have an individual whose personal problems he blamed on the political and when he decided to act upon it found a target that reflected his political concerns but also housed an individual he had a previous and highly acrimonious relationship with. In effect, a mixture of personal and political reasons led to his decision to act violently in the first place, and to act in that location specifically.

Another example is that of James Kenneth Gluck. The FBI interrupted his plot to develop ricin and attack Colorado's Jefferson County judiciary system in 1999. The investigation stemmed from a 10-page letter Gluck sent to a judge where he threatened to wage biological warfare. He refers to Ricin as 'a quintessential American weapon for "making a killing" (literally) without any responsibility because it cannot be determined who used it and cannot be determined where it came from'. Gluck previously experienced a couple of run-ins with Jefferson County officials. In 1989 he received a fine for the illegal possession of protected species. More recent to the plot (1997), Gluck served several weeks in jail on a contempt charge for ignoring zoning violations for the storage of junk on his property. Gluck contested the charge on the grounds that it was not junk but instead he was running a business selling scrap metal. The letter referred to Gluck's two years of planning for the attack, which corresponds with the cessation of his jail time. Just like in the case of Adkisson, we have an individual with personal problems that he blames on wider government (in this case the judicial system), which later turns to a grievance he wants to respond to with violence and he chooses particular targets he had previous personal problems with.

Turning away from actors with extreme right-wing views, we find the example of Ali Hassan Abu Kamal who conducted a mass shooting on top of the Empire State Building killing one and injuring six in 1997. Kamal committed suicide at the scene of the crime. In his possession was a two-page 'Charter of Honour' that outlined his justifications and various targets. The 'First Enemy' encapsulated those who he felt he was targeting at the Empire State Building namely Americans, Britons, French, and 'the Zionists'. Kamal's letter accused each of keeping the Palestinian people 'homeless'. The assignation of these people as enemies is clearly politically influenced. This is not the case with the others listed as a 'Second', 'Third', and 'Fourth' enemies. Included in these categories are individuals Kamal had a personal grievance against. They include a gang of individuals who attacked Kamal because he refused to help them cheat on an exam; an Egyptian Police officer and his brother who had insulted and 'beaten' Kamal 'savagely' during the 1980s; and three students who had blackmailed and attacked Kamal's son. Just like the Adkisson case, we can see an individual with some politically-inspired narratives alongside more personal grievance based narratives contained within the one suicide note.

Volkert van der Graaf is another interesting example. In 2002, he killed the Dutch political party leader Pim Fortuyn. Fortuyn's public rhetoric largely warned against the dangers of immigration, rising crime rates, and deteriorating health care. These issues appear unrelated to Van der Graaf's prior activism. Van der Graaf had a long history in the militant animal-rights movement in the Netherlands. In 1992, he founded a group called Environment Offensive that opposed all animal farming. It appears that this activism largely utilized the legal system such as fighting permits for factory farms and fur farms. This method proved successful, winning 70% of the 2,000 applications they fought against. Conflict exists over what motivated the killing of Fortuyn. The prosecution team, drawing on Van der Graaf's confession, stated:

> Van der Graaf said that he felt Fortuyn was an ever growing danger to vulnerable groups in society. He was concerned about Fortuyn's prejudiced political views and the incendiary way (he) presented them and the substantial political power (he) seemed to be gaining.

During the trial, Van der Graaf admitted he felt compelled to protect Muslim immigrants and that Fortuyn had made them scapegoats as the cause of crime in order to gain votes. He outlined he

> saw it as a danger ... [and] ... hoped that I could solve it myself.... You didn't see anybody who really knew how to take him on, not the media, nor politicians, nor demonstrators.... He had a talent for dealing with criticism. He knew how to make a circus out of it so that it didn't hurt him.... In my eyes, this was a highly vindictive man who used feelings in society to boost his personal stature ... I could see no other option than to do what I did.

On the other hand, a very senior member in Fortuyn's party claimed that Van der Graaf's actions were inspired not by antipathy towards Fortuyn's anti-immigration stance. Rather, the party member indicates Van der Graaf held a personal grudge against a colleague of Fortuyn who was also a pig farmer and had personal dealings with Van der Graaf. Before his trial he wrote to his girlfriend, 'Whenever I give a statement to the court or the media, I do not have to tell the truth necessarily. For the public at large the truth is not important'. The lead prosecutor in the case stated that 'the whole truth is only inside the suspect's head, and in my view he has not given us full disclosure of events' (cited in Spaaij, 2012: 38).

This book's sample of observations were all, to different degrees, driven by some form of political, social, or religious ideology. That being said, ideological motivation is not always easy to identify. For example, in April 2009 Karst Tates drove his car at high-speed into a Queen's Day parade in Apeldoorn, Netherlands. He targeted the open-top bus carrying the Royal family, missed, and killed seven civilians. According to van Buuren and de Graaf (2014: 172), the official investigation into Tates' act showed that although he seemed to be 'against everything' and possessed some affinity with the extreme right wing, he was not politically engaged and the actions were not ideologically inspired. Here is an example of someone carrying out an act that looks like terrorism, has some political interests that may slightly align with the action yet was not given the terrorist label by the Dutch authorities. Interestingly, and we return to this topic in Chapter 6, the investigation's report concludes by stating that this event 'was the individual act of a disturbed person, not inspired by any ideology and done without any significant preparations' (cited in van Buuren & de Graaf, 2014: 172). It seems that once mental illness was apparent, this became the master explanation for Tates' behaviour. The false dichotomy that an act of terrorism is either the actions of a rational terrorist or an irrational mental illness sufferer evidently remains in practitioner circles.

Another factor that makes understanding motivation difficult is the fact that some offenders change their justifications with the passing of time. For example, in 1994 Rashid Baz shot at a van containing 15 Orthodox Jewish students on the Brooklyn Bridge, killing one. In the initial interrogations, Baz claimed the shooting followed a traffic dispute with the van and claimed the attack was an act of road rage. Twelve years later, he conceded to FBI interrogators that the reason was 'because they were Jewish' (Celona, 2012).

To conclude on motivation, the case studies show ideological attainment to be only one component of the explanation. We must take care not to ascribe behaviour solely to an ideological motive. As Borum (2013: 105) highlights:

> When mass casualty violence occurs, because we assume terrorist-like acts to be politically motivated, we are poised to look for evidence of some kind of extremist ideas, associations or beliefs. When that evidence appears, the political explanation becomes the master explanation. We easily assume the political ideas caused the action. The truth is typically more complicated. Neither 'radicalization' nor grievances alone are typically sufficient to cause an individual to engage in terrorism.

It is this more complicated crystallization of features and behaviours that we turn to in the next chapter.

Notes

1 Although these findings appear promising, given the relatively small sample size ($n=53$), the researchers could only provide simple descriptive statistics from their questionnaire responses, and the findings could obviously be skewed by the composition (e.g. chances of two of the respondents being co-offenders) and non-random nature of their sample.
2 The note can be found here http://web.knoxnews.com/pdf/021009church-manifesto.pdf.

References

Adkisson, J. D. (2008). Claim of justification for actions. Retrieved from: http://web.knoxnews.com/pdf/021009church-manifesto.pdf. Accessed 6 October 2014.

Alarid, L. F., Buron, V. S., & Hochstetler, A. (2009). Group and solo robberies: Do accomplices shape criminal form? *Journal of Criminal Justice* 37(1):1–9.

Alison, M. (2003). Women as agents of political violence: gendering security. *Security Dialogue*, *35*(4), 447–463.

Arteaga, I., Chen, C. C., & Reynolds, A. J. (2010). Child predictors of adult substance abuse. *Children and Youth Services Review, 32*, 1108–1120.

Beasley, J. O., Hayne, A. S., Beyer, K., Cramer, G. L., Berson, S. B., Muirhead, Y., & Warren, J. I. (2009). Patterns of prior offending by child abductors: A comparison of fatal and non-fatal outcomes. *International Journal of Law and Psychiatry, 32*, 273–280.

Beautrais, A. L., Joyce, P. R., & Mulder, R. T. (1998). Unemployment and serious suicide attempts. *Psychological Medicine, 28*, 209–218.

Bedell, J. (2014a). [Blog] *Rothbardix – Technology for liberty and justice*. Retrieved from: http://rothbardix.blogspot.ie. Accessed 6 October 2014.

Bedell, J. (2014b). [Blog] *Information Currency and Information Engineering*. Retrieved from: http://infoeng.blogspot.ie. Accessed 6 October 2014.

Berntzen, L. E., & Sandberg, S. (2014). The Collective Nature of Lone Wolf Terrorism: Anders Behring Breivik and the Anti-Islamic Social Movement. *Terrorism and Political Violence*, (ahead-of-print), 1–21.

Bijleveld, C., & Hendriks, J. (2003). Vicious circles: Accounts of stranger sexual assault reflect abusive variants of conventional interactions. *Journal of Forensic Psychiatry*, 12, 515–538.

Block, C. R. (1985). Race/ethnicity and patterns of Chicago homicide 1965 to 1981. *Crime & Delinquency*, *31*(1), 104–116.

Bloom, M. (2005). *Dying to kill: The allure of suicide terror*. Columbia: Columbia University Press.

Bloom, M. (2011). *Bombshell: Women and Terrorism*. Philadelphia: University of Pennsylvania Press.

Bloom, M., Gill, P., & Horgan, J. (2012). Tiocfaidh ar mna: Women in the Provisional Irish Republican Army. *Behavioral Sciences of Terrorism and Political Aggression* 4(1): 60–76.

Borum, R. (2013). Informing Lone – Offender Investigations. *Criminology & Public Policy*, *12*(1), 103–112.

Celona, L. (2012). Killer: Jews my target. *New York Post*. Retrieved from: http://nypost.com/2012/03/26/killer-jews-my-target/. Accessed 1 June 2014.

Cheatwood, D., & Block, K. J. (1990). Youth and homicide: An investigation of the age factor in criminal homicide. *Justice Quarterly*, *7*(2), 265–292.

Clark, R. D. (1995). Lone versus multiple offending in homicide: Differences in situational context. *Journal of Criminal Justice, 23*(5), 451–460.

da Silva, T., Woodhams, J., & Harkins, L. (2013). Heterogeneity within multiple perpetrator rapes: A national comparison of lone, duo, and 3+ perpetrator rapes. *Sexual abuse: a journal of research and treatment*, 1079063213497805.

de Cataldo Neuburger, L., & Valentini, T. (1996). *Women and terrorism*. New York: St. Martin's Press.

De Mesquita, E. B. (2005). The quality of terror. *American Journal of Political Science, 49*(3), 515–530.

Del Bove, G., & Mackay, S. (2011). An empirically derived classification system for juvenile firesetters. *Criminal Justice and Behavior, 38*, 796–817.

Delsol, C., & Margolin, G. (2004). The role of family-of-origin in men's marital violence perpetration. *Clinical Psychology Review, 24*, 99–122.

Ehrensaft, M. K., Cohen, P., Brown, J., Smailes, E., Chen, H., & Johnson. J. G. (2003). Intergenerational transmission of partner violence: A 20-year prospective study. *Journal of Counseling Psychology, 71*, 741–753.

Ellison, C. G., Trinitapoli, J. A., Anderson, K. L., & Johnson, B. R. (2007). Race/ethnicity, religious involvement, and domestic violence. *Violence Against Women, 13*, 1094–1112.

Fair, C. (2008). Who are Pakistan's Militants and their Families? *Terrorism and Political Violence* 20(1): 49–65.

Farrington, D. P. (1998). Predictors, causes, and correlates of male youth violence. *Crime and Justice, 24*, 421–475.

Felson, M., Baumer, E. P., & Messner, S. F. (2000). Acquaintance robbery. *Journal of Research in Crime and Delinquency*, 37, 284–305.

Fergussen, D. M., Boden, J. M., & Horwood, L. J. (2008). Exposure to childhood sexual and physical abuse and adjustment in early adulthood. *Child Abuse and Neglect, 32*, 607–619.

Florez-Morris, M. (2007). Joining Guerrilla Groups in Colombia: Individual Motivations and Processes for Entering a Violent Organization. *Studies in Conflict and Terrorism* 30(7):615–634.

Freedman, D., & Hemenway, D. (2000) Precursors of lethal violence: A death row sample. *Social Science and Medicine*, 50, 1757–1770.

Friedman, A. S. (1998). Substance use/abuse as a predictor to illegal and violent behavior: A review of the relevant literature. *Aggression and Violent Behavior, 3*, 339–355.

Fergusson, D. M., Boden, J. M., & Horwood, L. J. (2008). Exposure to childhood sexual and physical abuse and adjustment in early adulthood. *Child abuse & neglect*, 32(6), 607–619.

Gardell, M. (2014). Crusader Dreams: Oslo 22/7, Islamophobia, and the Quest for a Monocultural Europe. *Terrorism and Political Violence, 26*(1), 129–155.

Gill, P., & Horgan, J. (2013). Who were the Volunteers? The Shifting Sociological and Operational Profile of 1240 Provisional Irish Republican Army Members. *Terrorism and Political Violence* 25(3):435–456.

Gill, P., & Young, J. (2011). Comparing role specific terrorist profile, paper presented at the International Studies Association annual conference, March 2011.

Gonzalez-Perez, M. (2008). *Women and terrorism: Female activity in domestic and international terror groups*. Oxford: Routledge.

Gover, A. R., Kaukinen, C., & Fox, K. A. (2008). The relationship between violence in the family origin and dating violence among college students. *Journal of Interpersonal Violence, 23*, 1667–1693.

Gruenewald, J., Chermak, S., & Freilich, J. D. (2013a). Distinguishing 'loner' attacks from other domestic extremist violence. *Criminology & Public Policy, 12*(1), 65–91.

Gruenewald, J., Chermak, S., & Freilich, J. D. (2013b). Far-Right Lone Wolf Homicides in the United States. *Studies in Conflict & Terrorism, 36*(12), 1005–1024.

Guerine, P., Harrison, P. R., & Sabol, W. J. (2011). *Prisoners in 2010.* Washington D.C.: Bureau of Justice Statistics.

Hauffe, S., & Porter, L. (2009). An interpersonal comparison of lone and group rape offenses. *Psychology, Crime and Law*, 15, 469–491.

Hauge, L. J., Skogstad, A., & Einarsen, S. (2009). Individual and situational predictors of workplace bullying: Why do perpetrators engage in the bullying of others? *Work & Stress, 23*, 349–358.

Hershcovis, M. S., Turner, N., Barling, J., Aronold, K. A., Dupre, K. E., Inness, M., LeBlanc, M. M., & Sivanathan, N. (2007). Predicting workplace aggression: A meta-analysis. *Journal of Applied Psychology, 92*, 228–238.

Hickle, K. E., & Roe-Sepowitz, D. E. (2010). Female juvenile arsonists: An exploratory look at characteristics and solo and group arson offenses. *Legal and Criminological Psychology, 15*, 385–399.

Hill, J., & Nathan, R. (2008). Child antecedents of serious violence in adult male offenders. *Aggressive Behavior, 34*, 329–338.

Hindelang, M. (1976). With a little help from their friends: Group participation in reported delinquent behavior. *British Journal of Criminology* 16, 109–125.

Hirschi, T., & Gottfredson, M. (1983). Age and the explanation of crime. *American journal of sociology*, 552–584.

Hood, R., & Sparks, R. (1970). *Key Issues in Criminology.* New York: McGraw-Hill.

Horgan, J. (2008). From profiles to pathways and roots to routes: Perspectives from psychology on radicalization into terrorism. *The ANNALS of the American Academy of Political and Social Science, 618*(1), 80–94.

Horgan, J., & Morrison, J. F. (2011). Here to Stay? The Rising Threat of Violent Dissident Republicanism in Northern Ireland. *Terrorism and Political Violence* 23: 642–669.

Horgan, J. (2005). *The psychology of terrorism.* London: Routledge.

Jacques, K., & Taylor, P. J. (2009). Female terrorism: A review. *Terrorism and Political Violence, 21*(3), 499–515.

Jacques, K., & Taylor, P. J. (2013). Myths and realities of female-perpetrated terrorism. *Law and human behavior, 37*(1), 35.

Knight, A. (1979). Female terrorists in the Russian socialist revolutionary party. *Russian review*, 139–159.

Lester, D. (2010). Female Suicide Bombers and Burdensomness 1. *Psychological reports, 106*(1), 160–162.

Lim, S., & Howard, R. (1998). Antecedents of sexual and non-sexual aggression in young Singaporean men. *Personality and Individual differences, 25*, 1163–1182.

Lochner, L. (2004). The effect of education on crime: Evidence from prison inmates, arrests, and self-reports. *The American Economic Review*, 94, 155–189.

McDevitt, J., Levin, J., & Bennett, S. (2002). Hate crime offenders: An expanded typology. *Journal of Social Issues, 58*(2), 303–317.

McKay, S. (2005). Girls as 'weapons of terror' in Northern Uganda and Sierra Leonean rebel fighting forces. *Studies in Conflict & Terrorism, 28*(5), 385–397.

Nacos, B. L. (2005). The portrayal of female terrorists in the media: Similar framing patterns in the news coverage of women in politics and in terrorism. *Studies in Conflict & Terrorism, 28*(5), 435–451.

Ness, C. D. (ed.). (2007). *Female terrorism and militancy: agency, utility, and organization*. Oxford: Routledge.

Nivat, A. (2005). The black widows: Chechen women join the fight for independence – and Allah. *Studies in Conflict & Terrorism*, 28(5), 413–419.

Nordstrom, C. (2005). (Gendered) war. *Studies in Conflict & Terrorism*, 28(5), 399–411.

O'Rourke, L. A. (2009). What's Special about Female Suicide Terrorism? *Security Studies*, 18(4), 681–718.

Pedahzur, A., Perliger, A., & Weinberg, L. (2003). Altruism and fatalism: The characteristics of Palestinian suicide terrorists. *Deviant Behavior*, 24(4), 405–423.

Piquero, A. R., Farrington, D. P., & Blumstein, A. (2007). *Key issues in criminal career research: New analyses of the Cambridge Study in Delinquent Development*. Cambridge: Cambridge University Press.

Reif, L. L. (1986). Women in Latin American guerrilla movements: A comparative perspective. *Comparative Politics*, 147–169.

Reinares, F. (2004). Who are the terrorists? Analyzing changes in sociological profile among members of ETA. *Studies in Conflict and Terrorism*, 27, 465–488.

Reiss, A. J., & Farrington, D. P. (1991). Advancing knowledge about co-offending: Results from a prospective longitudinal survey of London males. *Journal of Criminal Law and Criminology* 82, 360–395.

Roberts, A. L., McLaughlin, K. A., Conron, K. J., and Koenen, K. C. (2011). Adulthood stressors, history of childhood adversity, and risk of perpetration of intimate partner violence. *American Journal of Preventive Medicine*, 40, 128–138.

Sageman, M. (2004). *Understanding Terror Networks*. Philadelphia: University of Pennsylvania Press.

Schieman, S. (1999). Age and anger. *Journal of Health and Social Behavior*, 273–289.

Schweitzer, Y. (2006). *Female suicide bombers: dying for equality?* (No. 84). Jaffee Center for Strategic Studies, Tel Aviv University.

Simon, R. W., & Nath, L. E. (2004). Gender and Emotion in the United States: Do Men and Women Differ in Self-Reports of Feelings and Expressive Behavior? *American Journal of Sociology*, 109(5), 1137–1176.

Spaaij, R. (2010). The Enigma of Lone Wolf Terrorism: An Assessment. *Studies in Conflict and Terrorism* 33: 854–870.

Spaaij, R. (2012). *Understanding Lone Wolf Terrorism*. London: Springer, 98, 80–95.

Speckhard, A. (2008). The emergence of female suicide terrorists. *Studies in Conflict & Terrorism*, 31(11), 995–1023.

Stern, J. (2003). *Terror in the name of God: Why religious militants kill*. New York: Ecco.

Stolzenburg, L., and D'Alessio, S. (2008). Co-offending and the age-crime curve. *Journal of Research in Crime and Delinquency*, 45, 65–86.

Ullman, S. E. (1999). A comparison of gang and individual rape incidents. *Violence and Victims*, 14, 123–133.

van Buuren, J., & de Graaf, B. (2014). Hatred of the System: Menacing Loners and Autonomous Cells in the Netherlands. *Terrorism and Political Violence*, 26(1), 156–184.

Van Mastrigt, S. B., & Farrington, D. P. (2011). Prevalence and characteristics of co-offending recruiters. *Justice Quarterly*, 28(2), 325–359.

Vaughn, M. G., DeLisi, M., Beaver, K. M., & Howard, M. O. (2008). Toward a quantitative typology of burglars: A latent profile analysis of career offenders. *Journal of Forensic Sciences*, 53, 1387–1392.

Vaughn, M. G., Fu, Q., DeLisi, M., Wright, J. P., Beaver, K. M., Perron, B. E., &

Howard, M. O. (2010). Prevalence and correlated of fire-setting in the United States: Results from the national epidemiological survey on alcohol and related conditions. *Comprehensive Psychiatry, 51*, 217–223.

von der Pahlen, B., Ost, B., Lindfors, B., & Lindman, R. (1997). Early antecedents of spouse abuse. *Aggressive Behavior, 23*, 239–243.

Wright, R., & West, D. J. (1981). Rape – A comparison of group offenses and lone assaults. *Medicine, Science and the Law* 21, 25–30.

Zedalis, D. (2008). Beyond the Bombings: Analyzing female suicide bombers. *Female Terrorism and Militancy: Agency, Utility, and Organization*, 49–68.

3 The behavioural underpinnings of lone-actor terrorism

Understanding who lone-actor terrorists are is useful but perhaps only becomes operationally relevant when we understand how these factors interact with developmental trajectories into taking action in violent terrorist behaviours. This chapter focuses upon three behavioural facets. First, we focus upon behaviours and experiences that may be related to the individual's violent radicalization but are not necessarily a cause of it. These types of behaviours may be likened to distal influences that typically correlate with particular activities but do not alone cause them. Bouhana and Wikstrom (2011) frame these distal influences as 'the causes of the causes of action'. They can encompass demographic factors (like the issues we focused upon in the previous chapter) but they also include aspects concerning personality factors, peer networks, and past behaviours (e.g. criminal history, substance abuse, encounters with the law). Second, we focus upon proximal factors. Though long-term risk factors are important to research (and are often far more researched because they are more easily observable) situational and short-term risk factors are probably more important from an operational perspective. Situational theories highlight the importance of short-term risk factors by positing that anyone can be motivated to commit an offence, because the motivation to do so lies in the situation (Briar & Piliavin, 1965; Cohen & Felson, 1979; Osgood, Wilson, O'Malley, Bachman, & Johnston, 1996). It is unlikely that situational risk factors are the only ones contributing to violent or criminal behaviour. Rather, it is more likely that long-term risk factors lead to a higher predisposition to engage in criminal or violent behaviours, but short-term risk factors such as situation-specific motives and emotions lead to whether or not the event comes to fruition. We consider this crystallization of risk at great length. Finally, we focus upon behaviours related to both attack planning and attack commission.

Distal factors

Previous criminal history

In 2007, Jason Roach published a research article called 'Those who do big bad things also usually do little bad things'. Roach promotes the concept of 'self-selection' to catch serious offenders. The basic concept is that serious offenders are often identified and captured by police after the commission of a lesser offence. We return to the implications of this in the concluding chapter but the main take-home point for now is that 'serious offenders are often crime versatile, committing an array of different crimes, including minor as well as serious offences. People who do big bad things, will not cavil at doing little bad things' (Roach, 2007: 67). It should be no surprise therefore that much academic work on volume crime shows that a large predictor of future engagement with criminal and illicit behaviours is whether the individual has a previous history of criminal or illicit activities. For example, Beasley and colleagues (2009) found that the large majority (~75%) of their child abductor sample had previous arrests, across both fatal and non-fatal outcomes. Interestingly, only 14% had previously been arrested for kidnapping; the most common prior arrest reasons offences were larceny (40%), burglary/breaking and entering (35%), and forcible sex offences (33%). Soothill, Francis, and Liu (2006) found that 77% of kidnappers in their sample had previous convictions; approximately 33% had acquisitive convictions (e.g. theft, robbery, burglary, or deception offences), 41% had sexual or violent (but non acquisitive) convictions, and 3.4% of the individuals were convicted of 'other' crimes. Individuals convicted of arson, blackmail, kidnapping, and death threats are more likely to have committed a homicide after a 20-year period compared to the general population (Soothill et al., 2008). Those convicted of more than one type of serious offence are more likely to be convicted of homicide. Further, offenders with prior convictions including child molestation, robbery, or multiple probation sentences are more likely to engage in a spree of homicidal offending (DeLisi, Hochstetler, Scherer, Purhmann, & Berg, 2008). Fein and Vossekuil's (1999) study of individuals who took part in or at least attempted to take part in an assassination of a public figure illustrated that 56% of the sample had one or more arrests for a non-violent offence while 20% had one or more arrests for a violent offence.

When we turn to the lone-actor terrorist sample, we find similarly high figures. Just under half (49%) possessed a previous criminal conviction. Of this sub-sample, 55% served time in prison indicating the seriousness and/or prolific nature of their offending. Of those who served time, 20% adopted their violent extremist ideology in prison. This latter finding shows how previous criminality can be construed as a 'cause of the cause'. Imprisonment changed the individuals immediate environment and opened up a space in which the individual could consume and take on a violent ideology. Together these figures are certainly higher than we may intuitively expect from group-based terrorist offenders who may weed out individuals with criminal records in the recruitment process. Offences included attempted murder, threats to life, first degree robbery, criminal damage, custodial and second degree assault, affray, firearms offences including possession, arson, kidnapping, child pornography possession, drunk driving, grand larceny, vehicle theft, blackmail, drug possession/use, non-violent protests, counterfeiting, criminal use of explosives, vandalism, child neglect, lewd and disorderly conduct, contempt of court, obstructing law enforcement officers, hooliganism, restraining order violations, theft, income tax issues, graffiti and somewhat strangely possession of a carcass of a protected barn owl. We therefore see a very wide range of illegal activities and certainly no concentration of one crime type that we can identify as a 'trigger' for later behaviour in lone-actor terrorism.

What is clear however, is that there are three types of prior offenders amongst the lone-actor sample. The first are individuals whose offence history is very infrequent and when it did occur, was very minor. The second are those whose offence history is largely connected to their political activism with the terrorism offences coming at the end of a very long trajectory. An excellent example is that of James Kopp, who in 1998 fatally shot an abortion clinic doctor. In the 15 years prior to the shooting, police arrested Kopp on numerous (according to some sources possibly hundreds of) occasions. Most, if not all, of these arrests were for crimes related to abortion clinic protests such as trespassing and criminal damage. His first recorded arrest occurred in April 1984 in San Francisco. Between then and July 1988 he was subsequently arrested many more times in San Francisco but also in Florida and Georgia (for which he served jail time of several weeks). Between 1988 and 1993, he widened his area of offending further and was arrested in New York (on a couple occasions), Pennsylvania, West Virginia, and Vermont and areas in California other than San Francisco. He then went three full years (1994–1996) without an arrest before being picked up by police in New Jersey in 1997. The following year he committed his shooting offence. While Kopp's offending was very focused on discrete targets and conducted prolifically, this is not the case with others whose offending is linked to their later lone-actor terrorist attack. Take the example of Richard Baumhammers. In April 2000, Baumhammers committed a racially motivated shooting spree killing five and injuring one. He had a history of engaging in racially motivated crime before this. The trial's prosecutors outlined that in the mid-1980s, Baumhammers took part in cross burnings and threatened fire bombings against the homes of members of the black community in Mount Lebanon, Pennsylvania. During this time he also took part in threatening confrontations with several black students during his freshman year at Kent State University. He also stood accused of intimidating and threatening two Pakistani doctors and punching a female café owner because he believed she was Jewish.

The third type of previous criminal offender is that of the career prolific offender. The seriousness and flexibility in their offending differ substantially however. Adbulhakim Mujahid Muhammad is an excellent example of a prolific offender of serious crimes. In 2009, Muhammad engaged in a drive-by shooting on U.S. soldiers standing outside of a military recruiting office in Little Rock, Arkansas. The shooting killed one and injured another individual. Muhammad's problematic behaviour started early. He left school at twelfth grade after receiving a number of suspensions for fighting. After leaving school, Muhammad joined a gang and the scale and rate of his offending jumped substantially (Competency Evaluation for Abdulhakim Mujahid Muhammad). Gartenstein-Ross' (2014) in-depth case study of Muhammad utilized police and court records. The study illustrated how Muhammad previously came into contact with authorities in relation to:

- a fight with another former gang member;
- an altercation that involved a knife being pulled;
- a car crash to which Muhammad reacted by first running to the other driver's vehicle and 'hitting the rear passenger window with chrome-plated brass knuckles. Muhammad yelled, "Bitch I'm gonna kill you, get out, I'm going to kill you when I get your address"' (Gartenstein-Ross, 2014:113) and;
- an incident in which police found Muhammad in a car alongside a SKS assault rifle and a single-shot shotgun that Muhammad claimed he was selling to an individual who successfully fled from police. He was also found in possession of a bag of marijuana.

All of these events occurred before he turned 20. He converted to Islam soon after being charged and receiving a 14-year suspended sentence for the unlawful weapons and drug possession offence. Following his arrest for the fatal shooting at Little Rock, Muhammad's violence continued in jail. On one occasion he stabbed a fellow inmate. On another, he stabbed a prison guard. He used a shank both times. Muhammad has also been associated with a number of threats against prison staff and repeatedly vandalizing his cell (Gartenstein-Ross, 2014).

A remarkably similar case is that of Mohamed Merah. Merah conducted three shooting attacks against French soldiers and Jewish civilians in 2012, killing eight and injuring five. Again his problems started at an early age. He was expelled from many schools for various misdemeanours. At 17, police arrested Merah for stoning a bus alongside other youths. Later, police detained Merah on 18 separate occasions for vandalism and theft. In December 2007, Merah was imprisoned for 18 months for the violent theft of an elderly lady's handbag. He was also physically abusive towards his mother. After his failed suicide attempt a year later, his psychiatrist outlined that Merah had a 'disposition towards anti-social behavior'. Following his release from prison, Merah experienced a dispute with a local family because Merah forced one of their children into watching beheading videos from Afghanistan. In response to the family reporting him to the police, Merah turned up at the family's home 'in full military clothes, waving a sword and chanting "Al Qaeda, Al Qaeda"'.

This type of prior offender is not the sole confines of the younger al-Qaeda inspired cohort. For example, police interrupted Martyn Gilleard's plot when they searched his property in relation to child pornography possession. Police uncovered 39,000 indecent images of children including films and photographs. Gilleard also had a history of violence including being fined for possession of an offensive weapon, throwing his young son against a wall, killing the family dog with an axe and killing the neighbour's cat when it entered his garden (Sharpe, 2008).

Other distal factors

There are a number of other behaviours logged within the lone-actor terrorist dataset that provide an understanding of the offender's behavioural background (but not a full or even partial explanation of why they engaged in terrorism). These are rank ordered in terms of their prevalence within the sample in Table 3.1. We return to many of these in a later section when we discuss how 'risk' crystallizes.

Proximal factors

This section provides an overview of the prevalence of behaviours the individual engaged in very near to the terrorist event or planned event. None of these behaviours are attack-related specifically but again provide a more holistic view of the immediate life-situation various actors found themselves in just prior to planning their lone-actor terrorist attack. Table 3.2 rank orders these behaviours

Table 3.1 Prevalence of distal factors

Variable	Prevalence (%)
Socially isolated	55
Criminal conviction	49
History of violent behaviour	42
History of mental illness	41
Lived alone at time of event	40
Experience of long-term stress	32
History of substance abuse	27
Military experience	23
Combat experience	8

Table 3.2 Prevalence of proximal behaviours (%)

Variable	Occurred within 2 years	Occurred within 1 year	Occurred within 6 months
Religious beliefs noticeably intensified	8.1	7.2	4.5
Changed address	42.3	36	26.1
Ideological beliefs noticeably intensified	30.6	23.4	14.4
Recently unemployed	22.5	15.3	8.1
Experienced work-related stressor	9	7.2	2.7
Target of a perceived act of prejudice	15.3	9	4.5
Problems with personal relationships	14.4	11.7	9
Financial problems	19.8	13.5	8.1
Elevated level of stress	29.7	26.1	15.3

in terms of their prevalence within two years of the attack taking place or the plot being interrupted. The corresponding figures for one year and six months are also displayed.

The turn to violence

Strategically, lone and group actors' use of terrorism appears identical. Take this example from Paul Ross Evans who engaged in mail bombings against abortion clinics. Evans outlines that:

> Through the use of mail bombs, I desired to accomplish several objectives: 1. to generate media attention toward Christianity's dissatisfaction with the offending parties. 2. to display Christianity's initiative to fight for the lives of the innocent. 3. to coerce the government of the United States to renounce its present agenda – as unveiled as it is – in abandoning Christianity as its predominant moral influence. 4. to confound the agents and employees of the United States government. 5. to kill those targeted. Determined to keep any collateral damage to a bare minimum, I chose my targets scrupulously. As I compiled a list of potential targets, I focused only on those having addresses such that minimum numbers of non-targeted individuals, especially children, would be anywhere nearby. Targets who stood out from the rest and seemed to beg for retribution were those who generated disgrace toward the morally upright, and those who operated with flamboyance, arrogance, and smugness.
>
> (Evans)

Next we turn to issues regarding attack preparation and attack planning and how they may differ behaviourally from group-based plots.

Attack preparation

As the next chapter highlights in great detail, despite lone-actor terrorists engaging in their attack alone, very rare is the case of the individual who self-radicalized, had no contact with other militants whatsoever, conceived the plot with no influence/encouragement/inspiration from other persons or organizations, conducted all planning and preparation (including materials acquisition, making the devices, choosing targets) without influence/encouragement/inspiration from others, received no direct or indirect material support, executed all of the attack with no direct or indirect support and did not discuss their views or plans with anyone (Betley, 2013). The results (in Table 3.3.) reflect the fact that typically the offender was accompanied by somebody either face-to-face or virtually for some aspects of the radicalization, attack facilitation, or attack preparation. The results run completely counter to what those who promote the lone wolf strategy espouse. For example, Metzger's *Laws of the Lone Wolf* states that:

Table 3.3 Network related behaviours (%)

Other people aware of the individual's grievance	74
Other people aware of individual's extremist ideology	69
Read propaganda from a wider movement	60
Made verbal statements to friends/family about intent or belief	51
Claimed to be part of a wider group/movement	46
Learnt from virtual sources	42
Interacted face-to-face with members of a wider network	41
At least one other knew of the individual's research/planning/prep for an attack	35
Recently joined a wider group/organization/movement	32
Interacted virtually with members of a wider network	30
Family/close associates involved in political violence/criminality	24
Read propaganda about other lone actors	24
Received hands-on training	23
Tried to recruit others	22
Read propaganda written by other lone actors	18
Received help in procuring weaponry	16
Sought legitimization from epistemic authority figures	14
Rejected or ejected from a wider group or movement	14
Raised funds for a wider network	10
Evidence of command and control links	8
Spouse/partner part of a wider movement	5
Received help in building an IED	5

> The less any outsider knows, the safer and more successful you will be. Keep your mouth shut and your ears open. Never truly admit to anything.... Communication is a good thing, but keep your covert activities a secret. This will protect you as well as others like you.
>
> (Metzger)

Planning

Without a prolific terrorist group's social, financial, and human capital to support the lone actor, what does the planning process look like behaviourally and temporally? Those who see these actors as being crazy, delusional, or irrational may have a tendency to think of them as being spontaneous and acting out of perceived slights. However, in the vast majority of cases in which good data is available, the planning process appears to be a long one. We take a look at five cases in-depth in Chapter 9 but let's look at some illustrative examples for now.

Three years before the FBI interrupted Khalid Aldawsari's plot,[1] he wrote in his journal:

> I excelled in my studies in high school in order to take advantage of an opportunity for a scholarship to America ... I chose [a specific Saudi sponsoring corporation] for two reasons. First [it] sends its students directly to America ... second [its] financial scholarship is the largest, which will help tremendously in providing me with the support I need for Jihad.... Now

after mastering the English language, learning how to build explosives, and continuous planning [to] target the infidel Americans, it is time for Jihad.

In September 2008 Aldawsari entered the U.S. on a student visa and enrolled as a chemical engineering student at Texas Tech University. In March 2010, he vowed to pursue jihad and martyrdom on his blog. In July 2010, he wrote about his desire to create an Islamic group under the banner of al-Qaeda in his personal journal. In September 2010, he emailed himself a list of targets of three individuals (alongside their addresses) that previously served in the U.S. military at Abu Ghraib prison in Iraq. Two days later, his journal entry noted he is getting nearer to his goal of jihad by working toward obtaining weapons. In October 2010, he emailed an explosives recipe to himself. Six days later, he emailed another list of targets. This time the targets are structural like 12 reservoirs, hydro electrical dams, and nuclear power plants. Around this time, he downloaded 17 videos that 'are complete and detailed instructions for how to make a bomb'. In December 2010 and January 2011, he began ordering components for an IED including three gallons of concentrated sulphuric acid, soldering iron kit, 30 litres of concentrated nitric acid, miniature Christmas lights, a stun gun, a battery tester, alarm clock, Pyrex flasks, a glass stir rod, a professional chemistry lab equipment set, gas mask, hazmat suit, and screwdrivers. During this time he also emailed himself instructions on how to turn a mobile phone into a remote detonator and how to booby-trap a vehicle. Through January and February 2011, he watched the previously downloaded videos a total of 198 times. Aldawsari took over 50 pages of 'notes, diagrams, and instructions' based on these videos. In February 2011, Aldawsari found information on the assassination of the Spanish Prime Minister in 1973 with an IED planted underneath the street. Aldawsari's next online search involved the phrase 'how to excavate a street'. The next search sought information on former President George W. Bush's residence. He then emailed himself the address. Two days later, FBI agents question Aldawsari about his attempted phenol purchase (something that he had research for online with 134 separate searches). A week later FBI agents searched his apartment and found his purchased goods and notebook. Within two days of the final search, Aldawsari scaled down his ambitious targeting and searched the internet for the following terms: 'party in Dallas', 'can you take a backpack to a nightclub', 'bakepack' [sic], 'Dallas night clubs'.

In this example, just over two years passed between Aldawasari applying to go to the United States with the expressed intention of committing an act of jihad and actually beginning to plan for an attack. Once his aspirations transitioned into attack preparation, the tempo quickened. Although there was some overlap, the behaviours largely transitioned from gaining the capability to attack (IED construction) to consuming ideological material to choosing a specific target. This appears a slightly counter-intuitive pattern where one may instead expect ideological material to further inspire action, to choosing a specific target to then choosing an attack type (and gaining the corresponding capability) to match the demands of the target.

It is unsurprising that such plots take so much time in isolation. We may often imagine one step in the plan being quite easy when in reality it involves a great deal of effort and planning. Take the prosecutions closing comments in the Aldawsari case:

> Let's take as an example the nitric acid order. It is not just a matter of going out and wishing for nitric acid to appear. There has to be steps done to acquire that product. It requires downloading the video. It requires watching the video. It requires taking notes. It requires Google queries as to where to buy nitric acid. It requires clicking on the Boiler and Water Cooling website and looking at the information on nitric acid. It requires making the purchase, spending money to buy the product. It requires the use of emails; that when Mr. Zajac emails Mr. Aldawsari and says, 'I can't ship to a residence, I need an updated address,' it requires doing a query on Google maps and finding a place where he can have the nitric acid shipped. It requires telephone calls and emails to Mr. Zajac. It requires calls to Con-Way Freight to coordinate for the pick-up of the nitric acid. It requires getting in the car. It requires driving to Con-Way Freight. It requires picking the nitric acid up. So as you hear and as we talk about these substantial steps, understand it is just not one step. There are several steps that you have to take in order to even get to that step.
>
> (Trial Transcript of Closing Argument and Jury Charge Reading)

In other cases, the planning process was a lot quicker and was usually aided by either the plot's primitive nature or the offender's access to weaponry. Take the anti-abortion activist Paul Hill as an example. The below passages outline his thoughts in great detail. Hill writes that the thought of taking up violent action

> first occurred to me eight days earlier [to the eventual shooting] ... I was working ... wondering who would act next [after Michael Griffin had killed an abortion clinic doctor], when the idea of taking action myself struck; it hit hard. During the next two or three hours, as I continued to work in a distracted manner, I began to consider what would happen if I were to shoot an abortionist ... I finished my work that Thursday afternoon and drove home. Although at the time my thinking on these things had not crystallized, no matter how I approached the subject, everything seemed to fall together in an amazing manner. I continued to secretly consider shooting an abortionist, half hoping it would not appear as plausible after I had given it more thought. The next morning, Friday, as was my practice, I went to the abortion clinic (the Ladies Center).[2] I arrived at about eight o'clock, the time that many of the mothers began arriving. I was usually the first protester there, but that day another activist had arrived first. What was even more unusual was, after discrete questioning, I learned that he had been there when the abortionist arrived: about 7:30. More importantly, I discovered that the

abortionist had arrived a few minutes *prior* to the police security guard. This information was like a bright green light, signaling me on. For months my wife had planned to take our children on a trip to visit my parents, and to take my son to summer camp. She planned to leave that coming Wednesday morning and return the following week. I would have the remainder of the day that she left, and all of Thursday, to prepare to act on Friday, just eight days after the idea first struck me. All I had to do was hide my intentions from my wife for a few days until she left. If I did not act during her planned trip (since I could not have kept my feelings from her for long) she would almost certainly develop suspicions later, and my plans would be spoiled for fear of implicating her. I could not hope for a better opportunity than the one immediately before me. God had opened a window of opportunity, and it appeared that I had been appointed to step through it.... When Monday arrived, I knew I had to decide. When I went from mentally debating whether to act, in general, to planning a particular act, I felt some relief.

(Hill, 2003)

This example shows that the typically lengthy planning process can be drastically shortened in the case of offenders who (a) have prior experience with the attack location and (b) have ready access to firearms. Hill was also heavily immersed with anti-abortion activism so there was no real need for a further period of ideological intensification in the same manner Aldowasari experienced.

Floyd Lee Corkins is another interesting example of a rather quick planning process largely aided by access to firearms in the United States. On 15 August 2012, Corkins entered the offices of the conservative lobbying group, the Family Research Council (FRC) with the intention of 'killing as many people as I could'.[3] Corkins managed to injure a security guard before being overpowered and held at gunpoint until the police arrived. A list found on Corkins suggested he also planned to target three other social conservative advocacy groups. The government's sentencing memorandum highlights that Corkins acknowledged that he wanted to engage in violent activism for a long time. His parents told the FBI that he 'has strong opinions with respect to those he believes do not treat homosexuals in a fair manner'. It is also known that Corkins suffered with mental health issues (including major depressive disorders and psychotic features) throughout his adult life. Six months prior to his violent action, Corkins voluntarily committed himself to a mental hospital because he suffered from hallucinations and 'thoughts of killing his parents and conservative right-wing Christians'. He left a month later and continued counselling and medication. This is not to suggest however that there is a clear link between this illness and his decision to engage in violence. There are also no publicly available details on what helped transition Corkins from years of thinking about conducting violence, to actually preparing a violent act.

Floyd Lee Corkins originally planned to conduct a bombing attack but told police he 'didn't have the patience for it'. The vast majority of planning and preparation occurred in the week prior to the attempted attack. On 7 August, while browsing online Corkins identified Blue Ridge Arsenal in Chantilly, Virginia as a suitable location to purchase firearms. On 9 August, Corkins perused for firearms at the Blue Ridge Arsenal. The following day he returned and purchased a semi-automatic pistol and received two-hours of free firearms training. On 12 August, he visited the Southern Poverty Law Center's website and identified the FRC as being anti-gay. He also visited the websites of the FRC and the other three advocacy groups. The FRC's website states that its mission is to 'shape the public debate and formulate public policy that values human life and upholds the institutions of marriage and the family'. He then printed MapQuest and Google map directions to the FRC and one of the other groups. Upon his later arrest Corkins made various statements like 'I don't like the organization and what it stands for' and 'I don't like these people, and I don't like what they stand for'. On 13 August, he rehearsed the journey to the FRC. In his own words, he was 'basically tying to go over exactly what I was gonna do' on the day of the attack. He managed to access the lobby of their office by telling the receptionist he was there to meet an FRC employee and provided a fake name. The receptionist checked the employee directory, failed to find someone with the provided name, informed Corkins and he, in turn, exited the lobby. On 14 August, Corkins visited a branch of Chick-fil-A and bought 15 chicken sandwiches. He intended to smear these sandwiches in the face of his victims

> to make a statement against the people who work in that building ... and with their stance against gay rights and Chick-fil-A. They endorse Chick-fil-A and also Chick-fil-A came out against gay marriage so I was going to use that as a statement.[4]

Later that day, Corkins purchased a black backpack at Kmart that was eventually used to conceal his firearm and ammunition on the day of the attack. On the evening before his attack, Corkins returned to the Blue Ridge Arsenal and took part in another two hours of firearms training with the weapon he purchased days earlier. Later that night, he loaded three magazines for the violent event he planned to conduct the following day.

Again, this is another example where the capability to engage in attack (purchasing a firearm) was conducted before a target was chosen. It is almost as if the individual became convinced of the need to turn toward violence, checked into the viability of conducting a violent attack, and once he found it was a viable option, began to optimize between potential targets. This may have some implications for countering lone-actor terrorism. Perhaps minimizing the perceived potential to engage in violence may be a more malleable part of the lone-actor terrorist attack script for counter-terrorism practices rather than trying to counter the content of the extremism itself.

Many of the lone actors also rationally thought through how security and intelligence agencies may detect and/or interrupt their plots. Abdulhakim

Mujahid Muhammad, the shooter at the Little Rock army recruitment office, bought a .22 rifle 'over the counter at Wal-Mart to test if I'd get caught or questioned'. It was a 'test to see if I was under surveillance'. Once the new gun was purchased, he thought to himself 'It's on.... Meaning, I'm not under surveillance. The FBI had not put a hold or checked' (Competency Evaluation for Abdulhakim Mujahid Muhammad). To obtain the materials for his IEDs, Eric Rudolph 'drove 100 miles to Gadsden, Alabama, where I bought pipes, alarm clocks, batteries, and circuit wire. Then I drove a little more, hoping to make my activities hard to track' (Rudolph, 2013: 7). Rudolph also slept rough the nights before the bombing hoping to avoid the CCTVs installed at hotels. Paul Ross Evans engaged in a number of counter-intelligence practices. His online writings note:

> I stumbled upon a tangled ball of human hair of all colors. I picked it up and put it inside the cellophane wrapper of my cigarettes. I included bits of this hair in the letter [bombs] in order to 'throw off' agents working for the regime in Washington.

Attack signaling

One of the most surprising behavioural trends was the extent to which the sample tended to leak information to significant others regarding their attack plan (See Table 3.3). Studies of similar actors have however found similar results. For example, Meloy, Hempel, Mohandie, and Gray's (2001) study of adolescent mass murderers in North America illustrated that 44% of the sample discussed the act of murder with at least one other person prior to the event itself. Also, 58% had made threatening statements alluding to mass murder prior to the event and this was usually to a third-party audience. In 81% of Vossekuil, Fein, Reddy, Borum, and Modzeleski's (2002) sample of U.S.-based school shooters, at least one other individual had known of the offender's intentions or specific plans for the school attack. In 59% of the cases, more than one non-attack related person had prior knowledge. Unlike Meloy et al.'s study, there was a lower rate of school shooters (17%) who provided specific pre-event warnings. Vossekuil et al. (2002: 26) also found that although most of the offences were committed by individuals, in 44% of the cases the solo offender was 'influenced by other individuals in deciding to mount an attack, dared or encouraged by others to attack, or both'. In some of these cases, others aided the solo offender in acquiring the weapon and/or ammunition. Finally, Fein and Vossekuil (1999) studied individuals who committed or attempted to commit assassinations of public figures in the United States. They illustrate that although specific pre-attack warnings are a rare event, often others close to the offender were either aware of his/her interest in assassinations (44%), history of verbal/written communications about the eventual target (77%), or history of indirect, conditional or direct threats concerning the eventual target (63%).

Collectively these results show a large contradiction between the empirical reality and studies emphasizing the strategic utility of lone-actor terrorism. The latter posit that it is the very 'loneliness' of the offender that makes it such a threat because the lack of communication between co-offenders bypasses the sophisticated tools of the state. The former suggests however that even the most intimate of details regarding the plot are leaked to others. The analogous studies cited here offer a few clues as to why lone offenders leak this information. In some cases, they may be seeking to recruit co-offenders and/or looking for peer reassurance and/or providing warning to acquaintances not to turn up at school on a particular day. We may be able to add one further reason for the lone-actor terrorist sample. Without leaking information regarding your intent and its political/social/religious motivation, you risk the attack being depicted as part of a personally driven act of madness.

The leaking of intent is therefore a key indicator to keep in mind with regards to countering lone-actor terrorism. However, this information cannot be acted upon if the recipient of the leaked information does not pass this up to the relevant authorities. There could be clear barriers to this information being passed on. For example, Borum (2013: 108) posits that 'those with kinship bonds may not approve at all of the attacker's intent, but they may feel restrained from acting because of love and loyalty or concern about the consequences'. Borum further outlines that research on such reporting mechanisms shows that factors such as the presence of multiple reporting channels, anonymity, accessibility, safety, and credibility are key to successful transmission of this information. Of course, not all of the instances in which information is received about verbalized intent are viable threats or risks so instead of acting straight away, the logical next step is to engage in a risk assessment and look at the rest of the individual's behaviours with regard to their situation, capability, motivation, and opportunity to act.

Learning from other lone actors

Lone actors are often inspired by the actions of similar others. There is clearly some form of contagion effect as direct lines of lineage can be found on occasion. In 1993, Michael Griffin fatally shot an abortion clinic doctor, David Gunn. Griffin clearly inspired two co-ideologues to act similarly. The first was Shelley Shannon. A month after the shooting, Griffin received a letter from Shannon, who later went on to commit a series of arson attacks and also the shooting of an abortion clinic doctor. She wrote:

> I know you did the right thing. It was not murder. It was more like anti-murder. I believe in you and what you did, and really want to help if possible. I wish I could trade places with you.
> (Cited in Bray & Bray, 2009: 25)

The second was Paul Hill. In the immediate aftermath of Griffin killing Gunn, Hill announced himself as the new national spokesman for abortionist killers and appeared on a number of high-profile U.S. television shows. In this role, he predicted more violence would follow: 'This is going to be a watershed in the pro-life movement. I could envision a covert organization developing – something like a pro-life IRA' (cited in Liston, 1994). Hill also authored a 'Defensive Action Statement' asserting that 'if Michael Griffin did in fact kill David Gunn, his use of lethal force was justifiable provided it was carried out for the purpose of defending the lives of unborn children'.

A year later, Hill says he

> was working ... wondering who would act next [after Michael Griffin had killed an abortion clinic doctor], when the idea of taking action myself struck; it hit hard. During the next two or three hours, as I continued to work in a distracted manner, I began to consider what would happen if I were to shoot an abortionist.

Eight days after that Hill killed an abortion clinic doctor and his bodyguard.

At least two other lone-actor terrorists publicly lauded Paul Hill. During his trial for the murder of the abortion clinic doctor George Tiller,[5] Scott Roeder interrupted proceedings and loudly read from Hill's autobiography for 40 minutes. The second example is Eric Rudolph. Two years after Hill's actions, Rudolph began his bombing campaign at the Atlanta Olympics. In his autobiography, Rudolph begins the Olympics bombing chapter with two paragraphs telling the story of Paul Hill. For Rudolph, Hill

> seemed like a perfect anomaly, a genuine American hero in an age of cowardice. I'd read about such people in history books, but I didn't think they existed anymore. I knew then that the era of hot air was over. People were finally bridging the gap between their rhetoric and their actions. I knew then it was time for me to act as well.
>
> (Rudolph, 2013: 3)

Rudolph's actions, in turn, inspired another future lone-actor terrorist who did not share his ideological beliefs but was fascinated by the violence he caused. David Copeland's nail bombing campaign occurred between 17 and 30 April 1999. In total, three bombs targeted minority communities across London. The bombings occurred over three successive weekends, killing three (including a pregnant woman), and injuring a further 129. Copeland told police that he first came up with the idea of using violence when a bomb went off at the Olympic Games in Atlanta in 1996. The Notting Hill carnival[6] occurred around the same time as that bombing. According to Copeland he 'thought why, why, why can't someone blow that place up? That'd be a good one, you know, that would piss everyone off' (BBC, 2000: 9). Copeland noted that this initial thought

> kept going round, floating round my head, day after day after day. And then after a while I became that thought, you know, I was going to do it. I was going to get it out of my head, and the only way to get rid of it was to do it.
>
> (p. 3)

Copeland's actions as well as Timothy McVeigh's bombing in Oklahoma inspired other right-wing extremists also. A number of years after Copeland's campaign, police interrupted Neil Lewington's bombing plot in the U.K. At his home, police found compilations of news items and documentaries on both David Copeland and Timothy McVeigh. Similarly, on the day of Pavlo Lapshyn's bombing of a mosque in Walsall, he posted on his Facebook page that McVeigh was a 'lone hero' alongside a video and song celebrating McVeigh.

As mentioned previously, Shelley Shannon and Scott Roeder targeted the same abortion clinic doctor. In a way, George Tiller (the target) was a crime attractor that motivated lone actors sought out and became fixated upon. This type of dynamic resonates within group-based plots also (Ramzi Yousef's 1993 attack on the World Trade Center and the 9/11 attacks eight years later). Another example within the lone-actor terrorism sphere is that of Fort Hood. On 5 November 2009, Nidal Malik Hasan killed 13 people and injured over 30 others in a mass shooting at Fort Hood in Texas. Hasan served in the military as a psychiatrist and Medical Corps officer. In the build-up to Hasan's attack, he had been in touch with the radical cleric Anwar al-Awlaki over various matters. In June 2011, six months after Hasan's attack, al-Awlaki featured in an AQAP video. He stated his hope for Hasan's shootings to inspire others:

> Nidal Hasan is one of my students and I am very honoured for that.... What he did is a heroic act, a formidable operation ... I support what he did and I call upon each and everyone who claims to belong to Islam and who is serving in the American Army to follow the path of Nidal Hasan.... We ask Allah ... to make it an opportunity for Muslims to follow his lead.

In July 2012, police interrupted another plot involving a Muslim serving in the U.S. Army. Naser Abdo plotted to conduct a bombing and shooting attack against soldiers from the same army base that Hasan previously attacked. Abdo purchased weaponry in the same store Hasan had previously used. As police led Abdo away from his initial courtroom appearance, he shouted 'Nidal Hasan, Fort Hood'.

On other occasions, rather than being an inspiration, lone-actor terrorist attacks are a direct response to other similar attacks. On 25 February 1994, Baruch Goldstein shot and killed 29 worshippers at a mosque in Hebron, Palestine. The shooting occurred at the Cave of the Patriarchs, a holy site to both the Jewish and Islamic faiths. Four days later, Rashid Baz shot at a van containing 15 Orthodox Jewish students on the Brooklyn Bridge, killing one. Baz grew up in Lebanon and his mother came from Palestine. Baz's associates relayed that in the wake of the killings, Baz 'yelled' that revenge should be sought for the killings. A psychiatrist at the trial outlined that the shooting at the Cave of the Patriarchs had an 'enormous impact' on Baz's 'state of mind during that time.... He was enraged. He was absolutely furious ... I think Hebron put him from condition yellow to condition red ... I believe that were it not for Hebron this whole tragedy wouldn't have occurred' (Heilman, 2001).

Attack commission

Targeting

Some lone-actor terrorists make a clear distinction between legitimate and illegitimate targets. Seegmiller (2007: 519–520) outlines the account of Eric Rudolph who is most infamous for bombing the Atlanta Olympics in 1996. This bombing killed one civilian and injured 111. In the proceeding months, Rudolph also bombed two abortion clinics and a lesbian bar. The second abortion clinic bombing killed a security guard and critically injured a nurse. In his sentencing remarks for the abortion clinic fatalities, Rudolph commented 'I did not target them for who they were – but for what they did. What they did was participate in the murder and dismemberment of upwards of 50 children a week'. In Rudolph's eyes, these were legitimate targets. In his sentencing remarks for the Olympics bombing and in his autobiography, Rudolph refers to the victims as 'innocent civilians' and that he felt 'much remorse' because of the 'fatal decision', 'horrible mistake' and 'dangerous tactic' of planting the bomb in a crowded area, calling in an advanced bomb warning, and hoping that the area would be cleared of civilians. Reverend Michael Bray is another example. Bray conducted 10 bombings against women's health clinics and liberal advocacy groups in the mid-1980s, and later became the 'intellectual father of the extreme radical fringe of the anti-abortion movement that engages in terrorism' (Stern, 2003). In an interview with Juergensmeyer (2000: 24), Bray distinguished between the legitimacy of killing a retired abortionist ('retributive' action) and a practicing one ('defensive' action). This sense of rationally choosing between legitimate and illegitimate targets is also true of some lone actors who displayed aspects of mental illness. For example, Ted Kaczynski outlined that 'people who wilfully and knowingly promote economic growth and technical progress, in our eyes they are criminals, and if they get blown up they deserve it'.

Most of the time targeting is not random. Take Andrew Joseph Stack for example. In 2010, Stack deliberately crashed a single-engine light aircraft into an Internal Revenue Service (IRS) field office in Austin, Texas. Stack had a number of conflicts with the IRS, the earliest dated back to the mid-1980s. During this time, Stack and his wife formed a Universal Life Church Incorporated branch. The Internal Revenue Service (IRS) declared it an illegal tax shelter. In turn, the Stacks sued the U.S. government in order to defend the church's tax-exempt status. In the six-page manifesto that Stack published online the day of his attack, he recounts these initial conflicts:

> We carefully studied the law (with the help of some of the 'best', high-paid, experienced tax lawyers in the business) ... and then began to do exactly what the 'big boys' were doing (except that we weren't steeling [sic] from our congregation or lying to the government about our massive profits in the name of God). The intent of this exercise and our efforts was to bring about

a much-needed re-evaluation of the laws that allow the monsters of organized religion to make such a mockery of people who earn an honest living.

In effect, Stack was arguing against the constitutionality of the tax code. These attempts to diminish his tax liability altogether, ended up with a large fine and imprisonment for Stack. Within his note, he outlines that this 'little lesson in patriotism cost me $40,000+, 10 years of my life, and set my retirement plans back to 0.' Around the same time as the IRS challenged his church's tax status, the U.S. federal tax code was changed in such a way that software engineers (amongst other professions) like Stack were now classified as employees rather than self-employed workers which deprived certain tax deductions. Stack took this personally.

> The bottom line is that they may as well have put my name right in the text [of the legislation]. Moreover, they could only have been more blunt if they would have came out and directly declared me a criminal and non-citizen slave. Twenty years later, I still can't believe my eyes.

During the 1990s, Stack's relationship with state and federal tax did not improve. He failed to file a state tax return in 1994. His companies were suspended for this reason.

> To survive, I was forced to cannibalize my savings and retirement.... This came in a year with mammoth expenses and not a single dollar of income. I filed no return that year thinking that because I didn't have any income there was no need. The sleazy government decided that they disagreed. But they didn't notify me in time for me to launch a legal objection so when I attempted to get a protest filed with the court I was told I was no longer entitled to due process because the time to file ran out. Bend over for another $10,000 helping of justice.

Stack turned to professional accountants to help him through these difficulties. He refers to this as 'a very big mistake' as they failed to report his wife's income.

> I spent my entire life trying to believe it wasn't so, but violence not only is the answer, it is the only answer. I saw it written once that the definition of insanity is repeating the same process over and over and expecting the outcome to suddenly be different. I am finally ready to stop this insanity. Well, Mr. Big Brother IRS man, let's try something different; take my pound of flesh and sleep well.

Naser Abdo plotted to attack Fort Campbell in Kentucky, the location that he had previously been based before going AWOL following his charge for child pornography possession. On 3 July 2011, Abdo's attempt to buy firearms from a store near Fort Campbell proved unsuccessful. He planned to 'kidnap and video tape the execution of a high ranking member of my chain of command, who participated in the Afghan mission'. The president of the chain of stores outlined that Abdo 'exhibited behavior that alerted our staff and our staff refused to, based upon that behavior, sell him a firearm' (Stengle, 2011). Abdo felt that this information would leak back to his military superiors so he went AWOL. Later that month and 800 miles away, Abdo successfully purchased firearms at a gun store close to Fort Hood in Texas but again his behaviour was so suspicious that the clerks at the store tipped off police.

For others, their targeting is sparked by opportunity. Sean Gillespie filmed himself firebombing a Jewish Temple. Prior to the bombing, the video captures Gillespie driving around Oklahoma City looking for a target of opportunity. When interviewed by the FBI, Gillespie told them that he initially planned to bomb the address belonging to a Jewish-sounding surname that he found in the phonebook. This plan was abandoned when he couldn't find the address.

Poor tradecraft

A common theme running through some of the more alarmist books or articles on 'lone wolf terrorism' inflates their technical capabilities. While undoubtedly, some lone-actor events displayed much malevolent creativity and innovation, many show poor tradecraft. Stuart Christie, the man who tried to assassinate General Franco, received his explosive device from a bomb-maker in Paris. Christie's autobiography outlines the moments he spent in the bomb-makers apartment:

> Being thirsty, I went to the sink for water, and was about to put a glass to my lips when the chemist [the bombmaker) turned round and saw what I was doing. He shouted at me to stop and rushed across, removing the glass carefully from my hands, explaining that it had just been used for measuring pure sulphuric acid. Shaken, I stood back to lean on the sideboard and went to light a cigarette. This triggered another equally volcanic reaction from the chemist as he explained that the sideboard drawer was full of detonators.

Another example is Paul Ross Evans who attempted a series of bombings against various targets he deemed to be anti-Christian. When he set out to engage in violence, Evans acknowledges that he

> possessed very little knowledge concerning the improvised construction of explosives, improvised incendiary powder mixes, and various triggering mechanisms (especially for mail bomb devices). I did, however, have a basic knowledge of chemistry, and had even created some small explosive devices in my mischievous late teen years.

He first targeted the First Church of Satan in San Francisco with a mail bomb device. Evans relays that:

In the following weeks, I paid close attention to the media, via the Internet, especially in the San Francisco area.... But no news came from the west coast about the bombing. It was as if nothing had ever happened. I became frustrated by the silence.

A second attempted mail bombing also generated no media interest. Both IEDs apparently became redirected to a postal recovery centre and became defused. Next, Evans experimented with a timed detonator and targeted a sex shop. After he placed it in a rubbish bin outside the shop, Evans believes that 'some of the wiring had torn loose when I left it'. The IED failed to detonate. Next Evans attempted to utilize a fuse-detonated IED on a pornographic cinema. What follows is Evans' full account of this attempt:

> The massive IED that I placed near the corner of the building had a fuse detonator. I lit a cigarette, taking care to keep the butt free of any DNA, and attached it to the fuse. This was a tactic used by Special Forces in the Vietnam war. I hoped to cripple a corner of the building and to rain shrapnel on the cars parked beside it. It did not take, and as I walked back to my car, which I had parked a short distance up the road, a police officer passed by me close. It was very late at night, and upon reflection, I'm certain that had the bomb exploded, I would have been caught immediately. The next day I returned, planning to light the fuse directly with a cigarette lighter and destroy the building, but when I got there, the bomb was gone. I saw the packaging, but it looked light, and had been moved. Agents later told me that they "think the bomb was stolen by the homeless living in that area" to make fires. That seems rather humorous, but at the time it didn't. My guess is as good as theirs. I was quite surprised to find the bomb disturbed as I approached that day to finish what I had started. Bic lighter in hand, I stood near the scene, frozen for a moment. I could only suspect that a night watchman had discovered the bomb and had called in agents, and that a team of them were now studying me from the nearby forest. I left the scene and spent a paranoid next few days wondering if I were being followed and kept under surveillance.

Finally Evans targeted an abortion clinic in Austin but 'something inside that package had obstructed the wiring, causing the timer to stop three to five minutes before the inevitable massive explosion' (Evans). These examples, coupled with the fact that many fail to carry out their 'Plan A' is indicative of the fact that typically most lone-actor plots should be deemed a 'low probability, low impact' risk rather than the 'low probability, high impact' risk promulgated by some corners (see Simon, 2013).

Crystallization of risk

In trying to explain acts of lone-actor terrorism, there is a tendency to reach for mono-causal master narrative explanations. Take President Obama's words on the subject as an illustration:

66 The behavioural underpinnings

> The biggest concern we have right now is not the launching of a major terrorist operation ... the risk that we're especially concerned over right now is the lone wolf terrorist, somebody with a single weapon being able to carry out wide-scale massacres.... You know, when you've got one person *who is deranged or driven by a hateful ideology*, they can do a lot of damage.
>
> (Obama, 2001, emphasis added)

'Deranged or driven by a hateful ideology' is a perfect example of two master narratives that are often proffered and treated as being mutually exclusive. The individual actor is either deranged, unbalanced, unhinged, disturbed, mad, crazy, nuts, and unstable (take your pick) OR he/she is driven by a hateful ideology, radicalized, politically focused, determined to effect political change. In the days that follow a lone-actor event, the framing of the individual's motivation usually takes on one of these two narratives. The chosen narrative depends upon the easy availability of information regarding their ideological content, mental health history, or personal background details. The take home point from the last two chapters is to avoid such master narratives. Lone-actor terrorism is usually the culmination of a complex mix of personal, political, and social drivers that crystallize at the same time to drive the individual down the path of violent action. Whether the violence comes to fruition is usually a combination of the availability and vulnerability of suitable targets that suit the heady mix of personal and political grievances and the individual's capability to engage in an attack from both a psychological and technical capability standpoint. We now turn to seven short case studies that illustrate these points clearly. These examples span the ideological spectrum and include al-Qaeda inspired actors (one U.K., one U.S.), a black nationalist, a pro-Palestinian actor, an environmentalist, and an anti-abortionist.

In July 2011, police interrupted Naser Abdo's plot to engage in a multiple IED and shooting attack against serving U.S. Army members close to Fort Hood, Texas. Abdo was 21 at the time of his arrest. Abdo's parents divorced when he was three years old. Abdo grew up with his father. In 2004, police arrested Abdo's father for soliciting sex online from a police officer posing as a 15-year-old girl. Neighbours referred to Abdo as 'weird', someone who 'didn't fit in' (Stengle, 2011). In 2007, Abdo converted to Islam aged 17. At age 18, he enrolled in a mass communication programme at the American University of Dubai but dropped out after a year. Around this time, he spent a lot of time at the Dallas Central Mosque and was briefly employed there. He was quickly fired for 'abnormal' behaviour (Finn & Fordham, 2011). Without alternative job prospects, he joined the U.S. military soon after in March 2009. Over the coming months he endured insults and threats from fellow soldiers during his basic and advanced training because of his religious beliefs. He became more reclusive as a result. He also struggled to make his daily prayers and observe Ramadan fasting during this time. In November 2009, Nidal Malik Hasan, a fellow Muslim serving in the U.S. military engaged in mass casualty shooting attack at Fort Hood. In the aftermath of this shooting, Abdo sent an essay to Associated Press in which he said that such violence ran 'counter to what I believe in as a Muslim'. In February 2010, Abdo's father was deported to Jordan following his prior conviction. Around the same time, Abdo began to study Islam more closely looking for an answer as to whether his deployment in battle could be justified. In an interview with couragetoresist.com, a website that supports troops refusing to deploy, Abdo stated that: 'As I studied Islam and Islam's commitment to peace, I developed an entirely new perspective on war and conscience.... That's when I realized my conscience would not allow me to deploy'. In June 2010, Abdo sought conscientious objector status to deployment in Afghanistan, which eventually proved successful. While seeking this status, Adbo displayed 'very anti-American, anti-Western, anti-Army' views to an NGO whose help he sought (Finn & Fordham, 2011). In May 2011, he was charged with possession of child pornography on his government-issued computer. On 21 June, Abdo announced on Facebook that 'after this update I will be leaving'. On 3 July, Abdo attempted to buy firearms in a gun store close to Fort Campbell (where he had been stationed) but workers at the store refused to sell anything to him based on his strange behaviour. If the purchase was successful his plan was to 'kidnap and video tape the execution of a high ranking member of my chain of command, who participated in the Afghan mission'. On 4 July, Abdo went AWOL. Later that month, Abdo travelled 800 miles to buy firearms close to Fort Hood whereupon police arrested him soon after. At some point from January 2010 onwards, Abdo consumed al-Qaeda propaganda including *Inspire* magazine, which showed him how to make IEDs.

In Abdo's case, we almost see a path dependent situation. The decisions he faces at any given point in this chain are limited by the decisions he made in the past. Abdo suffered from family problems that in turn led to social problems, which in turn led to a religious conversion, dropping out of University, and losing his job. Without a job, he joined the military. There, he endured insults for his religious beliefs, which in turn led to further social problems. He becomes aware of a very successful lone-actor terrorist that shares many of his current life circumstances. He intensifies both his religious and political views soon after and his political grievances become overt. Around the same time, and possibly linked to his social problems, he is caught engaging in illegal activity (child pornography) and now has a deeper personal grievance against those who charged him. He attempts to gain capability for a copycat attack of the lone-actor that preceded his religious and political intensification. After that fails, he tries travelling to Fort Hood, the scene of the previous lone-actor attack. In effect, personal problems led to his conversion, the intensification of his beliefs and the timing of his attack plans. The intensification of these beliefs and the awareness of Hasan's actions provided Abdo with a script of who to target and how to carry it out.

On 7 December 1993, black nationalist Colin Ferguson fatally shot six passengers on-board the Long Island Rail Road and injured a further 19. A *New York Times* feature on Ferguson's life noted that law-enforcement officials trying to penetrate his mind and motives say he apparently planned the attack for weeks, working out the fine details.... It was, in a kind of twisted logic, one of the few events in his life that went off as planned.

(McFadden, 1993)

His slide toward violence was long and characterized by the crystallization of a number of factors. Born in Kingston, Jamaica, to a wealthy family, Ferguson suffered the unexpected loss of both parents in early adulthood. The deaths ruined the family's wealth and privilege. In 1982, at the age of 24, he moved to California. Acquaintances remembered him as 'brash, arrogant, disdainful of the menial jobs he found, and critical of whites and even blacks who were not militant enough. Easily offended ... he often twisted meanings to create racial issues where none was intended' (McFadden, 1993). He soon took to carrying a gun with him at all times after being victimized in a robbery. In 1986 he moved to Long Island and soon married. There, Ferguson became more fixated on the racism he felt he experienced in all situations. In 1988, his wife divorced him 'in what acquaintances called a crushing blow to a psychologically fragile man' (McFadden, 1993). In 1989, Ferguson suffered a serious injury at work and lost his job. He received $75 a week compensation. In 1990, he enrolled in a Community College, made Dean's list three times but was later forced to leave due to being overly aggressive toward a teacher. He then enrolled with Adelphi University and was suspended within a year for a series of racial threats. Over the proceeding couple of years, his ex-wife, his lawyers, and officials at the New York State workers' compensation board also took steps to protect themselves against Ferguson's increasingly erratic behaviour. In April 1992, police officers arrested Ferguson for an altercation with a white woman on the New York subway that involved Ferguson making pejorative racial comments and physically hurting the victim. Ferguson was found guilty of harassment. A year later, when he was arrested for the fatal shootings a note in his pocket outlined the 'reasons for this' act of mass violence. One of the reasons cited 'the false allegations against me by the filthy Caucasian racist female on the #1 line'. Around the same time as this arrest, Ferguson sought a larger lump sum payment to replace the $75 a week cheques he received as compensation. In September 1992, a settlement was achieved and he was awarded $26,250 minus the $4,800 he already received in weekly amounts. Within seven months, he sought to reopen the case looking for more money. Around the same time (April 1993), he moved back to California searching for new career opportunities but was unsuccessful. In California, he bought the Ruger pistol he later utilized in the mass shooting. Within a month, he moved back to New York. His landlord noticed that Ferguson's rants about racism became more strident and resembled 'some apocryphal-type doom scenario' (McFadden, 1993). In September 1993, Ferguson received word that his application to reopen his case was being processed. He pressed the matter further, calling two to three times a day. In October 1993, the board reopened the case and asked Ferguson to go for a medical re-evaluation. Ferguson refused and the board denied the application. He began taking five showers a day and neighbours repeatedly heard him chanting 'all the black people killing all the white people'. Concerned about this behaviour, Ferguson's landlord (who he was close to) asked him to move out. Two months later, Ferguson engaged in a mass shooting at the scene of one of his previous offences.

In Ferguson, we have a different trajectory to that of Abdo but one that still mixes a number of personal life problems and the development of a grievance against society. Ferguson's ideological adoption and intensification largely came about through his early experiences of victimization in the United States, which would never have occurred if he had not moved there because of a mixture of familial and financial difficulties. The move to Long Island preceded a fixation with the racism he felt he experienced. This in turn led to a divorce, which quickly followed injury and job loss. Only then did his beliefs become threatening to others, which led to further problems (being expelled from two universities and the altercation on the train that he cites in his justification message). Further financial problems occurred parallel to a growth in his ideological intensification which also led to a further downturn in his personal circumstances when he was kicked out of his apartment. Soon after, he engaged in the shooting spree.

Hesham Mohamed Hadayet carried out the July 2002 shooting at Los Angeles International Airport. An Egyptian national, he targeted the ticket counter of Israel's national airline, killing two and injuring four. In 1997, Hadayet set up a Limousine service that ran services from a number of airports including Los Angeles International Airport. Some colleagues and associates remember Hadayet making anti-Israeli and anti-Semitic remarks. Neighbours say Hadayet complained about the large U.S. flag hung outside their apartment complex. The FBI investigation into the killings pictured Hadayet as an increasingly militant supporter of the Palestinian cause and that he openly supported the killings of civilians in furtherance of the cause. In August 2001, state authorities revoked the company's license because Hadayet failed to provide proof of insurance. Hadayet continued trading until at least October 2001. Hadayet also struggled to cover the public liability insurance payments during this time. Two weeks before the shooting, his wife and two children moved back to Egypt. Hadayet was $10,000 in debt at the time of the shooting and the FBI report outlines Hadayet's depression on his birthday, the day of the shooting attack.

The Hadayet example runs almost contrary to the previous two cases. The previous two cases show how personal problems led to a turn towards ideological intensification. Here, we have an individual who is seemingly very well functioning and successful. Alongside this success, he holds extremist ideas (but not necessarily the compulsion to act violently upon them). These extremist ideas intensified over a period of time but the intent to act upon them violently only occurred following financial, familial, and personal difficulties. The attack location was not random. Instead it occurred at a location that Hadayet had personal experience of through his former company before state authorities discontinued it.

Police interrupted Andrew 'Isa' Ibrahim's (at the time 19 years old) production of a suicide bombing vest in 2008. Despite coming from a wealthy background, Ibrahim engaged in a series of troublesome behaviours from a young age. By the age of 12, Ibrahim had been expelled from two schools. The latter expulsion was for smoking cannabis on school property. He was later expelled from a third school for drinking alcohol. He eventually left school altogether at 16. By then he was using heroin and crack cocaine. Soon after he received three police warnings (two for shoplifting and one for heroin possession). In mid-2006, he converted to Islam. In late 2006, he declared himself homeless. In early 2007, he began wearing the traditional Islamic dress and changed his name from Andrew to Isa by deed-poll. He returned to full-time education and attempted to finish his secondary schooling. One of his teachers reported him to school authorities for asking what kind of bacteria could be used to kill people. In a newspaper interview, the chief investigating officer on the case argued that Christmas 2007 was a turning point for Ibrahim: 'He might have had an argument with his Mum and Dad, there seems to be a watershed where he had dabbled and had a look at things on the internet, to where it suddenly rises sharply after Christmas' (cited in Ballinger, 2009). Ibrahim moved into a one-bedroom flat and used this as the location to search for information on bomb-making and eventually to build the suicide bomb vest.

Ibrahim's case is more similar to that of Ferguson and Abdo. He experienced a lot of behavioural problems, which in turn led to problems within his family life and at school. He converted to Islam and things appeared to be improving for him. Suspicious behaviour upon his return to school and a family argument directly preceded a sudden rise in his intensification and attack planning.

On Christmas Day 2009, Umar Farouk Abdulmutallab failed to blow up a plane destined for Detroit from Amsterdam. In internet postings during his teenage years while he attended a boarding school, Abdulmutallab confessed:

> I am in a situation where I do not have a friend. I have no one to speak too, no one to consult, no one to support me and I feel depressed and lonely. I do not know what to do and then I think this loneliness leads me to other problems ... I get lonely sometimes because I have never found a true Muslim friend.

During these years, he became more pious and earned the nickname of 'Muslim scholar' amongst classmates. In 2005, he moved to England to study mechanical engineering at University College London. It is alleged that his turn towards radical Islam became more entrenched during this time. He became the president of the University's Islamic Society within a year and hosted a series of radical preachers and former Guantanamo Bay inmates. He graduated in 2008 and then attended a graduate level business course in Dubai, which he dropped out of in August 2009 against his father's wishes. He tried to return to England but the relevant authorities turned down his visa request. He then travelled to Yemen. In

November 2009, while Abdulmutallab spent time in Yemen, his father alerted the intelligence services of his son's growing radicalization.

Abdulmutallab's story should, by now, appear familiar. Early personal problems led to a growing sense of social isolation followed by a deeper immersion in religious beliefs, a move to a new location, an intensification of these beliefs, and a growing network of co-ideologues.

In September 2010, James Lee, an environmental activist, took hostages at the Discovery Channel with starter pistols and homemade pipe bombs. Lee's activism began two years prior, immediately after losing his job in San Diego and reading a novel authored by Daniel Quinn entitled *Ishmael*. The book tells the story of a gorilla who recounts how the plundering of natural resources affected his life in captivity. In an interview following a prior arrest Lee recounted the reading of this book as an 'awakening'. After watching Al Gore's *An Inconvenient Truth* he decided he was not doing enough to protect the environment. During this time, Lee was also periodically homeless following the loss of his job. Around this time, he also set up a website that promulgated his views, highlighted TV show ideas of his, and encouraged others to participate in pitching shows to Discovery. Here, Lee also published an essay aimed at the Discovery Channel telling them: 'The world needs TV shows that DEVELOP solutions to the problems that humans are causing, not stupefy the people into destroying the world. Not encouraging them to breed more environmentally harmful humans'. In this essay, Lee makes 11 demands. The first demand is as follows:

> The Discovery Channel and it's affiliate channels MUST have daily television programs at prime time slots based on Daniel Quinn's 'My Ishmael' pages 207–212 where solutions to save the planet would be done in the same way as the Industrial Revolution was done, by people building on each other's inventive ideas.

In February 2008, police charged Lee with disorderly conduct after he staged a protest at the Discovery Channel. He was later convicted and served two weeks jail time. He was also ordered to keep 500 feet away from the Discovery headquarters as part of his probation. This court order lapsed two weeks prior to his eventual violent attack.

In Lee, we have a case where an unfortunate change in personal life circumstance coincided with the consumption of material that helped frame his later activism. Unlike the other cases where a long series of events appeared to chain together, this is a very simple case. However, we still see this mixture of personal and political circumstances combining that eventually become more radical over time in their outward expression.

On 31 May 2009, Scott Roeder fatally shot Dr. George Tiller who was known as one of the few doctors in the United States that performed late-term abortions. Roeder was 51 at the time of the shooting. Over 30 years prior, doctors diagnosed him with schizophrenia. In a highly publicized television interview, Roeder's wife outlined the tipping point into Roeder's activism.

It was about 1991–92 when he basically couldn't cope with everyday life. He couldn't make ends meet, he couldn't pay the bills and didn't know why he couldn't do that. And someone told him that if he didn't pay his federal taxes, if those taxes were left in his check, he could make ends meet. And then he started investigating that and someone told him that it wasn't ratified properly in the Constitution, that it was illegal. And he went from there and got into the anti-government, got into the militia, got into the Freeman, and along those lines anti-abortion issues came up and he started becoming very religious in the sense that he ... was reading the Bible. But then, after we were divorced, his religion took on a whole new right wing of itself.

After this point, he became very active in a number of different movements including anti-government Montana Freeman group and the Sovereign Citizen Movement. His ex-wife continues: 'And that's when he really began to meet people. It was shortly after that that he started talking about Paul Hill and how Paul Hill had killed a doctor in Florida and [how] that was great. That was wonderful'. Roeder also started visiting the convicted Shelley Shannon in prison. Some reports say he visited Shannon up to 25 times. Shannon, of course, injured Dr. George Tiller in 1993 – around the same time that Roeder became more deeply embedded within anti-abortion circles. His wife recounts that:

He started talking about how it was murder. That these doctors were murdering babies. If they're going to murder the babies, well, we're going to murder them. If they kill, then they should be killed. It was hard to live with. Nick went to school one morning. I went to work. I came home and Scott was gone. Money was gone. His clothes were gone. He was just gone.

Roeder then became more immersed with the Montana Freeman group.

This account is far more nuanced than the one Roeder himself provided during his trial. 'Yes. I had been watching "The 700 Club" regularly, a Christian program. I was alone in my living room, and that day I kneeled down and I did accept Christ as my savior'. In 1995, his family grew concerned for his mental health and tried to have him committed but Roeder refused. In 1996, he received 24-months probation after police found explosives charges, a fuse cord, a pound of gunpowder, and nine-volt batteries in his car. Very soon after, he became divorced from his wife. A year later, his failure to pay taxes led to the probation being revoked and he was sentenced to 16 months in prison. He successfully appealed the original conviction on the basis of the search on his vehicle being illegal.

In 2007, a poster called 'Scott Roeder' left the following message on an anti-abortion website: 'Tiller is the concentration camp "Mengele" of our day and needs to be stopped before he and those who protect him bring judgment upon our nation'. In 2009, Tiller stood trial for violating state abortion laws. He faced 19 misdemeanour counts connected to an alleged illegal financial relationship with a physician who had approved a number of late-term procedures conducted by Tiller. Roeder attended the trial almost every day. After less than half an hour deliberations, the jury acquitted Tiller. Roeder called this decision a 'sham' and claimed that 'There was nothing being done and the legal process had been exhausted and these babies were dying every day. So, I felt that I needed to act and quickly for those children'.

Unlike the previous cases, Roeder had a long history of involvement with co-ideologues. The initial non-violent involvement came through a mixture of financial problems that Roeder turned into a political grievance against the government. Within those circles, Roeder's religion became more important to him and he began his anti-abortion activism. One of the individuals he met with frequently was Shelley Shannon who previously tried to kill Tiller. It is clear from Roeder's internet postings, he fixated on Tiller as a target. It was only after Roeder witnessed Tiller being freed by the courts, that Roeder decided to act violently.

Each of these cases share a mixture of unfortunate personal life circumstances coupled with an intensification of beliefs that later developed into the idea to engage in violence. What differed was how these influences were sequenced. Sometimes personal problems led to a susceptibility to ideological influences. Sometimes long-held ideological influences became intensified after the experience of personal problems. This is why we should be wary of mono-causal master narratives. The truth is usually far more complex. An understanding of this complexity and the multiplicity of potential factors could help inform how risk assessments of particular lone actors should be carried out. When we talk about 'risk', we need to ask the question – 'risk of what?' The illustrations highlight that the target and/or target location of the violence was usually associated with something to do with the individual's personal grievance. This may help give us a sense of the capabilities the individual needs to become a threat. These illustrations also highlight the fact that we need to view risk dynamically. Given a set of circumstances and conditions, an individual may appear to be no or low risk. However, small changes in their life-course, personal circumstances, or opportunity to offend can have a force-multiplier effect and propel the individual into a higher category of risk. Risk assessments should therefore be carried out periodically on people of interest even if the initial assessment is low risk.

Notes

1 All of the following information is available in Aldawsari's indictment documentation and the trial's closing statements.
2 Abortions were only carried out on Fridays at this location.
3 Cited in the government's sentencing memorandum – http://msnbcmedia.msn.com/i/MSNBC/Sections/NEWS/z-pdf-archive/20130919_Corkins_Sentencing.pdf.
4 A Chick-fil-A executive, two months earlier, had expressed his opposition to same-sex marriage.
5 Shelley Shannon herself had previously targeted Tiller also.
6 This carnival celebrates London's multicultural diversity.

References

Ballinger, L. (2009). How a Public Schoolboy was Turned into a Muslim Terrorist by Online Hate Preachers. *Daily Mail*, 17 July 2009.

Beasley, J. O., Hayne, A. S., Beyer, K., Cramer, G. L., Berson, S. B., Muirhead, Y., & Warren, J. I. (2009). Patterns of prior offending by child abductors: A comparison of fatal and non-fatal outcomes. *International journal of law and psychiatry, 32*(5), 273–280.

Betley, P. (2013) The Continuum of Aloneness, Direction, Ideology and Motivation: Identifying the Behaviours in the Dimensions of Islamic Lone Actor Terrorism. Unpublished Dissertation.

Borum, R. (2013). Informing Lone-Offender Investigations. *Criminology & Public Policy, 12*(1), 103–112.

Bouhana, N., & Wikstrom, P. O. (2011). Al Qai'da-Influenced Radicalisation: A Rapid Evidence Assessment Guided by Situational Action Theory. Retrieved from: www.gov.uk/government/uploads/system/uploads/attachment_data/file/116724/occ97.pdf. Accessed 1 June 2014.

Bray, M., & Bray, J. (2009). Tiller's Unheeded Warning: The Shelley Shannon Story. Retrieved from: www.armyofgod.com/POCShelleyShannonBookMikeBray.html. Accessed 1 June 2014.

Briar, S., & Piliavin, I. (1965). Delinquency, situational inducements, and commitment to conformity. *Social Problems, 13*, 35.

Cohen, L. E., & Felson, M. (1979). Social change and crime rate trends: A routine activity approach. *American sociological review*, 588–608.

Competency Evaluation for Abdulhakim Mujahid Muhammad. Retrieved from: www.commercialappeal.com/jihad/competency-evaluation/. Accessed 5 April 2014.

Delisi, M., Hochstetler, A., Scherer, A. M., Purhmann, A., & Berg, M. T. (2008). The Starkweather Syndrome: exploring criminal history antecedents of homicidal crime sprees 1. *Criminal Justice Studies, 21*(1), 37–47.

Evans, P. R. (Unspecified Year). Methodical Terrorism: How and Why. Retrieved from: www.armyofgod.com/POCPaulRossEvansMethodicalTerrorism.html. Accessed 6 October 2014.

Fein, R. A., & Vossekuil, B. (1999). Assassination in the United States: an operational study of recent assassins, attackers, and near-lethal approachers. *Journal of Forensic Sciences, 44*(2), 321–333.

Gartenstein-Ross, D. (2014). Lone Wolf Islamic Terrorism: Abdulhakim Mujahid Muhammad (Carlos Bledsoe) Case Study. *Terrorism and Political Violence, 26*(1), 110–128.

Heilman, U. (2001). Murder on the Brooklyn Bridge. *The Middle East Quarterly.* Retrieved from: www.meforum.org/77/murder-on-the-brooklyn-bridge. Accessed 1 June 2014.

Hill, P. J. (2003). Defending the Defenseless. Retrieved from: www.armyofgod.com/PHill_ShortShot.html. Accessed 6 October 2014.

Juergensmeyer, M. (2000). *Terror in the Mind of God*. California: University of California Press.

Liston, B. (1994, 7 March). After Conviction, Still Fears of Clinic Violence. *USA Today.*

Meloy, J. R., & O'Toole, M. E. (2011). The concept of leakage in threat assessment. *Behavioral sciences & the law, 29*(4), 513–527.

Obama, B. (2011). Biggest terror fear is the lone wolf. Retrieved from: http://security.

blogs.cnn.com/2011/08/16/obama-biggest-terror-fear-is-the-lone-wolf/). Accessed 1 June 2014.

Osgood, D. W., Wilson, J. K., O'Malley, P. M., Bachman, J. G., & Johnston, L. D. (1996). Routine activities and individual deviant behavior. *American Sociological Review*, 635–655.

Roach, J. (2007). Those who do big bad things also usually do little bad things: Identifying active serious offenders using offender self-selection. *International Journal of Police Science & Management*, 9(1), 66–79.

Rudolph, E. (2013). Between the Lines of Drift: The Memoirs of a Militant. Retrieved from: www.armyofgod.com/EricRudolphHomepage.html. Accessed 1 June 2014.

Seegmiller, B. (2007). Radicalized Margins: Eric Rudolph and Religious Violence 1. *Terrorism and Political Violence*, 19(4), 511–528.

Sharpe, M. (2008, 6 July). Mum Slams Caged Child Porn Beast. *Sunday Star*.

Simon, J. D. (2013). *Lone Wolf Terrorism: Understanding the Growing Threat*. New York, NY: Prometheus Books.

Soothill, K., Francis, B., & Liu, J. (2008). Does serious offending lead to homicide? Exploring the interrelationships and sequencing of serious crime. *British Journal of Criminology*, 48(4), 522–537.

Stengle, J. (2011, 29 July 2011). Army: AWOL Soldier Admits to Fort Hood Attack Plan. *The Associated Press*.

Stern, J. (2003). *Terror in the name of God: Why religious militants kill*. New York: Ecco.

Trial Transcript of Closing Argument and Jury Charge Reading. (Unspecified Year). Retrieved from: http://multimedia.lubbockonline.com/pdfs/aldawsari/aldawsariclosingtranscript.pdf. Accessed 6 October 2014.

Vossekuil, B., Fein, R. A., Reddy, M., Borum, R., & Modzeleski, W. (2002). The final report and findings of the Safe School Initiative. Washington D.C.: US Secret Service and Department of Education.

4 Why go it alone?

The evidence suggests that the assumed image of the lone-actor terrorist conducting every aspect of his/her radicalization, attack planning, and preparation without any aid or interaction is largely misguided. The true loners are few and far between. Although they engage in the violence by themselves, most of the sample consumed and accepted a broad legitimating ideology and call to arms of others, were enabled by the provision of safe spaces to psychologically and physically prepare for engagement in violence, and a smaller number received some form of training or material support. So, if the majority had some form of interaction at one point in their ideological adoption, ideological intensification, or attack planning/preparation, it begs the question why are they doing the actual attack alone? Why would an individual purposefully cede the 'easier' option of a collaboration that could be more advantageous in terms of additional skill sets and increased efficiencies (Felson, 2003)? These questions are all the more important because the existing data suggests that the usual strategic answer that is offered ('they attack alone to maximize personal security and thereby avoid detection') is invalid because the majority of these actors readily interact with others (face-to-face and virtually) and regularly leak key details of the actual attack itself. Other possible answers regarding going it alone such as the fear or betrayal or the lack of trust in potential co-offenders are invalid for the same reason. So what other dynamics could be at play here?

Situational drivers

Some clues to the answer may be available within the wider study of crime where the study of co-offending (or lack thereof) has witnessed a recent resurgence (Stolzenberg & D'Alessio, 2008; D'Alessio & Stolzenberg, 2010; Van Mastrigt & Farrington, 2009, 2011; McGloin & Stickle, 2011; McGloin & Nguyen, 2012, 2013; Carrington & Van Mastrigt, 2013; Tillyer & Tillyer, 2014; Schaefer, Rodriguez & Decker, 2014). A very common finding is that the peak years of co-offending are in early adolescence. Co-offending then slowly ebbs away over the life-course. Remember that our lone-actor terrorist sample is on the older side of the offending equation with the mean age in the mid-30s so this factor could be one very simple yet non-obvious explanation. It may simply be the case that the older cohort did not have the same opportunities afforded to younger would-be offenders and are not influenced by the same dynamics such as charismatic leaders and/or peer pressure. In the remaining sections, we outline a series of illustrations showing that the degree to which lone actors had the ability to co-offend (through the level of interaction with co-ideologues) differed widely. The reasons for why they remained a lone actor differ substantially. As we will see, many never sought out to be a lone actor in the first place, many framed their actions as part of a wider group or movement and many others claimed their act of violence in the name of a group of which they themselves were the sole member.

Framing issues

There is of course the possibility that many of the sample viewed themselves as group actors. Perhaps their conception of what a 'group' entails is far wider than the sort of one-man operational cell that brought them into the dataset in the first place. Indeed, 46% characterized their actions on behalf of a group and 41% did interact face-to-face with members of a wider network; 23% received training from an established terrorist group. One example is that of Umar Farouk Abdulmutallab, who boarded a plane from Amsterdam to Detroit carrying an IED. The device ignited but failed to detonate fully before staff and other travellers managed to subdue Abdulmutallab and quenched the flames. Abdulmutallab's court testimony highlights the degree to which he was networked; yet acted alone.

> I agreed with at least one person to carry an explosive device onto an aircraft and attempt to kill those on-board and wreck the aircraft as an act of jihad ... I was greatly inspired to participate in jihad by the lectures of the great ... Anwar al-Awlaki.

In the aftermath of his failed attack, AQAP released a video of a desert training camp in Yemen. Abdulmutallab is recorded on a firing range shooting targets such as a Jewish star and the British Union Jack flag.

Others received some form of facilitative help. Taimour Abdulwahab al-Abdaly blew himself up on a crowded Stockholm street in December 2010. Some doubts exist whether this was an intentional suicide bombing or not. Evidence suggests that the technology for a remote detonation of the devices on his body were found closeby. Prior to this attack, al-Abdaly resided in England and attended a mosque in Luton in late 2006 and early 2007. During this time, he made statements focused on 'suicide bombings, pronouncing Muslim leaders to be disbelievers, denouncing Muslim governments' and was confronted by mosque elders (Lawless & Rising, 2010). He also depicted his actions of that of a group. The audio message sent minutes before the bombing announced: 'We now exist in Europe and Sweden. We are a reality. I don't want to say more about this. Our actions will speak for themselves'. The day after his apparent suicide bombing, his martyrdom video appeared online. This suggests he possessed some form of facilitative help. Early investigations focused upon the role of his wife. He also received bomb-making training in Iraq for months. The training occurred a year before the bombing (Cruickshank, Lister, & Nyberg, 2011).

Some of the sample were deeply embedded within a wider movement of individuals before engaging in violence by themselves. Take the actions of Eric Rudolph for example. Over the course of 18 months, Rudolph bombed two abortion clinics, the Atlanta Olympics, and a lesbian bar. He carried out all of the planning, preparation, and actions alone. Yet, in his numerous writings throughout the bombing campaign, during his sentencing and while in prison, Rudolph depicts himself as part of a wider movement of anti-abortion activists. As noted by Seegmiller (2007), between 1973 (when abortion was legalized in the U.S.) and 2007, over 200 abortion clinics were bombed or set on fire and over 4,000 acts of violence were carried out or threatened against abortion providers. Rudolph sees himself as just one component of what is a wider movement of committed action. He 'frames his activism and identity as connected to an amorphous milieu of violent, radical anti-abortion activists who largely draw upon religious authority, biblical language, and apocalyptic narratives to frame and justify their activities' (Seegmiller, 2007: 521). Indeed, Rudolph's writings are hosted on the Army of God website including his 240-page autobiography that suggests they view him as one of their own also. The autobiography states that Rudolph's goal was to overthrow an illegitimate government but he acknowledges

> Naturally, I couldn't do it alone. I had no delusions on that score. I had to somehow encourage others to help.... The hope was that my actions would push other pro-lifers and Patriots to bridge the gap between their rhetoric and their actions.
>
> (Rudolph, 2013: 5–6)

Rudolph had also grown quite sceptical of how effective the pro-life movement had become while it remained on a non-violent course.

> The masters of the media have censored the pro-life movement out of the mainstream society. The protestors ... might as well be on the moon as far as most Americans are concerned. I was planning my own protest for the anniversary of *Roe* v. *Wade*. Unlike other protests, mine wouldn't be ignored. I planned to blow Northside Family Planning off the map.
>
> (Rudolph, 2013: 27)

Shelley Shannon is a similar example. She engaged in a high number of non-violent, yet criminal, resistance activities prior to her fatal shooting of the abortion clinic doctor George Tiller. Her biography on the Army of God website lists the following actions for which she was convicted of trespassing on abortion facilities a number of times. For example she received the following punishments:

1   June 1988 – sentenced to 24 hours community service;
2   December 1988 – sentenced to 30 days in jail;
3   April 1989 – commanded to perform community service;
4   March 1990 – sentenced to 30 hours of community service;
5   June 1990 – sentenced to 15 days in jail;
6   September 1990 – sentenced to 30 days in jail;
7   November 1991 – sent to jail for 19 days.

According to the same biography, Shannon began corresponding in 1986 with the imprisoned John Brockhoeft who had been responsible for committing arson on two abortion clinics. 'She collected his handwritten folksy writings, typed them, and published them to a list of about 200 addresses in a series of jocular, country-Kentuckian flavoured stories and reflections' (Bray & Bray, 2009: 13). She also corresponded with two other lone-actor terrorists: Curt Beseda and Michael Bray. Much later, she corresponded with Michael Griffin and made financial contributions to his defense fund. One letter read:

> I know you did the right thing. It was not murder; you shot a murderer. It was more like anti-murder. I believe in you and what you did and really want to help, if possible. I wish I could trade places with you.

Griffin, like Shannon, was also deeply involved in non-violent activism. He grew gradually disillusioned with these tactics. In a public letter to a U.S. newspaper, Griffin notes the moment he crossed the Rubicon towards violent action:

> I stood holding a sign that said 'Abortion Kills Children.' It was facing the traffic. I turned it around and read it. I looked at my child next to me, then back at the sign. 'Abortion Kills Children.' Was it true? Of course it was true; that wasn't the question. The question was, why was I standing here across the street from the abortion clinic instead of doing something?
> (Humphreys, 2007)

Something similar occurred with Shannon.

It was during the 1988 prison time that Shelley became exposed to the idea of more violent methods. She says: 'The first mention of it was in Atlanta ... when Jayne Bray came into the City Prison where pro-lifers were being held' (Bray & Bray, 2009: 12). Jayne Bray's husband was Michael Bray who conducted 10 bombings against women's health clinics and liberal advocacy groups in the mid-1980s. Shannon recalls being 'very impressed' by this meeting. By the summer of 1991, Shannon was, in her own words, 'convinced that violence was the way to further her goals' (Bray & Bray, 2009: 12). On top of these interpersonal drivers, the state of Oregon also increased the maximum sentencing for non-violent blockading of abortion clinics to five years. The new policy did not deter Shelley, instead it encouraged her to get more 'bang for her buck' (Bray & Bray, 2009: 15).

This type of behaviour was not the sole reserve of anti-abortion activists. In 2012 a jury found Dennis Mahon guilty of the 2004 mail bombing that injured a black city official in Phoenix. During the trial, prosecutors argued that the Mahon brothers bombed the official on behalf of a group called the White Aryan Resistance, which they say encourages members to act as 'lone wolves' and commit violence against non-whites and the government. Mahon had a long history of activism within these circles. In a letter filed as evidence in federal court, Dennis Mahon wrote that he led the White Knights of the KKK from 1987 to 1991. A 1991 story in the Associated Press outlined that Mahon had made a 'propaganda tour in Germany in late summer' that included a cross burning event. During this tour, Mahon commented on a series of attacks and firebombings against political asylum-seekers in Germany: 'I'm very pleased to see this.... Every means are justified, I mean every, to rescue your nation.' Mahon was also a leading member of Tom Metzger's White Aryan Resistance. Metzger himself is largely responsible for the diffusion of the 'lone wolf' ideal within the U.S. extreme-right. In 1992, he ran unsuccessfully for mayor of Tulsa under the slogan 'Help the White Working Man'. The journalist Jon Ronson interviewed Mahon for a television documentary entitled 'Secret Rulers of the World'. Mahon conducts his interview with a Nazi flag hanging on the wall behind him and dismisses the concerns surrounding the number of civilians killed in the Oklahoma bombing and hails Timothy McVeigh as a 'true hero'. This was not an individual who shied away from espousing his ideology publicly. In the years before his bombing attack, the newspaper *Alarming City* published Mahon's letter. This newspaper is largely described as racist, anti-Semitic, and anti-immigrant. Mahon also gave a public lecture at Aryan Fest, a white power music festival where he advocated the 'nuking' of Washington D.C.

Others were deeply embedded within an activist network via their family connections. Mohamed Merah, the French shooter, is a case in point. Merah's father adopted radical Salifism in the early 1990s. Two brothers and his sister followed suit. The sister networked within extremist circles. Investigators identified one brother in a 2008 investigation into a recruitment network in Belgium that sent foreign fighters to Iraq via Cairo. The same brother stabbed another brother seven times when he refused to leave his Jewish girlfriend. The image depicted in Merah's brother's book is of Mohamed being immersed in anti-Semitism from a young age. It was also apparent in his wider family tree. Relatives in Algeria supported the Islamic Salvation Front, which wanted to establish an Islamic state under sharia law. Some relatives joined the Islamic Group of Algeria, a terrorist organization (Andre & Harris-Hogan, 2013). One of his brothers and his sister separately announced their pride at Merah's actions after Merah died in a stand-off with French security services. Merah's mother had also got married for a second time, to a man who was later arrested in Syria in 2006 at an al-Qaeda safe house on his way to Iraq. Merah visited his stepfather in prison and sent him money. Merah regularly visited a Syrian Salifist preacher based in France (Andre & Harris-Hogan, 2013). He spent some time in Afghanistan in 2010, and told police that Al-Qaeda trained him in Waziristan and that 'brothers in Pakistan' funded his weapons acquisition (Cruickshank et al. 2012). During the final stand-off with French police, Merah claimed to be acting on behalf of al-Qaeda also. He signed off his final tweets before his death with the words 'Mohamed Merah-Forsane Alizza'. Forsane Alizza are a radical Salifist group that lists its targets as the French military, the Jewish people, Jewish institutions, and Israel. 'Considering the targets chosen by Merah, it would appear the group's ideology had a significant influence on his actions' (Andre & Harris-Hogan, 2013: 316).

All of the above examples are of individuals who could (and did) frame their actions as part of a wider group despite having little or no help in their preparation and certainly no help in actually carrying out their violence. Some lone actors however had no direct contact at all but still claimed their actions on behalf of a wider group. Abdulhakim Majahid Muhammad, for example, claimed an association with al-Qaeda in the Arabian Peninsula (AQAP). In his justification statement, Muhammad states:

> There's an all out war against Islam and Muslims in Afghanistan, Pakistan, Waziristan, Chechnya, Somalia, Palestine, Phillipines, Yemen etc. And Muslims have to fight back.... We believe in an eye for eye not turn the other cheek. Now it's all out war on American and I'm on the other side. The side of the Muslims – Yes! The side of Al-Qaeda – Yes! Taliban – Yes! Al-Shabaab – Yes! We are all brothers under the same banner. Fighting for the same cause which is to rid the Islamic world of Infidel and Apostate Hypocritic [sic] regimes and Crusader Invaders and re-establish the Caliphate, the Islamic Empire and Islamic Law as was ended officially in 1924 by the fall of the Ottomans.
>
> (Cited in Gartenstein-Ross, 2014: 118)

Here, Muhammad not only aligns with and portrays himself as being the same as Al-Qaeda, the Taliban, and Al-Shabaab, he also places himself in a long historical narrative of resistance that has been ongoing since 1924. He wrote further that:

> Our goal is to rid the Islamic world of Idols and Idolators, Paganism and Pagans, Infidelity and Infidels, hypocrisy and hypocrites, apostasy and apostates, democracy and democrats and relaunch the Islamic caliphate, the Islamic Khalifah and to establish the Islamic Law (Shari'ah) – Allah's Law on Earth and anyone who strives for his is affiliated with the movement. So yes, I'm al-Qaeda and proud to be.

As noted by Gartenstein-Ross (2014: 120),

> the most noteworthy aspect of Muhammad's claim to be affiliated with al Qaeda is that he explains it based on shared values.... He does not claim any sort of formal affiliation, such as having taken an oath of *bayat* (a formal oath of allegiance) to the jihadi group.

This is a very common trait amongst the non-connected lone-actor terrorist sample.

Others may inflate either their ideological motivations or links with co-conspirators. For example, 15-year-old Charles Bishop killed himself when he flew a Cessna jet into the Bank of America Tower building. He left behind a suicide note that begins with the statement:

> I have prepared this statement in regards to the terrorist[1] acts I am about to commit. First of all, Osama bin Laden is absolutely justified in the terror he has caused on 9–11. He has brought a mighty nation to its knees!… Al Qaeda and other organizations have met with me several times to discuss the option of me joining. I didn't. This is an operation by me only. I had no other help, although, I am acting on their behalf.

Others claimed the attack on behalf of a group that they created and of which they were sole members. One example is that of Mark Bulman who firebombed a U.K. mosque in 2006. At the time of the arson attack, Bulman was the registered fund holder for the local British National Party office. He campaigned for the party in the local elections four months before the arson. Shortly before the arson, he left the BNP and formed the 1290 sect that was named after the year the Jewish people were expelled from England. Another U.K.-based extreme right-wing lone actor also claimed to set up his own group. Neil Lewington authored a 'mission statement' describing his plans for two-man bomb squads to launch random attacks across Britain. He also drew up a notebook entitled the 'Waffen SS UK members' handbook'. The handbook said:

> A new group has been formed, the Waffen SS UK. We have 30 members split into 15 two-man cells. We are highly trained ex-military personnel and will use incendiary and explosive devices throughout the UK at random until all non-British people as defined by blood are removed from our country. This is no joke. In this country the most serious domestic terrorist threat is the ALF, start rewriting the books? Finally our motto: You cannot stop what can't be stopped.

The notebook also contained handwritten sections with titles such as 'picking target areas', 'transportation of devices', 'parcel bomb' and 'counter surveillance'. Under another title, 'targeting/attacking Pakis' was written 'general surveillance, names and addresses, observing Asians in cars, planting motion-sensitive bombs, hate mail, hit-and-run by vehicles'. Despite these projects, all the evidence counts towards Lewington being very socially isolated. He left school at 16 with no qualifications before working for 16 years as an electrician. At the age of 34, his employers fired him for drunkenness. In court his parents described him as an alcoholic loner who would often drink 16 pints of beer a day and had twice attempted suicide (once with a paracetamol overdose and once by drinking bleach). At the age of 44, Lewington still lived at home with his parents although he had not spoken to his father in 10 years. He spent most of his time alone in his bedroom. Lewington often blocked the keyhole with Blu-Tack to prevent his parents seeing him.

Similarly, Richard Baumhammers was a self-appointed chairman of an anti-immigration political party called The Free Market Party. This group opposed (a) all immigration from developing countries (b) affirmative action (c) strong state criminal laws (d) high taxes (e) foreign aid provision, and (f) multi-lingualism in schools. Baumhammers developed a website for the group and published his self-authored manifesto through the website. During the trial, approximately 100 pages of material taken from Baumhammers' computer listed the contacts and communications Baumhammer had with a dozen white supremacist organizations. Prosecutors also showed evidence that in the weeks before the shooting spree, Baumhammers downloaded several treaties on the benefits of 'lone wolf' terrorism including Tom Metzger's (outlined in the introduction).

Looking farther afield than the U.K. and the U.S., the available evidence suggests that Anders Breivik's Knights Templars did not exist. The same is also true for Franz Fuchs' Bajuvarian Liberation Army.

Of the lone actors, 14% were rejected from joining a wider group. Faisal Shahzad, the Times Square bomber, initially sought to join the insurgency in Afghanistan. His father blocked these plans. A few of these lamented their failure to be recruited. Adbulhakim Maujahid Muhammad outlined that he initially wanted bomb-making training in Yemen or Somalia. He outlines:

> I wanted training in explosives, on how to make bombs and in particular, carbombs, and had I got this training my story would have ended a lot differently than it's going to end now. My drive-by would have been a drive-in, with none escaping the aftermath.[2]

Eric Rudolph, the Atlanta Olympics bomber, held similar laments. He outlined that he had 'been around long enough to know the pitfalls of collaboration' (Rudolph, 2013: 6) and he lamented the lack of help during his fourth bombing: 'Oh, how easy it would be if I had a partner.... Though working alone had its advantages, namely, there was nobody to rat me out, it also made a quick execution and getaway more difficult' (Rudolph, 2013: 42).

Some frame themselves as being the tipping point for others to follow and explain their lone actions as a result of others not yet being ready to act out violently. David Adkisson, who shot and killed members at a Unitarian-Universalist Church congregation because of their liberal beliefs, saw himself as the vanguard for others to follow. Adkisson concludes his four-page suicide note:

> Someone had to get the ball rolling. I volunteered. I hope others do the same ... I'd like to encourage other like-minded people to do what I've done. If life ain't worth living anymore just kill yourself. Do something for your country before you go. Go kill liberals.
>
> (Adkisson, 2008)

Martyn Gilleard (who was convicted of weapons possession) wrote in his notebook that 'there had been too much bar-stool nationalism and not enough courageous action to save this country [the U.K.] from the multi-racial peril' (Caulfield, 2008).

To return to the original question; why go it alone? The cases outlined here display a wide range of justifications. The vast majority just see their actions no differently from those of their co-ideologues who operate either in cooperation with others or not. Formal group membership may mean relatively nothing for social movements whose structure is quite nebulous or where no formal groups actually exist in the first place. The fact remains that the vast majority either do not see themselves as lone actors in terms of trying to affect political change or wanted to either become a formal group member or framed their actions on behalf of a group (some that existed others that did not) or took the decision to go it alone for others to follow in their footsteps. Rare is the case of the completely idiosyncratic lone actor acting on behalf of an ideology devoid of co-ideologues or informal social support networks.

Notes

1 The word terrorist was faintly crossed out.
2 Scanned copies of these Muhammad's correspondence with Katrina Goetz can be found at www.commercialappeal.com/jihad/.

References

Andre, V., & Harris-Hogan, S. (2013). Mohamed Merah: From Petty Criminal to Neojihadist. *Politics, Religion & Ideology*, *14*(2), 307–319.

Bray, M., & Bray, J. (2009). Tiller's Unheeded Warning: The Shelley Shannon Story. Retrieved from: www.armyofgod.com/POCShelleyShannonBookMikeBray.html. Accessed 1 June 2014.

Caulfield, A. (2008, 16 June). Court Told Racist Planned Terrorist Acts. Press Association.

Cruickshank, P., Lister, T., & Robertson, N. (2012, 8 May). Al-Qaeda's Bomb-Makers Evolve, Adapt and Continue to Plot. CNN. Retrieved from: http://edition.cnn.com/2012/05/08/world/al-qaeda-evolving-strategy/. Accessed 22 September 2014.

D'Alessio, S. J., & Stolzenberg, L. (2010). Do cities influence co-offending?. *Journal of Criminal Justice*, *38*(4), 711–719.

Felson, M. (2003). The process of co-offending. *Crime prevention studies*, *16*, 149–168.

Gartenstein-Ross, D. (2014). Lone Wolf Islamic Terrorism: Abdulhakim Mujahid Muhammad (Carlos Bledsoe) Case Study. *Terrorism and Political Violence*, *26*(1), 110–128.

Lawless, J., & Rising, M. (2010, 13 December). Stockholm Bomber was seen as Radical by UK Muslims. *The Associated Press*.

McGloin, J. M., & Nguyen, H. (2012). It was my idea: Considering the instigation of co-offending. *Criminology*, *50*(2), 463–494.

McGloin, J. M., & Nguyen, H. (2013). The importance of studying co-offending networks for criminological theory and policy. *Crime and Networks*, 13.

McGloin, J. M., & Stickle, W. P. (2011). Influence or convenience? Disentangling peer influence and co-offending for chronic offenders. *Journal of Research in Crime and Delinquency*, *48*(3), 419–447.

Rudolph, E. (2013). Between the Lines of Drift: The Memoirs of a Militant. Retrieved from: www.armyofgod.com/EricRudolphHomepage.html. Accessed 1 June 2014.

Schaefer, D. R., Rodriguez, N., & Decker, S. H. (2014). The Role of Neighborhood Context in Youth Co-offending. *Criminology*, *52*(1), 117–139.

Seegmiller, B. (2007). Radicalized Margins: Eric Rudolph and Religious Violence 1. *Terrorism and Political Violence*, *19*(4), 511–528.

Stolzenberg, L., & D'Alessio, S. J. (2008). Co-offending and the age-crime curve. *Journal of Research in Crime and Delinquency*, *45*(1), 65–86.

Tillyer, M. S., & Tillyer, R. (2014). Maybe I Should Do This Alone: A Comparison of Solo and Co-offending Robbery Outcomes. *Justice Quarterly*, (ahead-of-print), 1–25.

Van Mastrigt, S. B., & Carrington, P. (2013). Sex and Age Homophily in Co-offending Networks. *Crime and Networks*, 28.

Van Mastrigt, S. B., & Farrington, D. P. (2009). Co-offending, age, gender and crime type: Implications for criminal justice policy. *British Journal of Criminology*, azp021.

Van Mastrigt, S. B., & Farrington, D. P. (2011). Prevalence and characteristics of co-offending recruiters. *Justice Quarterly*, *28*(2), 325–359.

5 The role of the internet

Over the past few years, a number of concerns have been raised about both the nature of the internet's relationship with terrorism and the threat posed by lone-actor terrorists. Despite these growing concerns, both literatures have lacked an empirical focus. The tendency to focus upon theory-building and illustrative examples means that we lack an understanding of how generalizable aspects of both concerns tend to be. Instead, what we are left with is a series of disjointed anecdotes (some rigorously researched, others not), with very little attempt at testing explanations or predictions or replicating previous case studies. As an increasing number of studies argue that the so-called rise of lone-actor terrorism is linked to the internet (Feldman, 2013), it is important to take a closer look at what role it actually plays, if any. This chapter investigates whether those who interact virtually with like-minded activists display markedly different experiences (e.g. radicalization, event preparation, and attack outcomes) than those who do not. The key findings from the statistical analysis will be presented alongside illustrative examples. Finally, I also examine how some of these actors have used the internet to overcome the difficulties inherent in committing a terrorist offence absent the logistical support network and expertise of a terrorist organization.

The internet and lone-actor terrorism

Neumann (2013) mapped the evolution of virtual communication in the context of terrorism. Static websites were primarily used in the 1990s, which communicated unfiltered news and ideological texts, circumventing legitimate media channels. Discussion forums became more popular at the peak of static websites. These social areas permit users to examine and disseminate the increasing range of violent extremist content. Forums permit a variety of user types to engage, each with different levels of support and commitment to the ideological cause. This anonymous virtual community allows for the breeding of extremist ideas, their reinforcement, and normalization (Brynielsson, Horndahl, Johansson, Kaati, Mårtenson, & Svenson, 2013). Due to the fast-paced, constant evolution of internet capabilities, online forums are now only one of many communication outlets available. Social networking sites such as Facebook, MySpace, and Second Life (Weimann, 2012; O'Rourke, 2007) act as forums with the benefit of having access to personal demographic data. Micro blogging site Twitter (O'Callaghan, Greene, Conway, Carthy, & Cunningham, 2012) is also exploited to garner support alongside redirecting users to content on external websites. Following further evolution of technology, video-based discussions on platforms such as YouTube (Conway, 2012; Bowman-Grieve & Conway, 2012) are utilized to disseminate previously unreachable and emotive propaganda. Evolutions in subtitling have led to dissemination of media to previously unreachable sympathizers as language barriers are removed (Conway, 2012). It might be expected therefore that as virtual technologies increase, there may also be a significant linear increase in lone-actors because of the proliferation of resources online. Empirically, however, this has not been the case. Figure 5.1 illustrates that the number of lone-actor terrorists has remained quite stable over time, with a typical range of five to 11 actors per year.

While the growth of the internet has not correlated with a rise in lone-actor terrorist activity year-on-year, Figures 5.2 and 5.3 illustrate that there is a growing trend amongst lone-actors to make use of virtual interactions and virtual learning techniques. In other words, the internet has not brought about a growth spurt in lone-actor terrorist activity but has significantly shaped the pre-attack behaviours of those lone-actors that do emerge. Instead, these new platforms allowed an incremental evolution in lone-actor extremist activity (Hummel, 2008).

In the next two sections, I discuss the content and nature of these virtual interactions and virtual learning methods.

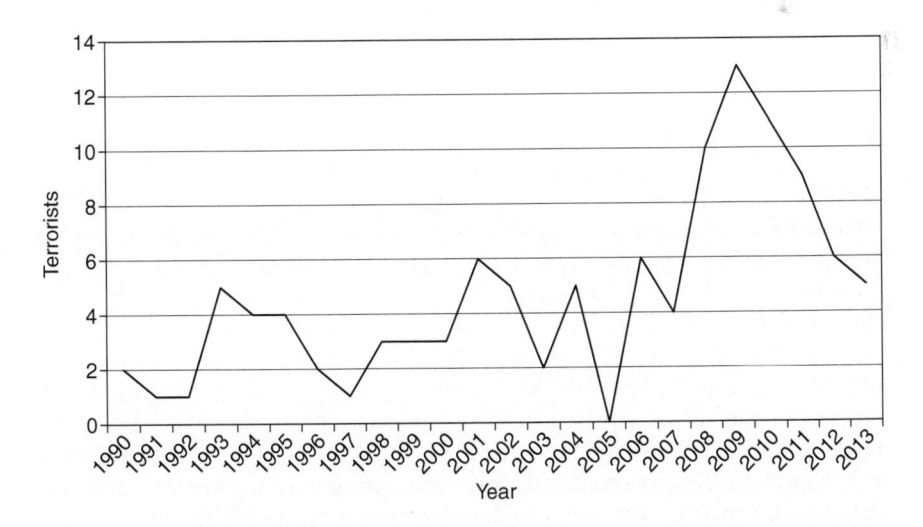

Figure 5.1 Lone-actor terrorists per year.

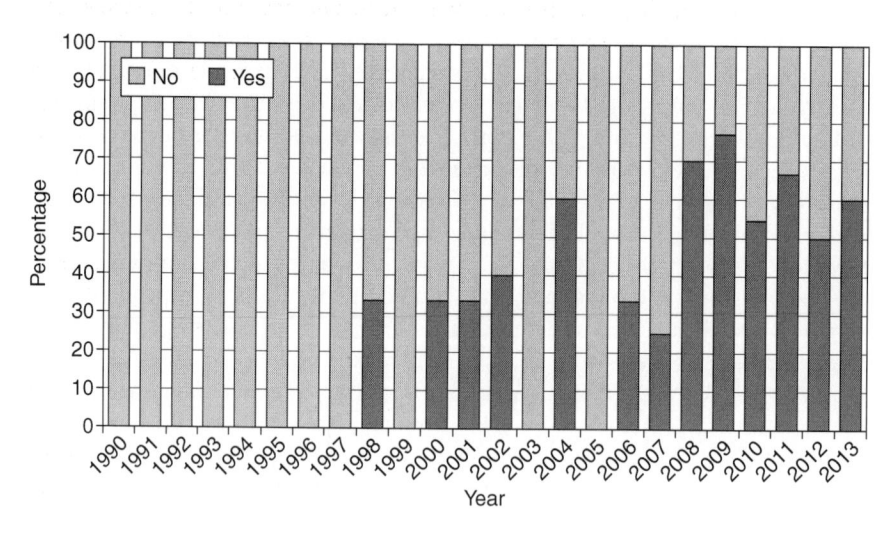

Figure 5.2 Has the individual learnt through virtual sources?

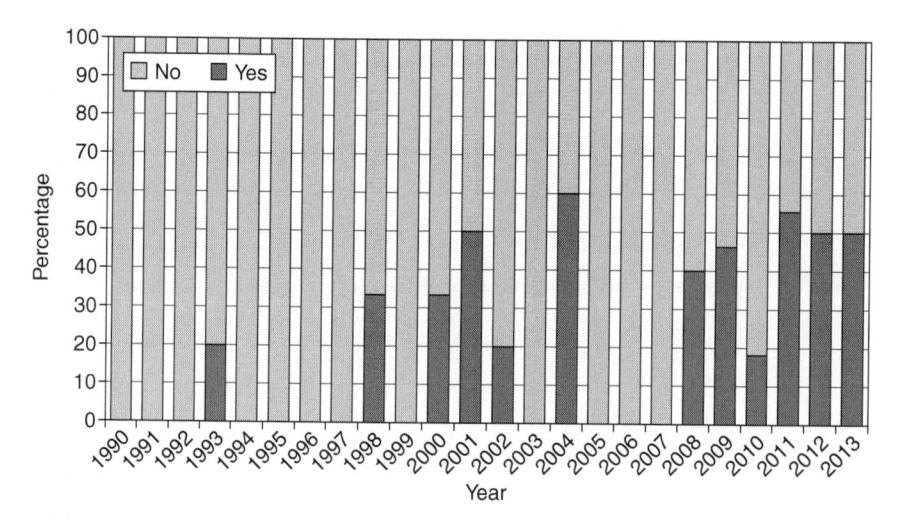

Figure 5.3 Has the individual communicated with others virtually?

The nature of virtual interaction

Lone-actors are often depicted in academic literature as being social isolates (Fein & Vossekuil, 1999; Meloy, Hempel, Mohandie, Shiva, & Gray, 2001). However investigations concerning internet usage consistently argue these same actors to be socially active online (Brynielsson et al., 2013; Sageman, 2008; Weimann, 2012). Feldman (2013) highlights that 47% of White Revolution's website users identify themselves as lone actors. Pantucci (2011) presents four lone-actor types. Each ideal type includes a case study in which the actor utilized the internet to communicate with others online. Indeed, while our sample is defined by the fact that they 'acted' alone, there is a lot of evidence to suggest that many of these lone-actors interact with co-ideologues during their radicalization and/or attack-planning process. Just less than half (41%) interacted face-to-face with members of a wider network of political activists, and 30% did so virtually. The number of those making use of virtual interactions is perhaps unsurprising. One of the benefits the internet provides is the capability and ease of access to individuals on an international scale. Stevens and Neumann (2009) argue that the internet makes it easier to locate those holding similar interests, and create networks of such individuals across international boundaries. These opportunities have been seized by extremist organizations as a way of expanding and reaching out to previously unknown sympathizers (Conway & McInerney, 2008). Indeed, for those would-be extremists not living in a conflict zone and not having direct access to terrorist groups, there is a need to access extremist material online (Conway, 2012).

While there is an implicit tendency within the literature that dichotomizes offenders into those who interact virtually from those who interact face-to-face with co-ideologues, our data suggests that once an offender does one type of interaction, he/she is significantly more likely to also do the other. Not only are those who interact virtually more likely to interact face-to-face with co-ideologues, they are also more likely to make verbal statements about their intent to engage in terrorist activity (and sometimes divulge details of the actual attack). One such example, Abdulhakim Mujahid Muhammad, engaged in a drive-by shooting on soldiers at a U.S. military recruitment centre in Arkansas. He accessed various materials online and also, according to testimony delivered at a House Homeland Security Committee, was facilitated in his radicalization by other Muslims in the Nashville area.

The more pertinent question therefore may be not why individuals choose to interact virtually or physically, but rather why they choose to interact at all? The evidence suggests that much of this virtual interaction involved (a) reinforcing of prior beliefs (b) seeking legitimization for future actions (c) disseminating propaganda and providing material support for others (d) attack signalling, and (e) attempting to recruit others. The following sections provide illustrative examples of each.

Reinforcement of beliefs

Evidence suggests that many went online not to have their beliefs changed but rather reinforced. In the aftermath of Ian Davison's trial (in which his son was also convicted on other offences), for developing ricin, police sources noted that Davison's 'views developed over time. After going online he accessed websites and started to look at places where those kinds of views were shared with other people' (Sims, 2010). Another case is that of Kevin Harpham who attempted to bomb the Martin Luther King Jr. Day parade in Spokane in 2011. Over the course of seven years, Harpham posted 1,000 comments to the Vanguard News Network, an anti-Semitic, white supremacist website. His initial posts discussed issues such as quitting smoking and chewing tobacco, and computer software problems. Over time, the posts became more extreme as he discussed ways to dismantle society, stockpile ammunition, acquire guns, and provide material support to white supremacists currently on the run from law enforcement. He also discussed using his background as an electrician to help stage an attack and was one of the top five financial donors to the website itself.

Seeking legitimization for their actions

Many lone-actors interact virtually with co-ideologues in order to seek legitimization or social sanction for their intended terrorist attack. Whereas the previous sub-section pertains to beliefs, this section relates to intended action. For example, prior to killing two U.S. Airmen at Frankfurt Airport in 2011, Arid Uka contacted Sheik Abdellatif and other potential extremists online. Many of these contacts were made in the two weeks prior to his attack. Perhaps a more famous example of this action is that of the Fort Hood shooter, Nidal Malik Hasan's emails to Anwar al-Awlaki. In the earliest email released by the FBI, Hasan asks al-Awlaki if a Muslim in the U.S. army were to kill his colleagues, whether it would be considered an act of jihad and whether the perpetrator would be considered a martyr if they died in the commission of the act. After corresponding with al-Awlaki on other issues such as financial donations, finding a wife, and setting up an essay writing contest in al-Awlaki's honour, Hasan returned to the issue of whether dying in the cause of saving others is permissible or not. After referring to the arguments of others, Hasan concludes:

> I would assume that [the] suicide bomber whose aim is to kill enemy soldiers or their helpers but also kill innocents in the process is acceptable[?] Furthermore, if enemy soldiers are using other tactics that are unethical/ unconscionable then those same tactics may be used[?]
>
> (cited in Berger, 2012)

Disseminating propaganda

Many lone actors were not just passive consumers of ideological content. Many disseminate propaganda to either signal their seriousness as an extremist or to try to convince others of the ideology. For example, Arid Uka's (mentioned previously) Facebook page was full of links to extremist materials, rants against members of the Jewish faith, quotes from former Islamic fighters, and anti-Western songs. The Stockholm suicide bomber, Taimour Abdulwahab's Facebook page was similar and included graphic videos of human rights abuses in Iraq and Chechnya. Khalid Aldawsari ran a blog in which he posted (amongst other things) extremist messages, vowing jihad, and martyrdom due to his dissatisfaction with the current condition of Muslims worldwide.

On other occasions, lone-actor terrorists disseminated propaganda they developed themselves. Sometimes, the act of violence is seen as the marketing tool for the self-produced propaganda itself. Anders Breivik's coordinated attacks occurred on 22 July 2011 in Oslo and Utøya Island, Norway. In total, 77 were killed and approximately 320 were injured. Between February 2007 and November 2009, Breivik wrote his manifesto, which he viewed as a radicalizing tool.

> All it takes is access to the compendium. If you read it from the first word to the end, you will be radicalized. The [compendium] is both a tool and an application. The entire standard difficult recruitment process is being replaced. This is much more effective because the compendium is structured so that you are automatically radicalized.
> (Husby & Sorheim, 2011: 101)

Further, Breivik alleged, 'the work is the first step, a groundbreaking start. It cannot be read without the reader being radicalized' (Husby & Sorheim, 2011: 109). In the manifesto, he refers to the attacks as the 'marketing operation' (Breivik, 2011: 8). The initial plan for the day of the attack was to distribute his manifesto at 3 a.m., conduct the bombing at 10 a.m., and be on Utøya Island at 11 a.m. in order to execute Gro Harlem Brundtland, a Norwegian politician who was due to give a talk to the young people at Utøya. The plan was delayed, however. According to Breivik, 'This delay was disastrous for the whole thing' (Husby and Sorheim, 2011: 28). The original delay occurred because his installation of a high-speed modem and the configuration of Microsoft Outlook on his PC took longer than expected.

After these installations were complete, he drove the getaway car into Oslo and parked it. He then took a taxi back to his mother's house. There, he uploaded a film he had made to YouTube and wrote the last message in his manifesto at 2:45 p.m. At 3:05 p.m., Breivik distributed his more than 1,500-page manifesto to approximately 8,000 people via email. Breivik largely cultivated these email addresses through Facebook between October 2009 and March 2010. According to Breivik, 'Utøya Island and the government building was all about publishing the manifesto, to reach the 350,000 militant nationalists who are the audience' (Husby & Sorheim, 2011: 100). The use of virtual dissemination therefore acted as a force multiplier. It was far easier to distribute such a large body of work virtually.

There are other less famous examples that engaged in similar behaviours. Examples include the eco-terrorist James Lee whose website included a list of demands for the Discovery Channel to meet in order for him to free the hostages he had taken at the channel's headquarters. John Patrick Bedell, who shot and wounded two Pentagon police officers, published countless audio tapes and postings online where he propagated ideas as far ranging as 9/11 conspiracy theories ('the work of a criminal organization controlling the U.S. government'), anti-government diatribes, computer programming, a call for the Pentagon to fund his research on smart weapons, libertarian economics, the science of warfare, and marijuana laws. Prior to a spree shooting that killed five people, Richard Baumhammers was a self-appointed chairman of an anti-immigration political party called The Free Market Party. This group opposed all immigration from developing countries. Baumhammers developed a website for the group and published his self-authored manifesto through the website.

Other lone-actor terrorists proactively uploaded videos that could help others engage in a terrorist attack. For example, Ahmed Abdellatif Sherif Mohamed recorded a 12-minute video in which he demonstrated and explained how a remote-control toy car could be reassembled, rewired, and converted into an IED detonator. This video was uploaded to YouTube and was accessed hundreds of times by others, according to court documents. Mohamed stated that the purpose of the video was to teach 'martyrdoms' and 'suiciders' how to continue the fight against the U.S. military and their allies. Mohammed Atif Siddique was convicted of setting up websites providing links to documents providing instructions on how to operate weaponry and make explosives, and circulating terrorist publications on the web to encourage, induce, or assist the commission, preparation, or instigation of actors of terrorism.

Recruitment

Many lone actors (or isolated dyads) do not originally set out to be lone actors. Instead, they try to recruit others but for various reasons are unsuccessful. Some attempt to recruit online. The Davisons (mentioned previously) set up an organization called the Aryan Strike Force that had an active online presence. This website was used to disseminate ideological content, training videos, practical guides, and also documents discussing the effectiveness of lone wolf terrorism and leaderless resistance. Through this website, the Davisons had apparently contacted over 300 extremists.

Attack signalling

Many lone-actor terrorists signal their attack plans to others online beforehand. At times, this attack signalling can be quite vague. For example, Charles Bishop emailed friends in the build-up to his eventual attack telling them to watch the news because he would be on it. At other times, the signalling can be very specific regarding the necessity to target a particular place or individual. For example, Scott Roeder had a long history of internet postings across many websites regarding his eventual target, George Tiller (who ran a clinic that specialized in late-term abortions). Some of the initial posts regarding Tiller advocated non-violent resistance but later became more extreme, referring to Tiller as the 'concentration camp Mengele of our day' and someone who 'needs to be stopped'.

On other occasions, this form of behaviour is a signal of the attack itself. Taimour Abdulwahab, emailed Swedish police and a news agency minutes before his suicide bombing, warning of reprisals for the stationing of Swedish soldiers in Afghanistan and the depiction of the Prophet Muhammad as a dog by a Swedish artist. The anti-abortion activist Clayton Lee Waagner left posts on the Army of God website announcing his forthcoming escalation of activities on abortionists in June 2001 stating; 'I am going to kill as many of them as I can.... It doesn't matter to me if you're a nurse, receptionist, bookkeeper, or janitor, if you work for the murderous abortionist I'm going to kill you'. (Waagner cited in Jacoby, 2002).

The nature of virtual learning

Within the sample, 42% learned through virtual sources. We found many forms of learning that informed different stages of the attack planning and attack commissioning process. They include (a) accessing ideological content (b) opting for violence (c) choosing a target (d) preparing an attack, and (e) overcoming hurdles.

Accessing ideological content

In a previous section, I outlined how one aspect of virtual interaction allows users to strengthen previously formed beliefs. This sub-section instead outlines how some of our cases found and took on a new ideological identity through virtual learning absent of virtual interactions with co-ideologues.

In May 2010, Roshonara Choudhry stabbed British MP Stephen Timms. The subsequent investigation established that Choudhry began downloading Anwar al-Awlaki's videos and sermons in the autumn and winter of 2009. She began spending an abundance of time in her bedroom; her parents believed that she was studying, but in reality she was downloading extremist material, including more than 100 hours of al-Awlaki's sermons. It was supposedly during this time that Choudhry decided to engage in a violent attack. During her police interview, Choudhry responded to a question concerning the transition from immersing herself in religion to committing violence. Choudhry's response stated:

> Because as Muslims we're all brothers and sisters and we should all look out for each other and we shouldn't sit back and do nothing while others suffer. We shouldn't allow the people who oppress us to get away with it and to think that they can do whatever they want to us and we're just gonna [*sic*] lie down and take it.[1]

Choudhry referred to a specific YouTube video of Sheikh Abdullah Azzam that made her understand that 'even women are supposed to fight' and that she had an obligation to turn towards violence. According to the police interviews, Choudhry made this realization at some point in April and soon after began her preparations for the attack.

Isa Ibrahim is another similar case. Ibrahim was said to have developed 'a mindset of martyrdom' over the course of five months of listening to radical preachers (including Oetmar Bakri and Abu Hamza) over the internet. Ibrahim himself referred to his online activities as 'an obsessive interest' in suicide bombing activities. In a similar vein, the radical cleric Abu Qatada once boasted that one of the Glasgow airport bombers, Bilal Abdullah, was heavily influenced by listening to Qutada's taped sermons. Taimour Abdulwahab's radicalization allegedly occurred through consuming Dr. Omar Abdel Kafi's preachings, whose sermons he downloaded. This form of virtual learning is not only applicable to al-Qaeda inspired terrorism, however. For example, white supremacist spree shooter Keith Luke apparently developed his racist views over the course of a six-month period where he consumed a large number of videos hosted by the white nationalist website Podblanc. The Southern Poverty Law Center claimed that these videos included Russian neo-Nazis assaulting orthodox Jews and non-Whites as well as killing (sometimes by beheading) Asian immigrants.

Opting for violence

A smaller number of lone-actor terrorists decided to turn towards violent activities after virtually learning through non-ideologically-oriented materials. According to court documents submitted by the prosecutors, Abdulhakim Mujahid Muhammad (mentioned previously) told police that after watching a particular video online 'pertaining to subversive activities' it 'spurred him to commit' a violent act. Arid Uka (also mentioned above) made similar statements regarding a video allegedly depicting members of the U.S. military raping a young girl from Afghanistan.

Choosing a target

Once they have decided to act violently upon their extremist beliefs, the next stage in the attack planning process is to choose a target. Some lone actors utilized the internet to opt between a plethora of available targets. Roshonara Choudhry (mentioned previously) devised a list of Members of Parliament who voted for the 2003 invasion of Iraq. She researched the backgrounds of London-based Members of Parliament using the website 'They Work For You', which includes information on voting records. She appears to have concentrated her research on Labour ministers Jim Fitzpatrick, Margaret Hodge, Nick Raynsford, and Stephen Timms. Detectives later declared that Timms was her 'sole and easiest target'. The decision to attack Timms was made three to four weeks prior to the attack itself. Timms was Choudhry's local Member of Parliament. Her online research showed that Timms regularly voted with his political party (which held power at that time). Choudhry later told detectives that,

> he just voted strongly for everything, as though he had no mercy. As though he felt no doubts that what he was doing was right even though it was such

an arrogant thing to do and I just felt like if he could treat the Iraqi people so mercilessly, then why should I show him any mercy?

In a similar vein, Abdulhakim Mujahid Muhammad researched potential targets online including military facilities, Jewish centres, a post office, a Baptist church, and a childcare centre. Charles Bishop, who flew a plane into a Bank of America office tower, originally planned to target a military site and sought maps of military bases online. Khalid Aldawsari sent himself an email with the subject line 'Targets' that allegedly included the names of three Americans who had returned from service and had been stationed in Abu Ghraib for a period of time. In another email titled 'Nice Targets 01', Aldawsari sent himself the names of 12 reservoir dams in Colorado and California and in a third email titled 'Nice Targets', he listed two categories of targets: hydroelectric dams and nuclear power plants. Each of these targets had been researched online. He also spent time researching online about the rules for backpacks in Dallas nightclubs and the location of George W. Bush's family home.

Clayton Lee Waagner engaged in a series of activities against abortion doctors and clinics. On an online post he suggested the utility in setting up an online 'Combat Information Center', which would store and share pertinent information regarding different abortion clinics that others could utilize in the commission of a terrorist attack. To this end, Waagner also researched clinic location, descriptions, and access issues of various abortion clinics but did not publish them publicly in the end.

Sometimes, the search for a target is not so discriminate. When asked why Naveed Haq had decided to target the Seattle Jewish Federation in particular, the lead investigator in the case answered that it came from a 'generic search' on Google and that any Jewish building would have done.

Attack preparation

Once a target is chosen, the next stage involves preparing for the attack method itself. Unsurprisingly, this is the most common usage of virtual learning. Amongst our lone-actor terrorist sample, police seized materials including recipes for sarin and cyanide, bomb-making recipes, videos of previous successfully executed terrorist attacks and training methods, body armour, and chemicals purchased online.

Overcoming hurdles

Without the benefit of a group's financial, human, and social capital, particular forms of terrorist attacks can involve multiple hurdles that are difficult to overcome for the lone actor. Here, the internet may play a key facilitative role. We can see how in two similar but different terrorist events. In April 1999, David Copeland engaged in a 13-day bombing campaign across London. Two years prior, Copeland originally tried to use a recipe from *The Terrorist's Handbook*, a manual that he downloaded in April 1997. He purchased ammonium nitrate and the required detonators; he also managed to steal a large canister of nitric acid. However, the manual failed to provide an exhaustive list of all of the necessary explosive compounds, and Copeland found it 'too complex' to manufacture and procure the missing chemical compounds by himself. Frustrated, Copeland temporarily gave up. In June 1998 he downloaded a second manual, *How to Make Bombs Part 2*. At first he tried to build a fertilizer bomb; he purchased liquid ammonium from a local medical supply store and ordered rocket fuses, but again he failed to manufacture a fully functioning device. Copeland then turned to smaller devices and again used the second manual to learn how to make a pipe bomb. Anders Breivik faced similar problems, 12 years later, while attempting to manufacture a series of car bombs. Breivik initially planned to build four IEDs. He began work on 3 May. On 5 May, Breivik ground aspirin tablets with a mortar and pestle and later with a dumb-bell. On 6 May, Breivik began to synthesize acetylsalicylic acid from the ground-down aspirin. This proved problematic because the instructions he followed in the bomb-making manual he had downloaded did not work. According to Breivik himself, he 'began to somewhat panic ... and began to lose heart' (Breivik, 2011: 1455). This delayed him for three days until a YouTube video provided a viable alternative solution that he tested successfully on 9 May. Rather than downscaling the nature and complexity of his IED like Copeland did, Breivik had recourse to YouTube and a solution to his problem.

Over the next few sections we statistically test whether there are aspects of the lone actor's demographic characteristics, network properties, antecedent event behaviours, or facets of event-commission that are significantly correlated with whether the individual communicated virtually with co-ideologues or learnt through virtual sources. In particular we assess whether there are statistically significant differences across socio-demographic characteristics, motivations, and event outcomes.

Demographic correlates and virtual activity

We tested a wide range of socio-demographic characteristics (age, education, profession, family characteristics, relationship status etc.) and their relationship with virtual activity. A couple of characteristics remained significant across both 'virtual learning' and 'virtual interaction' variables. Younger offenders were significantly more likely to engage in both types of activities than older offenders. Presumably, the age of the offender also explains why those actors who are (a) not married or divorced and (b) currently a student, are also significantly more likely to interact virtually with others and learn virtually for their upcoming attack. This relationship between offender age and virtual activities may be explained by the fact that younger people use the internet for a greater number of hours per day and for a wider range of tasks (Teo, Lim, & Lai, 1999). This finding may therefore be explained by the simple routine activities that young people engage in. For those younger would-be lone-actor terrorists, it is perhaps natural that they would rely upon their daily routine activities to help plan their attack in the same way an active soldier may rely upon his prior knowledge, skills, and awareness. Given the relatively recent spread of the internet, it is still too early to predict whether this relationship is actually an effect of 'age' that will remain constant over the next 20 years or whether in fact it is a cohort effect. If it is a cohort effect, what we are likely to see in the future is the current significant relationship between age and virtual interactions/learning dissipate as today's younger population grow older and an infinitesimally small number develop into lone-actor terrorist offenders later in their lives.

It is also interesting to note that the non-U.S.-based sub-sample were significantly more likely to learn through virtual sources. This might be explained by the constraints imposed upon European lone actors where firearms are far more difficult to obtain. This constraint may push some offenders into learning online about bomb making. The fact that there was no relationship between virtual interactions with co-ideologues and offender location may also attest to this explanation. In other words, U.S. based and non-U.S. based offenders were just as likely to interact virtually with co-ideologues but it was the non-U.S. based sample who were significantly more likely to study for their impending attack online.

Ideological differences

Much of the work on internet radicalization has focused upon religious extremism (Hummel, 2008). However Feldman (2013) explains that members of far-right organizations are often early adopters of the technological advancements that the internet has brought, and Neumann (2013) describes the range of ideologies that utilize the internet to self-radicalize, garner support, and plan attacks. Violent extremists also take advantage of this contemporary platform, utilizing websites to further their cause, particularly targeting younger users (Weimann, 2012). Our results show some disparity across ideological divides. Those who are motivated by single-issues (anti-abortion, environmentalists etc.) were significantly less likely to learn or interact virtually. However, those espousing al-Qaeda-style ideology were significantly more likely to learn through virtual sources.

Event outcomes and virtual activity

Despite the many benefits from virtual learning and virtual activity described previously, the individuals who interacted virtually with co-ideologues were significantly less likely to actually carry out a violent attack. Indeed, the individuals who learnt through virtual sources were also significantly less likely to kill or injure anybody. This is all the more surprising when we consider the fact that they were significantly more likely to plot an attack against indiscriminate soft targets.

Why is this the case? Well, as the study of terrorism has become more empirically focused, the mantra 'terrorism is a group phenomenon' has become more commonplace. These studies typically tend to agree that this is mainly because groups provide the necessary operational capabilities to perform a terrorist attack while also providing individuals with a mechanism for moral disengagement (Gill, 2012). Military psychology suggests that there are many factors that inhibit individuals engaging in fatal violence against others. For example, Marshall concludes that

> the average and healthy individual ... has such an inner and usually unrealized resistance towards killing a fellow man that he will not of his own volition take life if it is possible to turn away from that responsibility ... at the vital point.
>
> (cited in Grossman, 1995, p. 29)

In the absence of a group setting, terrorist violence is difficult to commit for practical and psychological reasons. There is however a number of personal circumstances that may help overcome these barriers and they include a criminal background, a prior history of violent activities, mental illness, and previous military experience. Interestingly, individuals who experienced at least one of these three factors were significantly less likely to learn through virtual sources. Additionally, those with previous military experience were also significantly less likely to interact virtually with others. There are also situational factors that may initiate a proximal stressor, which could in turn manifest itself as a lone-actor terrorist incident including being the target of prejudice, being disrespected, or having their anger noticeably escalating. Again, each of these three variables were significantly less likely to co-occur with individuals who learnt through virtual sources. So while virtual learning and virtual interactions may provide some of the 'know-to' of engaging in a terrorist attack, the evidence suggests that the lone-actor needs additional qualities in order to transition this knowledge into 'know-how' and action (Kenney, 2010).

Conclusion

This chapter provided an insight into the content and nature of virtual learning and interaction from a sample of lone-actor terrorists. The results largely downplay the threat emanating from the internet with regard to lone-actor terrorists. The rise of the internet has not led to an exponential growth in lone-actor terrorism. Those who participate in online activities, the data suggests, have also been far less successful in committing attacks and causing fatalities and injuries. The results also attest to the fact that we should take other situational and personal circumstances and experience into account when assessing an individual's capability of engaging in a lone-actor terrorist attack. In sum, whether an individual engages in such virtual activities is often linked to either the individual's normal daily routine activities or because something is lacking in their personal abilities or awareness space that drives the need to go online and engage. Figure 5.4 illustrates that while some behaviours are closely correlated with both virtual

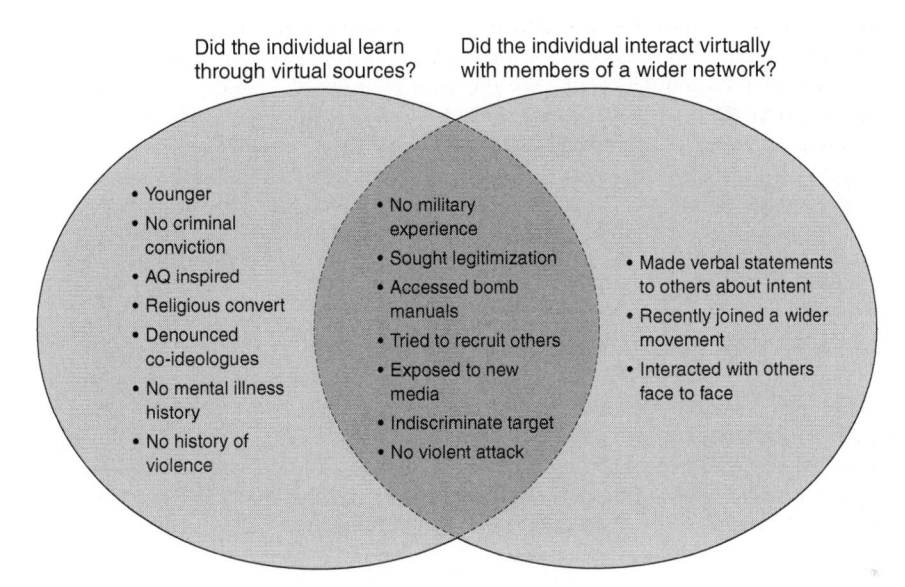

Figure 5.4 Behaviour covariates.

Left circle (Did the individual learn through virtual sources?):
- Younger
- No criminal conviction
- AQ inspired
- Religious convert
- Denounced co-ideologues
- No mental illness history
- No history of violence

Intersection:
- No military experience
- Sought legitimization
- Accessed bomb manuals
- Tried to recruit others
- Exposed to new media
- Indiscriminate target
- No violent attack

Right circle (Did the individual interact virtually with members of a wider network?):
- Made verbal statements to others about intent
- Recently joined a wider movement
- Interacted with others face to face

learning and virtual interaction, there are some behaviours that are specifically related to only one of these factors.

Overall, the results suggest that the nature of virtual interactions and virtual learning for lone-actor terrorists is far more complex than currently conceived but this chapter has only scratched the surface of online radicalization. A recent RAND publication analysed the registry keys of 15 terrorists and extremists and demonstrated level of data granularity that is incomparable in the existing literature (von Behr et al., 2013). This chapter and the RAND study will hopefully pre-empt a large growth in the data-driven study of online radicalization and the individual terrorist in the coming years.

Notes

1 Roshonara Choudhry's police interview extracts can be found here: www.theguardian.com/uk/2010/nov/03/roshonara-choudhry-police-interview. Accessed 22 September 2014.

References

Abu Qatada smuggles out letters to extremists. (2009, April 4). *The Telegraph*. Retrieved from: www.telegraph.co.uk/news/5102928/Abu-Qatada-smuggles-out-letters-to-extremists.html. Accessed 1 June 2014.

BBC (2000, 30 June). *Panorama*, The Nailbomber (Recorded from Transmission: BBC 1) [Programme transcript]. Retrieved from: http://news.bbc.co.uk/hi/english/static/audio_video/programmes/panorama/transcripts/transcript_30_06_00.txt. Accessed 1 June 2014.

Berger, J. M. (2012, 19 July). Anwar Awlaki e-mail exchange with Fort Hood shooter Nidal Hasan. *Intelwire.* Retrieved from: http://news.intelwire.com/2012/07/the-following-e-mails-between-maj.html. Accessed 22 September 2014.

Breivik, A. B. (2011). *2083: A European Declaration of Independence.* London, England. Retrieved from: http://unitednations.ispnw.org/archives/breivik-manifesto-2011.pdf. Accessed 1 June 2014.

Bowman-Grieve, L., & Conway, M. (2012). Exploring the Form and Function of Dissident Irish Republican Online Discourses. *Media, War & Conflict, 5(1)*, 71–85.

Bledsoe, Melvin. (2011). The Extent of Radicalization in the American Muslim Community and that Community's Response. Committee on Homeland Security. Washington D.C.: US House of Representatives. Retrieved from: http://homeland.house.gov/sites/homeland.house.gov/files/Testimony%20Bledsoe.pdf. Accessed 1 June 2014.

Brynielsson, J., Horndahl, A., Johansson, F., Kaati, L., Mårtenson, C., & Svenson, P. (2013). Harvesting and analysis of weak signals for detecting lone wolf terrorists. *Security Informatics, 2(11),* 1–15.

Conway, M. (2012). From al-Zarqawi to al-Awlaki: The Emergence of the Internet as a New Form of Violent Radical Milieu. *posted to ISODARCO website.* Retrieved from: www.isodarco.it/courses/andalo12/doc/Zarqawi%20to%20Awlaki_V2.pdf. Accessed 1 June 2014.

Conway, M., & McInerney, L. (2008). Jihadi video and auto-radicalisation: Evidence from an exploratory YouTube study. In D. Ortiz-Arroyo, H. L. Larsen, D. D. Zeng, D. Hicks, & G. Wagner (eds.) *Intelligence and Security Informatics: First European Conference EuroISI 2008* (pp. 108–118). Berlin Heidelberg: Springer.

Cuniff, M. M. (2011, March 13). Postings reveal bomb suspect's views. *The Spokesman-Review.* Retrieved from: www.spokesman.com/stories/2011/mar/13/postings-reveal-suspects-views/. Accessed 1 June 2014.

Dodd, V. (2010, November 3). Roshonara Choudhry: Police interview extracts. *The Guardian.* Retrieved from: www.theguardian.com/uk/2010/nov/03/roshonara-choudhry-police-interview. Accessed 1 June 2014.

Fein, R. A., & Vossekuil, B. (1999). Assassination in the United States: An Operational Study of Recent Assassins, Attackers, and Near-Lethal Approachers. *Journal of Forensic Sciences, 44(2),* 321–333.

Feldman, M. (2013). Comparative Lone Wolf Terrorism: Toward a Heuristic Definition, *Democracy and Security, 9(3),* 270–286.

Fizpatrick, L. (2009, June 2). Scott Roeder: The Tiller murder suspect. *Time.* Retrieved from: http://content.time.com/time/printout/0,8816,1902189,00.html. Accessed 1 June 2014.

Gill, P. (2012). Terrorist Violence and the Contextual, Facilitative and Causal Qualities of Group-Based Behaviors: A Case Study of Suicide Bombing Plots in the United Kingdom. *Aggression and Violent Behaviour 17(6),* 565–574.

Gill, P., & Horgan, J. (2013). Who were the Volunteers? The Shifting Sociological and Operational Profile of 1240 Provisional Irish Republican Army Members. *Terrorism and Political Violence 25(3),* 435–456.

Grossman, D. (1995). *On killing: The psychological cost of learning to kill in war and society.* Boston, MA: Little, Brown and Company.

Harney, G., & Kearney, T. (2010, May 1). Keyboard warriors or threat to the public? *The Northern Echo.* Retrieved from: www.thenorthernecho.co.uk/news/8132260.Keyboard_warriors_or_threat_to_the_public_/. Accessed 1 June 2014.

Hopkins, N. (2000, June 6). The bomber who tried to unleash a race war. *Guardian.*

Retrieved from: www.theguardian.com/uk/2000/jun/06/race.uksecurity. Accessed 1 June 2014.

Hummel, M. L. (2008). Internet Terrorism. *The Homeland Security Review, 2*(2), 117–130.

Husby, T., & Sorheim, S. (2011). *Anders Breivik Psychiatric Report 2011–11–29*. Case no.: 11–120995EN E-OTI R/o8. Retrieved from: http://issuu.com/js-ror/docs/111129_hs-psych-rep/1. Accessed 1 June 2014.

Jacoby, M. (2002, 4 August). Domestic Terrorist. *St. Petersburg Times* (Florida).

Kenney, M. (2010). Beyond the Internet: Mētis, Techne, and the Limitations of Online Artifacts for Islamist Terrorists. *Terrorism and Political Violence, 22*(2), 177–197.

Meloy, J. R., Hempel, A. G., Mohandie, K., Shiva, A. A., & Gray., T. (2001). Offender and Offense Characteristics of a Nonrandom Sample of Adolescent Mass Murderers. *Journal of the American Academy of Child & Adolescent Psychiatry, 40*(6), 719–728.

Neumann, P. R. (2013). Options and Strategies for Countering Online Radicalization in the United States. *Studies in Conflict & Terrorism, 36*(6), 431–459.

Waagner, C. L. (2001, June 18). Claton Waagner's message to the United States [Web log message]. Retrieved from: www.armyofgod.com/Claytonsmessage.html. Accessed 1 June 2014.

O'Callaghan, D., Greene, D., Conway, M., Carthy, J., & Cunningham, P. (2012). An Analysis of Interactions Within and Between Extreme Right Communities in Social Media. *arXiv preprint arXiv:1206.7050*.

O'Rourke, S. (2007). *Virtual Radicalisation: Challenges for Police*. Proceedings of the 8th Australian information warfare security conference (pp. 29–35). Edith Cowan University, Perth.

Pantucci, R. (2011). *A Typology of Lone Wolves: Preliminary Analysis of Lone Islamist Terrorists*. Report for the International Centre for the Study of Radicalisation and Political Violence.

Press Association. (2008, April 11). Kafeel Ahmed's email to his brother. *Guardian*. Retrieved from: www.theguardian.com/uk/2008/apr/11/uksecurity.scotland1. Accessed 1 June 2014.

Sageman, M. (2008). *Leaderless Jihad: Terror Networks in the Twenty-First Century*. Philadelphia, PA: University of Pennsylvania Press.

Sims, P. (2010, 1 May). Race-Hate Conspiracy Born in a Sleepy Village. *Daily Mail*.

Stacy, M. (2008, 18 December). Egyptian student gets 15 years in Fla. terror case. *Fox News*. Retrieved from: www.foxnews.com/printer_friendly_wires/2008Dec18/0,4675,ExplosivesArrest,00.html. Accessed 1 June 2014.

Stevens, T., & Neumann, P. R. (2009). *Countering Online Radicalisation: A Strategy for Action*. In ICSR (ed.). London, England: King's College London.

Teo, T. S. H., Lim, V. K. G., & Lai, R. Y. C. (1999). Intrinsic and Extrinsic Motivation in Internet Usage. *Omega, 21*(1), 25–37.

U.S. Department of Justice. (2011, February 24). Texas resident arrested on charge of attempted use of a weapon of mass destruction: Suspect allegedly purchased bomb materials and researched U.S. targets. *Federal Bureau of Investigation: Dallas Division*. Retrieved from: www.fbi.gov/dallas/press-releases/2011/dl022411.htm. Accessed 1 June 2014.

von Behr, I., Reding, A., Edwards, C., & Gribbon, L. (2013). *Radicalisation in the digital era: The use of the internet in 15 cases of terrorism and extremism*. Retrieved from: www.rand.org/content/dam/rand/pubs/research_reports/RR400/RR453/RAND_RR453.pdf. Accessed 1 June 2014.

Weimann, G. (2012). Lone Wolves in Cyberspace. *Journal of Terrorism Research, 3*(2), 75–90.

Woodward, J. (2009, June 4). Radical Muslim student developed 'mindset of martyrdom'. *Press Association Mediapoint*. Retrieved from: www.lexisnexis.com.libproxy.ucl.ac.uk/. Accessed 1 June 2014.

6 Mental illness and lone-actor terrorism

Within terrorism studies, efforts to comprehend the motivation and drives of the terrorist have a long history. Different dominant explanations have come and gone during this time. Pathological explanations held sway during the 1970s. They posited that the impulse to join a terrorist group, or the vulnerability to recruitment, is inherent within the individual. Various deviant characteristics of the terrorist personality were regularly offered despite the lack of rigorous research or reliable data. To this end, researchers postulate deviant characteristics of the 'terrorist'. For Victoroff, this field 'is largely characterised by theoretical speculation based on subjective interpretation of anecdotal observations' (2005: 3). Several researchers claim there is an identifiable terrorist personality that is 'spoiled, disturbed, cold and calculating, perverse, excited by violence, psychotic, maniac, irrational and fanatic' (Brynjar, 2000: 9). Hubbard's (1971) analysis of hijackers show that they typically possess a violent, often drunken father, a deeply religious mother, a personality that is sexually shy and passive, a protective feeling towards younger siblings, poor achievement, suicidal tendencies, and a limited chance of high wages in the future. Ferracuti and Bruno (1981) assert nine commonalities amongst their sample of 908 right-wing Italian militants. These are (1) ambivalence toward authority, (2) defective insight, (3) adherence to convention, (4) emotional detachment from the consequences of their actions, (5) sexual role uncertainties, (6) magical thinking, (7) destructiveness, (8) low education, and (9) adherence to violent subculture norms and weapons fetishes. They also assert that right-wing militants are more likely than their left-wing counterparts to possess personality disorders (cited in Victoroff, 2005: 9). Piven (2002) views terrorist behaviour as psychotic, lacking empathy and full of malignant rage. Hacker's (1976) typology of terrorists included the ideal type 'Crazies' who were motivated by false ideas arising from mental illness. Similarly, Hamden's (2002) typology includes the ideal type 'Psychopathic'. Pearce (1977) viewed terrorists as sociopaths due to gaps in self-monitoring. Pearce based his conclusion on an analysis of the tattoos adorning one particular militant's body. Cooper (1978) argued that terrorists possess psychopathic or sociopathic personalities and if it were not for engaging in political violence, they would find another outlet for their violent impulses. Tanay (1987) agrees and argues that the acts of terrorists are merely psychopathic tendencies hidden behind political rhetoric to provide the militant with an excuse to aggress. Adigun Lawal (2002) views terrorists as dogmatic and having a major sense of helplessness caused by low self-esteem, lack of independence, and a lack of assertiveness. Lester, Yang, and Lindsay (2004) suggest suicide bombers possess authoritarian personalities created by Islamic child-rearing practices. Without providing empirical evidence, Martens (2004) argues that numerous terrorists share many of the traits of antisocial personality disorders.

Psychoanalytical approaches took over during the 1980s. Psychoanalysis has been a particularly popular tool in the quest to understand individual motivation to become engaged in political violence. Psychoanalysis reveals the relationship between conscious and unconscious thought, and focuses upon psychological development from childhood. The findings from this research trend are reasonably similar to the previous assumptions of the terrorist personality being essentially abnormal but see this as determined by unconscious drives and urges originating from childhood rather than inherent personality flaws.

One particular concept in psychoanalysis, narcissism, has been very attractive to many researchers. Narcissists possess an over-inflated sense of self to the effect that they feel superior to others, possess volatile self-esteem, have interpersonal problems, and are prone to aggression in response to ego threats (Hogg & Vaughan, 2005: 136). Narcissistic injuries, caused by early emotional injuries, lead to a damaged sense of self in adulthood. Incapable of overcoming these early emotional injuries, the individual directs his/her anger towards other targets and holds them responsible for the narcissistic injuries incurred. Lasch (1979) and Pearlstein (1991) assert that narcissism is key to understanding the terrorist personality. For Pearlstein (1991), terrorists utilize their 'narcissistic rage' in undertaking their duties. He goes as far to claim that narcissism provides the most complete and 'intellectually satisfying theory regarding the personal logic of political terrorism'. Stern (2004) alleges a link between early failure and susceptibility with engaging in terrorism. According to Akhtar (1999), terrorists' narcissistic rage stems from childhood physical abuse and emotional humiliation. She states that terrorists are deeply traumatized, suffered from chronic physical abuse and emotional humiliation as children, and now mistrust others. Similarly, Billig (1985) correlates the inability to identify with a father figure with becoming engaged in militancy. De Mause (2002) and Hoffman Baruch (2003) offer similar analyses of Muslim militants. They assert that abusive and/or sexually repressive misogynist families set the eventual militant down the path of radicalization. Bollinger (1985) emphasizes deviance within the family system as symptomatic of militants' early life. De Cataldo Neuberger and Valentini (1996) suggest that Italian female militants' experiences of tyrannical fathers and weak mothers lead them to their career path. Berko (2007) constantly refers to the broken homes that suicide bombers grew up in. Kent and Nicholls (1997) posit that family backgrounds that create a murderous rage in the child are crucial to understanding early motivation. Crayton (1983) and Beck (2002) instead assert that group processes drive narcissism that in turn enhances collective self-image. Kaplan (1978) posits the role of low self-esteem and the sense of failure motivates individuals to join militant organizations. Membership enhances a feeling of masculinity. Crayton (1983) also argues that charismatic group leaders draw narcissistically exposed people toward militant organizations.

Studies that emerged through the late 1990s and early 2000s dismissed these approaches on methodological and empirical grounds (Horgan, 2005; Victoroff, 2005). A consensus soon emerged that group dynamics were key to understanding terrorist motivation. For example, one academic, who in the past championed psychoanalytical interpretations of terrorist motivation, argued that 'a clear consensus exists that it is not individual psychology, but group, organizational and social psychology, that provides the greatest analytical power in understanding this complex phenomenon' (Post 2005: 7). This consensus was largely shaped through improved data collection and primary interviews that refuted the above diagnoses. For example, research carried out on the IRA, Northern Ireland loyalists, Hezbollah, German terrorists, the FLN, ETA, Colombian terrorists, global jihadists, and captured Palestinian terrorists has provided evidence that group-based terrorists are psychologically quite normal (Crenshaw, 1981; Post, Sprinzak, & Denny, 2003; Heskin, 1984; Ferguson, Burgess, & Hollywood 2008; Rasch, 1979; Reinares, 2007; Sageman, 2005; Sanchez-Cuenca, 2007).

The role of mental illness and personality became so completely downplayed that one noted expert recently stated: 'we also tried to distinguish terrorists from violent lunatics. Crazies, by definition, could not be terrorists' (Jenkins, 2013: 9). Malkki (2014: 186) makes a similar distinction. 'One of the key issues in this debate is how to draw the line between politically motivated lone wolf terrorism and mass murderers acting primarily motivated by personal grievances or mental health problems'. Others make the case that there is too much focus on mental health issues. The introduction of a special issue of *Terrorism and Political Violence* on the topic of lone-actor terrorism complains of the overt focus on psychological problems of lone-actor terrorists (Kaplan, Lööw, & Malkki, 2013: 5–6). Pantucci (2011a: 37) agrees: 'a further complicating factor is how to separate and distinguish them from those individuals who for their own perverse reasons decide to act'. Sageman (cited in Pantucci, 2011b: 5) also expresses similar thoughts: 'There are two kinds of Lone Wolves, real lone wolves and mass murderers'. While the former, according to Sageman, are part of a virtual community, the latter works from their own 'personal insane ideology'. Burton and Stewart (2008) distinguish between 'lone wolves' and 'lone nuts'. The latter are 'mentally ill individuals motivations for other reasons ... not conducting politically motivated terrorist attacks'. This false dichotomy prevails in public and practitioner discourse also. As mentioned earlier, President Obama's 2011 remarks regarding the threat of lone-actor terrorism highlighted 'When you've got one person who is deranged *or* driven by a hateful ideology, they can do a lot of damage, and it's a lot harder to trace those lone wolves' (emphasis added). Similarly, an Air Force Colonel, speaking about the Hasan Akbar case stated: 'The question is whether this is a mental health issue *or* an issue with a fundamentalist in jihad who had some kind of conversion and believed this is a mission he needed to undertake' (Brown, Mecoy, & Martineau, 2003, emphasis added).

In other words, an act of targeted violence is either the action of a rational terrorist or an irrational mentally unstable civilian. Over the space of 40 years of research on terrorist motivation the literature has jumped from one extreme position ('they are all mentally ill') to the exact opposite ('by definition, a terrorist cannot be mentally ill'). This is also reflected in some major criminological research. For example, Hirschi and Gottfredson's (1983) control theory views 'regular criminals' as impulsive, whereas terrorists need higher levels of control and are implicitly more calculating and therefore less likely to be mentally ill. In reality, such distinctions are probably less clear-cut. A false dichotomy may exist that categorizes violent individuals as either a rational terrorist or an irrational and unstable individual.

This false dichotomy may therefore be driven by three factors – the search for master narratives, a misunderstanding of rationality, and the focus on group-based actors. First, once a history of mental health is identified within an individual offender, it is often incorrectly assumed that the mental illness is the primary driver of behaviour. Borum (2013) elucidates: 'If the subject … been given some diagnostic label, then there is a common tendency to regard that label as a master explanation of the subject's thinking, motives and behaviour. It is not'. Instead, we should be looking at how a multitude of variables and experiences (mental illness being one) crystallize within the offender at the same time.

Second, it is also often incorrectly assumed that just because there is a history of mental illness, the offender is 'completely irrational and incapable of planned or self-interested behaviour' (Borum, 2013: 107). Research demonstrates however that the supposed 'irrationality' experienced by the mentally ill is not as debilitating as previously thought (Gill, Horgan, & Deckert, 2014; Borum et al., 2012; Fein & Vossekuil, 1999). These studies have shown that individuals with mental illness can display rational motivations. For example, Gill et al. (2014) illustrate that lone-actor terrorists diagnosed with mental illness frequently display rational motives. Similarly, Borum (2013) highlights a number of terrorists with mental illness who were capable of sophisticated attack planning. In an operational study of assassins, attackers and near-lethal approachers, Fein and Vossekuil (1999), highlight cases of mentally ill individuals planning and executing behaviours as effectively as those lacking diagnosis.

Take Richard Baumhammers for example. On 28 April 2000, he went on a racially motivated shooting spree, killing five individuals. His political manifesto largely complained about the ills of immigration from developing countries. In 1993, he experienced a psychotic episode. He became convinced that the FBI, among others, monitored his everyday routine activities. He was admitted to the Western Psychiatric Institute and Clinic in Oakland. For a number of years afterwards, doctors proscribed him anti-psychotic drugs. Despite his mental health problems, Baumhammers targeting on that day was purposive. First, he fatally shot his next-door neighbour, a member of the Jewish faith. Next he drove three miles north to the Beth El congregation where his neighbour worshipped. There he fired at the windows of the synagogue and spray-painted two red swastikas onto the building's walls. Next he drove half a mile east to an Indian grocery shop where he fatally shot one and paralyzed another. Both individuals were of Indian descent. Baumhammers then drove another two miles north to another synagogue located in Carnegie. Again he shot the windows out before driving six and a half miles north-west to Robinson town centre. There he entered a Chinese restaurant, killing two Asian-American customers, a Vietnamese-American chef and the Chinese manager. Baumhammers also planned for a getaway by storing $4,000 in his sports-utility vehicle that he utilized to drive between the different targets.

Finally, existing studies of terrorist offenders typically focus on group not lone actors. The former population of recruits does not tend to be psychopathologically damaged, or for that matter highly uneducated and impoverished because of a selection effect. Organizational elites seek to recruit those most capable of undertaking assigned tasks. Most tasks require an element of secrecy, calibrated violence, and technological know-how. Educated, psychologically healthy and normal volunteers tend to be preferred for this particular reason. It was argued that those who seek to join but display signs of mental illness may be weeded out in the selection process (Silke, 2003).

Of the sample within this book, 41% experienced a history of mental health problems. This figure is comparable to analogous studies. For example, Fein and Vossekuil (1999) found 61% of lone assassins had previous contact with mental health services. Hewitt (2003) found 22% of American 'loners' psychologically disturbed. In perhaps the methodologically most sophisticated study, Gruenewald et al. (2013) compared far-right group and lone offenders, finding mental illness prevalence differed across offender types (group offender, 7.6%, and lone offender, 40.4%). Similarly, Hewitt (2003) describes differences in prevalence of mental illness across terrorist group and lone actors (8.1% compared to 22%). These results suggest psychopathological causation differs across terrorist type. This higher preponderance amongst lone-actor samples may be due to processes that the group-based terrorism literature has long hypothesized. Individuals displaying these traits will not be selected for recruitment. For example, De Mesquita (2005) utilizes a game theoretic model to demonstrate differences between recruits and sympathizers to terrorist causes. The rationale being that organizations screen recruits to select the most competent to become cadres. Similarly, Horgan (2005) notes that particular individuals may never meet recruitment criteria due to overt psychological characteristics rendering them unsuitable. Spaaij (2010) explains that due to psychological conditions, certain individuals fail to become recruited despite demonstrating willingness, and thus act independently instead.

The relatively high prevalence suggests a need for revisiting the issue of mental illness as a part of the process for some people becoming involved in terrorism. Psychopathological mechanisms remain systematically unexamined, and there may be grounds to pursue a more concrete understanding of how mental illness and psychological processes influence an individual's participation in and trajectory through terrorist behaviours. The wider criminology literature suggests that much promise exists in utilizing mental illness as a central variable with relation to criminogenic factors. As Anderson (1997) explains, the symbiotic relationship between mental illness and criminal behaviour is complex. Co-morbidity of mental illness with other behaviours is well documented across the literature and includes substance abuse (Todd et al., 2004), and violent and criminal convictions (Anderson, 1997).

The Corner and Gill study (2014)

In a recent study of lone-actor terrorists and lone dyads between 1990 and 2011, Corner and Gill (2014) analysed a number of factors related to mental illness and lone-actor terrorism. The results illustrated the need to recalibrate the literature's position on mental illness and terrorism in a number of ways. Their first analysis involved comparing the prevalence of mental illness between the lone actor/lone dyad sample with a matched sample of group-based actors. While such contentions have long been outside the realm of terrorism studies, these studies typically focused upon terrorist groups not lone actors. Because of the presence of co-offenders and the group manner in which terrorist events usually take place, it can be doubted whether terrorist group members possess the same personality characteristics and motivations as solo offenders. As the group terrorist member needs to cross fewer psychological barriers to commit violence against others (due to factors such as deindividuation, diffusion of responsibility, conformity to group elders, etc.) than a lone-actor terrorist, it may be likely that a group terrorist offender has on average a less problematic personality structure. Indeed, the results showed that the rates of mental illness were significantly greater in the former group. This reflects the findings of Gruenewald et al's (2013) analysis of extreme right-wing offenders who have caused fatalities in the U.S.

Next, Corner and Gill disaggregated the lone actor/lone dyad sample in two and compared the demographic traits and behaviours of those with and without a history of mental illness. They came to a number of highly interesting conclusions. First, those with a history were significantly less likely to have some form of command and control link. This further bolsters the argument that selection effects are at play; something that an increasing number of studies are finding. Future interview-based research should delve deeper into this domain. We have next to no first-hand accounts of the recruitment process from the group's perspective. Second, the study also revealed a significant association between mental illness and having a spouse/partner associated with a wider movement. This could possibly be suggestive of those with mental illness being susceptible to ideological influences in their immediate social environment. Such results again reflect the need to avoid 'master narrative' explanations and instead focus upon the sort of perfect storm the individual found him/herself in. In a similar vein, Corner and Gill also demonstrated significant associations between mental illness and the experience of stressors.

Third, a recurring theme in the literature concerning lone actors is social isolation. The results demonstrated those with a history of mental illness are no more likely to have an association with social isolation than those without. This result provides important implications for countering lone-actor terrorism, and suggests community services hold the potential to be the most effective discipline in combating this facet of behaviour.

Fourth, they found that lone actors with a history of mental illness were more likely associated with single-issue ideologies than al-Qaeda inspired or extreme right-wing ideologies. Those who hold a single-issue ideology are more typically fixated upon a target that they see as wholly responsible for their grievance. For example, Walter Leroy Moody Jr. mailed pipe bombs to specific targets affiliated with criminal courts and Scott Roeder targeted an abortion provider he extensively wrote about online. These behaviours are reflected in certain mental illnesses. Those with mental illness can experience intrusive thought processes, neuroticism, and psychotic episodes (Link & Stueve, 1994; American Psychiatric Association, 2000; World Health Organization, 2010) which cause fixations upon specific 'targets' who the individual view as responsible. This finding also follows Clarke and Newman's (2006) work on situational crime prevention. They hypothesize successful attacks to be more likely when opportunities are apparent. Individuals fixating upon singular targets will encounter a great range of opportunities. The above evidence also counters the school of thought that explains irrationality to negatively affect behaviour (Hiday & Burns, 2010: 479), thus impairing their capability of striking. The significant finding that those with a mental illness have an association with claiming responsibility publicly also fits diagnostic criteria of certain mental illnesses (grandiosity, extraversion, delusions, delirium, impulsivity, and attention seeking behaviours) (American Psychiatric Association; World Health Organization). The finding that those with a mental illness have an association with expressing a desire to hurt others may provide useful directions for prevention efforts.

Fifth, despite previous research showing definitive associations between individual's with mental illness and crime (Anderson, 1997; Holcom & Ahr, 1988; Singleton, Meltzer, & Gatward, 1998; Teplin, 1984), there were no significant associations found between mental illness and prior criminal behaviour. Those with a history of mental illness were no more likely to have a criminal history than those with no history. However, due to the type of data analysed, it was not possible to discern dates for previous criminal convictions and any psychiatric diagnoses. This could have helped determine whether the terrorist act immediately followed the onset of a disorder. Further investigations should consider such dynamics, to definitively conclude whether those with a mental illness are statistically more likely to possess criminal convictions. Although those with a history of mental illness were not more likely to have a prior criminal conviction, the cohort did have a strong statistical link with prior violent behaviours. These results support the preceding literature that those with a mental illness are more likely to be violent.

Rather than treating mental illness dichotomously (either the individual had a history of it or not), Corner and Gill's final analysis stratified mental illness across a broad spectrum. The analysis demonstrated that certain variables significantly impact upon certain mental illness diagnoses (despite the low number of individuals in each category). Schizophrenia and associated disorders was the only diagnostic group to be significantly associated with previous violence and this supports past research (Krakowski, Volavka, & Brizer, 1986; Shaw et al., 2006). Negative statistics (though not significant) were found concerning stress related disorders and violent behaviour (supporting Swanson, Holzer, Ganju, & Jono, 1990). Negative associations were also found between personality disorders and autism and having a spouse/partner related to a terror movement, which may be indicative of not having a spouse due to the detrimental nature of these disorders. Because mental disorders often share symptoms, further research may also focus upon analysing symptoms of mental illness rather than the diagnoses themselves (Douglas, Guy, & Hart, 2009). Unfortunately, this was not possible due to constraints in the available data. However, both authors are currently working alongside colleagues with the U.K.'s North West Counter Terrorism under Project Regulus to consider both differential diagnosis and symptoms as risk factors of violence in a sample of lone domestic extremists.

Finally, the findings of the Corner and Gill (2014) study provided evidence those lone actors with a history of mental illness were also more likely to engage in certain antecedent events and behaviours that security and policing agencies can utilize to monitor and prevent further developments in attack plotting. In essence, the correlated behaviours provide an image of how risk can crystallize within the individual offender and that our understanding of lone-actor terrorism should be multivariate in nature. The findings supported James et al. (2007) and Chermak, Freilich, and Simone (2010), who emphasize the need for cooperation between agencies and widespread sharing of information. The empirical evidence suggests mental health professionals may have a role in preventing lone-actor terrorist attacks. If mental health professionals were aware of these findings then screening processes can be carried out by security agencies on patients that present similar antecedents and behaviours in medical evaluations. Examples of multidisciplinary cohesion concerning criminal offences include the Multi-Agency Public Protection Arrangements (MAPPA) and the Fixated Threat Assessment Centre (FTAC). MAPPA involves multiple agencies (including mental health professionals, probation service, police forces, and the HM prison service) that are tasked with managing offenders, and focuses upon a range of offenders (Ministry of Justice, 2012). FTAC is an initiative aiming to protect politicians, the British Royal Family and other public figures from fixated individuals, by incorporating input from the department of health and the metropolitan police (Fixated Research Group, 2013). MAPPA focuses upon offenders following conviction and release, whereas FTAC assesses potential threats and aims to provide psychiatric services to offenders as a prevention mechanism. The results highlight that data-driven analyses can help provide an empirical knowledge base from which organizations like FTAC and MAPPA can make more informed decisions concerning risk and capability.

A limitation to this approach is that it typically treats all variables equally in terms of when the individual experienced them. We have no sense of the temporal trajectory and how these variables interacted with each other in space and time. We just now they co-occurred at some point in the individual's life-course. Horgan (2014: 63) correctly notes that although studies of lone actors often find high preponderance of mental health issues within the sample, 'detailed research would be needed to further clarify the precise nature and role (if any) of mental health problems in the development of their violent activity'. This debate is ongoing within the wider study of crime also. On the one hand, a strand of research assumes a consistent causal link between psychiatric symptoms (where they are found to be present) and criminal behaviour (Torrey, 2011). On the other hand, a more nuanced strand of research argues there are 'a (small) group of offenders whose symptoms relate directly to crime and a (larger) group whose symptoms and crimes are not directly related' (Peterson, Skeem, Kennealy, Bray, & Zvonkovic, 2014: 1). For example, various studies illustrate that the offender (across a range of crimes) was experiencing the symptoms of their diagnoses at the time of their (often violent) crime between 4% and 18% of the time (Monahan, Steadman, & Silver, 2001; Junginger, Claypoole, Laygo, & Crisanti, 2006; Peterson, Skeem, Hart, Vidal, & Keith, 2010; Peterson et al., 2014).

To get an indication of potential answers with respect to lone-actor terrorism, we now turn to three illustrative case studies.

Case studies

On 23 March 2003, Sergeant Hasan Akbar threw four hand grenades into three tents where members of the 101st Airborne Division of the U.S. Army slept. He also fired a series of shots in the chaos that ensued. The attack occurred at Camp Pennsylvania in Kuwait. Two people died and another 14 were injured. At his court martial, Akbar's defence lawyers indicated he suffered a number of mental health problems including depression, paranoia, irrational behaviour, and a series of sleep disorders including insomnia. Indeed, Akbar twice fell asleep at his pre-trial hearing. He suffered these problems since he was 14. His clinical psychologist from those early years testified he believed Akbar had a learning disability. Court records from one of Akbar's appeals reveals that (a) his father had a history of depression, sleep problems, and previous suicidal issues (b) his uncle was discharged from the Marines for psychiatric problems and (c) his half-brother suffered from significant paranoia.

He was 31 at the time of the incident; a 17-year gap between the initial diagnoses and the violent action. The defence claimed the symptoms worsened during his military service. The military clinical psychologist could not make a definitive diagnosis because of 'various symptoms, such as bizarre thinking, decompensation under stress, history of depression, paranoia, suspicion, inability to read social cues, sleep problems, psychometer agitation and impulsivity'. Instead he made three differential diagnoses, all on the schizophrenia spectrum (United States Army Court of Criminal Appeals, 2012). The defence lawyer argued these mental health issues stemmed from the time Akbar's stepfather sexually abused Akbar's younger sister. Akbar had been recently reprimanded for insubordination and was blocked from entering active duty in Iraq.

In his personal diaries written during his time at Fort Campbell, Akbar noted (cited in Thompson, 2005): 'I am not going to do anything about it as long as I stay here. But as soon as I am in Iraq, I am going to try and kill as many of them as possible'. However, the stated intentions to commit violence were nothing new. As far back as 1992, Akbar wrote: 'I made a promise that if I am not able to achieve success because of some Caucasians, I will kill as many of them as possible'. In 1993, he wrote: 'I do not like the military. They have too much control over people's lives. I suppose I am just anti-government.... A Muslim should see himself as a Muslim only. His loyalty should be to Islam only'. Two further entries from 1996 noted: 'Anyone who stands in front of me shall be considered the enemy and dealt with accordingly' and 'Destroying America was my plan as a child, and as a juvenile and in college. Destroying America is my greatest goal'. In 1997 he wrote: 'My life will not be complete unless America is destroyed'. He joined the military in 1998.

It appears in the case of Akbar that his mental illness certainly played a role in the violence he finally engaged in. His story is very reminiscent of many of the cases looked at in previous chapters. Akbar suffered from his mental illness and wrote of his intention to engage in violent activities over a long period of time. Because of the long time lag, mental illness cannot be the master narrative. It lacks specificity by itself and necessitates looking at Akbar's immediate situation to get a clearer picture of what lessened his resilience against engaging in violence. The stress of military life and later being deployed abroad appeared to have worsened many of his symptoms, which in turn helped feed the perceived legitimacy of his grievances and planned actions.

On 4 March 2010, John Patrick Bedell shot and wounded two Pentagon police officers at the security checkpoint in the Pentagon station of the Washington Metro transit system. Bedell had a long history of mental health issues. On at least three occasions, he was committed to mental institutions. According to his brother, Bedell held a long-standing scepticism toward the U.S. government that dated back to the 1991 Gulf War. Following the break-up of his relationship in 2002, this suspicion became more salient and turned to paranoia. Bedell would point skyward, convinced 'they were watching', he would listen to songs on the radio and believe secret warnings were coded in them. On other occasions, he insisted on associates removing their mobile phone batteries and believed the neighbours were spying on him. In 2004, he was diagnosed as suffering from bipolar disorder, depression, and anxiety. In 2006, Bedell cited bipolar disorder in relation to a charge of cultivating 16 marijuana plants and resisting arrest. A psychiatrist confirmed this diagnosis. Around this same time, Bedell began to rail against the U.S. government in a series of blog posts, podcasts, and Wikipedia entries. In one internet posting, he suggested the 9/11 attacks were the work of a criminal organization controlling the U.S. government. 'This organization, like so many murderous governments throughout history, would see the sacrifice of thousands of its citizens in an event such as the Sept. 11 attack as a small cost in order to perpetuate its barbaric control'. He continued: 'To prevent themselves from being enslaved, the powerful masters of our existing governments use every means at their disposal, including bribery, theft, and murder, to control those governments, which are, in imperfect institutions, operated by imperfect individuals'. In 2007, he received community service in lieu of jail time for a disturbance of the peace offence. The offence involved threatening a six-year-old and his/her father with a six-foot hockey stick when they refused him entry into the soccer practice game. In 2008, he registered for graduate school education. He failed to register for the Spring 2010 class sometime during fall 2009. On 3 January 2010, police stopped Bedell for speeding. He also received a citation for possession of drug paraphernalia.

On 4 January, Bedell's parents filed a missing person report for him. The report mentions that Bedell went missing soon after getting into a fight with his brother. On 10 January 2010, Bedell attempted a $600 purchase at a shooting range but was declined due to his mental illness history. Bedell made a brief return home within a couple of days. His parents mentioned to police that Bedell appeared 'impaired, delusional and agitated'. Much of this agitation sprung from questioning concerning the attempted $600 purchase and he quickly left the house. On 18 January, Bedell's parents revoked the missing person report upon his second return to the family home. On 29 January, Bedell purchased a Ruger handgun at a Las Vegas gun show. On 1 February, police stopped Bedell's vehicle and charged him with marijuana possession. Bedell failed to show up in court the following day.

In Bedell, we have another example of how mental illness should not be treated as a master narrative explanation. His symptoms appeared to worsen when other things in his life went wrong such as the breakdown of a relationship (personal and familial) and troubles with the law. Unlike Akbar, Bedell had a criminal history that spanned drug production on a very minor scale, to physical assaults to driving offences. If we are to apply the master narrative mental illness explanation to his terrorist offences, we would need to also apply it to his other crimes and find a reason for why these were the crimes he opted for first rather than terrorism.

The final example is Nicky Reilly whose failed bombing attack targeted a restaurant in Exeter, U.K. The next quote is lengthy and is testimony provided by his mother during the trial.

> He sort of lived in a bubble. He felt comfortable in his own company although he did have lots of friends in primary school – he mixed better at primary school than at secondary school.... When I actually got the diagnosis, I felt relieved because everything was answered then. This Asperger's – this autism – it all made sense then, because for years I was told there

was nothing wrong with him.... At around 15, Nicky started becoming very obsessive. I don't know if adolescence brought it out more, but something brought this illness out in Nicky, triggered it really badly.... He was so obsessive – with everything he did, every day. Nicky's behaviour was mentally draining, exhaustive.... It was pulling him down. He was frustrated. He was a very frustrated child.... He started self harming – but then self harming became the obsession.... He was contemplating suicide all the time and it was destroying us all. He was so young and he had everything to live for, but he was negative and frustrated. It was really hard.... He used to be very good at convincing me 'I'll be okay. I'm not going to do this', then you would let him go out and he would do something stupid. I think it was a cry for help. I asked myself if he really wanted to take his own life all the time – 'Does he really want to die?'

(cited in Cheston, 2009)

Age 16, Reilly was sent to a residential care centre for a few weeks. He missed the final weeks of that years schooling:

That was his biggest regret, missing the last few weeks of school, everybody leaving. Even up to when he did what he did he used to still talk about it. He always wishes he was back at school and he misses all his friends and everything ... Nicky tends to look back even though he's only 22. He says it's the good old days. I don't know whether he means that he wants to go back and start again, have his life again. He would look at photos and go 'remember that'. He was so happy then. But he just became so negative and in a rut. As he got older his anxiety attacks got worse and worse. He's been on medication for depression – the side effect was he put on a lot of weight – but he didn't get better through being on it.

Reilly found solace at the local mosque:

When he went to the mosque they welcomed him and accepted him for who he was. They gave him respect and that's where he felt comfortable ... Nicky could have got into any religion. I only wish he'd got into Buddhism now. In my heart I always believed that it (Islam) was another hobby, another fad, and he'd go onto something else, move on from it.

Reilly's is a more clear-cut case than the other two. Clearly his mental health issues were linked to a number of self-harming behaviours, suicidal ideation, and his fixation with different aspects of life that passed in fads. Reilly's mother is convinced he came into contact with people that led him towards acting violently:

I believe someone took Nicky under their wing, planted the seed of all these extremist views, nurtured it, set him on the path and then slowly fell back into the background themselves. And then that's where the internet took over.... Someone's loaded the gun for him to fire – loaded him up in his head – and that day, in that moment of madness, it's just ruined his whole life.

If this is true, it adds further weight to the fact that while mental illness may play a key role in an individuals trajectory towards lone-actor terrorism, it can only ever be treated as one distal risk factor that needs to interact with more proximal drivers like meeting with co-ideologues, and building the capacity to engage in an attack on a target perceived as vulnerable.

Regardless, these are purely illustrations limited by the lack of access to these offenders. What does shine through within these analyses of mental health issues and lone-actor terrorism is the need for researchers to be very specific about what population of actors they are addressing. For too long, aggregate analyses tried to understand the 'terrorist' and implicitly assumed that the drivers were similar across ideologies, time, role, and group (or lack thereof). As data (in all shapes and sizes, be it first-hand interviews or databases based on court records) becomes more and more available within terrorism studies, we can start to unpick the subtle differences between terrorist offenders on a range of measures. This in turn, can help lead toward more targeted measures aiming at controlling, disrupting, detecting, and mitigating against a stratified terrorist sample.

References

Adigun Lawal, C. (2002). Social-psychological considerations in the emergence and growth of terrorism, pp. 23–56 in C. E. Stout (ed.). *The psychology of terrorism: Programs and practices in response and prevention.* Westport, CT: Praeger Publishers.

Akhtar, S. (1999). The psychodynamic dimension of terrorism. *Psychiatric annals 29*(6): 350–355.

American Psychiatric Association. (2000). *Diagnostic and statistical manual of mental disorders* (4th ed., text rev.). Washington D.C.: American Psychiatric Association.

Anderson, M. (1997). Mental Illness and Criminal Behaviour: a Literature Review. *Journal of Psychiatric and Mental Health Nursing, 4*(4), 243–250.

Beck, A. T. (2002). Prisoners of Hate. *Behavior research and therapy 40*(3): 209–216.

Berko, A. (2007). *The path to paradise: The inner world of suicide bombers and their dispatchers.* New York: Praeger Publishers.

Billig, O. (1985). The lawyer terrorist and his comrades. *Political psychology 6*(1): 29–46.

Bollinger, L. (1985). Terrorist conduct as a result of a psychological process. *Psychiatry: The state of the art* 6: 387–390. New York: Plenum.

Borum, R. (2013). Informing Lone-Offender Investigations. *Criminology & Public Policy, 12*(1), 103–112.

Borum, R., Fein, R., & Vossekuil, B. (2012). A Dimensional Approach to Analyzing Lone Offender Terrorism. *Aggression and Violent Behaviour, 17*(5), 389–396.

Brown, M., Mecoy, L., & Martineau, P. (2003, 25 March). From UCD Graduate to GI Killing Suspect. *Metro Final Edition.*

Brynjar, L. (2000). *Why terrorism occurs: a survey of theories and hypotheses on the causes of terrorism.* Norway: Norwegian Defence Research Establishment.

Chermak, S. M., Freilich, J. D., & Simone, Jr, J. (2010). Surveying American State Police Agencies About Lone Wolves, Far-Right Criminality and Far-Right and Islamic Jihadist Criminal Collaboration. *Studies in Conflict & Terrorism, 33*(11), 1019–1041.

Cheston, P. (2009, 30 January). Muslim Convert is Jailed for 18 Years Over Nail Bombing. *The Evening Standard.*

Clarke, R. V. G., & Newman, G. R. (2006). *Outsmarting the terrorists.* Portsmouth, N.H.: Greenwood Publishing Group.

Cooper, H. H. A. (1978). Psychopaths as terrorists. *Legal medical quarterly* 2: 253–262.

Corner, E., & Gill, P. (2014). A False Dichotomy? Lone Actor Terrorism and Mental Illness. *Law and Human Behavior.*

Crayton, J. W. (1983). Terrorism and psychology of the self. pp. 33–41 in L. Z. Freedman, & Y. Alexander (eds.). *Perspectives on terrorism.* Delaware: Scholarly Resources.

Crenshaw, M. (1981). The causes of terrorism. *Comparative politics 13*(4): 379–399.

De Mause, L. (2002). The childhood origins of terrorism. *Journal of psychohistory* 29 (4): 340–348.

De Mesquita, E. B. (2005). The Quality of Terror. *American Journal of Political Science, 49*(3), 515–530.

Douglas, K. S., Guy, L. S., & Hart, S. D. (2009). Psychosis as a Risk Factor for Violence to Others: A Meta-Analysis. *Psychological Bulletin, 135*(5), 679–706.

Fein, R. A., & Vossekuil, B. (1999). Assassination in the United States: An Operational Study of Recent Assassins, Attackers, and Near-Lethal Approachers. *Journal of Forensic Sciences, 44*(2), 321–333.

Ferguson, N., Burgess, M., & Hollywood, I. (2008). Crossing the rubicon: Deciding to become a paramilitary in Northern Ireland. *International journal of conflict and violence 2*(1): 130–137.

Ferracuti, F., & F. Bruno (1981). Psychiatric aspects of terrorism in Italy, pp. 199–213 in I. L. Barak-Glantz, & C. R. Huffs (eds.). *The mad, the bad, and the different: essays in honor of Simon Dinitz.* Lexington, MA: Heath.

Fixated Research Group. (2013). Preventing harm and facilitating care. Retrieved from: www.fixatedthreat.com/. Accessed 22 September 2014.

Gill, P., Horgan, J., & Deckert, P. (2014). Bombing Alone: Tracing the Motivations and Antecedent Behaviors of Lone-Actor Terrorists. *Journal of Forensic Sciences, 59*(2), 425–435.

Gruenewald, J., Chermak, S., & Freilich, J. D. (2013). Distinguishing 'Loner' Attacks from other Domestic Extremist Violence: A Comparison of Far-Right Homicide. Incident and Offender Characteristics. *Criminology & Public Policy, 12*(1), 65–91.

Hacker, F. J. (1976). *Crusaders, criminals, crazies: Terror and terrorism in our time.* New York: Norton.

Hamden, R. H. (2002). The retributional terrorist: Type 4, pp. 162–192 in C. E. Stout (ed.). *The psychology of terrorism: A public understanding.* Westport, CT: Praeger Publishers.

Heskin, K. (1984). The psychology of terrorism in Northern Ireland, pp. 88–105 in Y. Alexander, & A. O'Day (eds.). *Terrorism in Ireland.* Kent: Croom Helm.

Hewitt, C. (2003). *Understanding terrorism in America.* New York, NY: Routledge.

Hiday, V. A., & Burns, P. J. (2010). Mental illness and the criminal justice system. In T. L. Scheid & T. N. Brown (eds.). *A handbook for the study of mental health: Social*

contexts, theories and systems (2nd ed., pp. 478–498). Cambridge, England: Cambridge University Press.
Hoffman Baruch, E. (2003). Psychoanalysis and terrorism: The need for a global 'talking cure'. *Psychoanalytic psychology 20*(4): 698–700.
Hogg, M., & Vaughan, G. (2005). *Social psychology*. London: Pearson Prentice Hall.
Holcomb, W. R., & Ahr, P. R. (1988). Arrest rates among young adult psychiatric patients treated in inpatient and outpatient settings. *Hospital and Community Psychiatry, 39*(1), 52–57.
Horgan, J. (2005). *The psychology of terrorism*. London: Routledge.
Hubbard, D. G. (1971). *The skyjacker: His flights of fantasy*. New York, NY: Macmillan.
James, D. V., Mullen, P. E., Meloy, J. R., Pathé, M. T., Farnham, F. R., Preston, L., & Darnley, B. (2007). The Role of Mental Disorder in Attacks on European Politicians 1990–2004. *Acta Psychiatrica Scandinavica, 116*(5), 334–344.
Jenkins, B. M. (2013). Foreword. In J. D. Simon (ed.). *Lone wolf terrorism: Understanding the growing threat* (pp. 7–11). New York, NY: Prometheus Books.
Junginger, J., Claypoole, K., Laygo, R., & Crisanti, A. (2006). Effects of serious mental illness and substance abuse on criminal offenses. *Psychiatric Services, 57*(6), 879–882.
Kaplan, A. (1978). The psychodynamics of terrorism. *Terrorism* 1: 237–257.
Kaplan, J., Lööw, H., & Malkki, L. (2014). Introduction to the Special Issue on Lone Wolf and Autonomous Cell Terrorism. *Terrorism and Political Violence, 26*(1), 1–12.
Kent, I., and W. Nicholls (1977). The psychodynamics of terrorism. *Mental health and society* 4: 1–8.
Krakowski, M., Volavka, J., & Brizer., D. (1986). Psychopathology and Violence: A Review of Literature. *Comprehensive Psychiatry, 27*(2), 131–148.
Lasch, C. (1979). *The culture of narcissism: American life in an age of diminishing expectations*. New York: Norton.
Lester, D., Yang, B., & Lindsay, M. (2004). Suicide bombers: are psychological profiles possible? *Studies in conflict and terrorism 27*(4): 283–295.
Link, B. G., & Stueve, A. (1996). Psychotic symptoms and the violent/illegal behavior of mental patients compared to community controls. In J. Monahan, & H. J. Steadman (eds.). *Violence and mental disorder: Developments in risk assessment* (pp. 137–160). Chicago: University of Chicago Press.
Malkki, L. (2014). Political elements in post-Columbine school shootings in Europe and North America. *Terrorism and political violence, 26*(1), 185–210.
Martens, W. H. J. (2004). Terrorist with antisocial personality disorder. *Journal of forensic psychology practice 4*(1): 45–56.
Ministry of Justice. (2012). MAPPA guidance: Version 4. Retrieved from www.justice.gov.uk/downloads/offenders/mappa/mappa-guidance-2012-part1.pdf. Accessed 22 September 2014.
Monahan, J., Steadman, H., Silver, E. (2001). *Rethinking Risk Assessment: The MacArthur Study of Mental Disorder and Violence*. New York: Oxford University Press.
Obama, B. (2011). Biggest terror fear is the lone wolf. Retrieved from: http://security.blogs.cnn.com/2011/08/16/obama-biggest-terror-fear-is-the-lone-wolf/). Accessed 1 June 2014.
Pantucci, R. (2011a). What Have We Learned about Lone Wolves from Anders Behring Breivik? *Perspectives on Terrorism*, 5(5–6).
Pantucci, R. (2011b). *A typology of lone wolves: preliminary analysis of lone Islamist terrorists*. London: International Centre for the Study of Radicalisation and Political Violence.

Pearce, K. I. (1977). Police negotiations. *Canadian psychiatric association journal* 22: 171–174.

Pearlstein, R. M. (1991). *The mind of the political terrorist.* Wilmington D.C.: SR Books.

Peterson, J., Skeem, J., Hart, E., Vidal, S., & Keith, F. (2010). Analyzing offense patterns as a function of mental illness to test the criminalization hypothesis. *Psychiatric Services*, *61*(12), 1217–1222.

Peterson, J. K., Skeem, J., Kennealy, P., Bray, B., & Zvonkovic, A. (2014, April 14). How often and how consistently do symptoms directly precede criminal behavior among offenders with mental illness? *Law and Human Behavior*. Advance online publication. Retrieved from: http://dx.doi.org/10.1037/lhb0000075. Accessed 1 June 2014.

Piven, J. S. (2002). On the psychosis (religion) of terrorists, pp. 119–148 in C. E. Stout, (ed.). *The psychology of terrorism: Theoretical understandings and perspectives.* Westport, C.T.: Praeger Publishers.

Post, J. (2005). When hatred is bred in the bone: psycho-cultural foundations of contemporary terrorism. *Political psychology*, *26*(4): 615–636.

Post, J., Sprinzak, E., & Denny, L. (2005). The terrorists in their own words: Interviews with 35 incarcerated Middle Eastern terrorists. *Terrorism and political violence*, *15*(1): 171–184.

Rasch, W. (1979). Psychological dimensions of political terrorism in the federal republic of Germany. *International journal of law and psychiatry* 2: 79–85.

Reinares, F. (2004). Who are the terrorists? Analyzing changes in the sociological profile among members of ETA. *Studies in conflict and terrorism*, *27*(6): 465–488.

Sageman, M. (2005). *Understanding terror networks.* Pennsylvania: University of Pennsylvania Press.

Sanchez-Cuenca, I. (2007). The dynamics of nationalist terrorism: ETA and the IRA. *Terrorism and political violence*, *19*(3): 289–306.

Shaw, J., Hunt, I. M., Flynn, S., Meehan, J., Robinson, J., Bickley, H., Parsons, R., McCann, K., Burns, J., Amons, T., Kapur, N., & Appleby, L. (2006). Rates of Mental Disorder in People Convicted of Homicide: National Clinical Survey. *British Journal of Psychiatry*, *188*(2), 143–147.

Silke, A. (2003). Becoming a terrorist. In A. Silke (ed.). *Terrorists, victims and society: Psychological perspectives on terrorism and its consequences.* Chichester, England: Wiley.

Singleton, N., Meltzer, H., & Gatward, R. (1998). *Psychiatric morbidity among prisoners: Summary report.* Government Statistical Service. Retrieved from Office for National Statistics website: www.ons.gov.uk/ons/rel/psychiatric-morbidity/psychiatric-morbidity-among-prisoners/psychiatric-morbidity-among-prisoners–summary-report/index.html. Accessed 1 June 2014.

Spaaij, R. (2010). The Enigma of Lone Wolf Terrorism: An Assessment. *Studies in Conflict & Terrorism*, *33*(9), 854–870.

Stern, J. (2004). *Terror in the name of God: Why religious militants kill.* London: HarperCollins.

Swanson, J., Holzer, C., Ganju, V. K., & Jono, R. T. (1990). Violence and Psychiatric Disorder in the Community: Evidence from the Epidemiologic Catchment Area Surveys. *Hospital & Community Psychiatry*, *41*(7), 761–770.

Tanay, E. (1987). Pseudo-Political terrorism. *Journal of forensic science*, *32*(1): 192–200.

Teplin, L. A. (1984). Criminalizing Mental Disorder: The Comparative Arrest Rate of the Mentally Ill. *American Psychologist*, *39*(7), 794–803.

Thompson, E. (2005, 20 April). Accused Sergeant's Father Says Son was Racially Harassed Before Attack on Fellow Soldiers. *The Associated Press*.

Todd, J., Green, G., Harrison, M., Ikuesan, B. A., Self, C., Pevalin, D. J., & Baldacchino, A. (2004). Social exclusion in clients with comorbid mental health and substance misuse problems. *Social psychiatry and psychiatric epidemiology*, *39*(7), 581–587.

Torrey, E. F. (2011). The association of stigma with violence. *American journal of psychiatry*, *168*(3), 325–352.

United States Army Court of Criminal Appeals (2012). United States, Appellee v. Sergeant Hasan K. Akbar United States Army, Appellant. 13 July. Retrieved from: http://www.caaflog.com/wp-content/uploads/akbar.pdf. Accessed 1 June 2014.

Victoroff, J. (2005). The mind of a terrorist: A review and critique of psychological approaches. *Journal of conflict resolution*, *49*(1): 3–42

World Health Organization. (2010). *ICD-10: International Statistical Classification of Diseases and Related Health Problems* (10th rev.). Retrieved from: www.who.int/classifications/icd/en/. Accessed 1 June 2014.

7 Comparing lone-actor terrorists

This chapter describes ways in which we can conceive and categorize types of lone-actor terrorists, characteristics, and behaviours. First, we should review the literature on the development of typologies within criminological and forensic psychological contexts.

In the limited literature that currently exists on lone-actor terrorists, offenders tend to be depicted in a binary fashion; subjects either 'are' or 'are not' a lone-actor terrorist. Lone-actor terrorists are therefore typically treated in a homogeneous manner.[1] Anecdotally, however, there are a number of easily distinguishable differences in lone-actor terrorists' characteristics, behaviours and connectivity with other groups. For example, there is a difference between Ted Kaczynski and Timothy McVeigh in terms of prior memberships in activist movements. Whereas Kaczynski had never been a member of an activist group, McVeigh had been a member of several. Differences are also apparent in Nidal Malik Hasan and Roshonara Choudhry's interactions with Anwar al-Awlaki. Whereas Choudhry downloaded and consumed al-Awlaki's sermons by herself, Hasan had been in direct email contact with al-Awlaki. As the analysis in both the internet and mental health-focused chapters earlier attest, there are also likely behavioural differences between different kinds of lone-actors in the developmental trajectory of their planned terrorist events.

The descriptive analysis of the data in Chapter 2 illustrates that there is no reliable profile of a lone-actor terrorist. Although this form of terrorist behaviour is heavily male-oriented, women have also taken part in it. Ages ranged widely, as did relationship status. Some had children while many did not. The educational attainment of our sample was evenly distributed. Many were unemployed, but many were students or in gainful employment. Some had criminal histories, military backgrounds, or had mental health issues while others had no such experiences. Target types and attack methods also differed across the sample. In sum, the data illustrate a complex and diverse sample population.

From such diversity, this chapter seeks to develop a typology of lone-actor terrorists. The key is finding the optimal grounds upon which subgroups of lone-actor terrorists can theoretically make sense and are empirically verifiable while remaining operationally useful from law enforcement perspectives (Hood & Sparks, 1970). Burgess, Commons, Safarik, Looper, and Ross (2007: 585) outline the usefulness of such classification models. First, classification systems may aid investigators in apprehending an offender through behavioural investigations. Second, classification systems may inform those working within the criminal justice system about issues concerning 'recidivism risk, risk of violence, appropriateness for probation, custody level (i.e. security risk), etc'. Third, classification systems may also inform treatment planning and clinical decision-making. Finally, classification systems help our understanding of the developmental trajectories into offending. Unique characteristics and developmental pathways into offending may be uncovered through such a scientific endeavour.

Categorizing offenders

There are multiple methods of classifying offender types. The optimal method for each classification depends upon both the data at hand and the purpose of the research itself (Brennan, 1987). Typologies can differ across (a) the qualitative and quantitative methods used to develop them, and (b) the specific factors that researchers use to distinguish between offender types.

Qualitative methods usually allow for theoretical conceptualizations focused on specific variables or sets of variables that distinguish between subgroups. They also regularly use illustrative prototypical case studies rather than building and analysing large datasets. For example, Pantucci's (2011) typology of lone Islamist terrorists disaggregates offender types across a spectrum of how connected they were to others. 'Loners' appear to have no actual connection to other extremists. A 'Lone Wolf' interacts with other extremists face-to-face or online in what often appears to be a reflection of some command and control structural influence. Members of 'Lone Wolf Packs' radicalize with fellow co-offenders in preparation for terrorist acts. 'Lone Attackers' on the other hand are formal members of terrorist groups but engage in their attacks alone (i.e. a 'one man terror cell').

Such qualitative approaches often have shortcomings, however. First, qualitative approaches largely rely on small sample sizes. As such, researchers can usually only provide illustrative examples, which are in turn problematic in terms of establishing generalizable validity and reliability. Second, qualitatively derived subgroups may be more similar than dissimilar and may in fact only differ on the variable chosen by the researcher (e.g. network connectivity).

Quantitative methods, on the other hand, uncover distinctive clusters of variables utilizing techniques such as smallest space analysis (SSA). Such analyses focus upon variable co-occurrence. Prominent examples include Canter and Heritage's (1990) work on serial rapists, and Canter, Alison, Alison, and Wentink's (2004) work on serial murder. The lone-actor terrorist typologies presented next utilize this specific method.

Typology research also differs in terms of whether offender-related characteristics or offence-related factors are in the analysis or not. Much research within the criminology field categorizes offenders solely according to offence-specific factors. The most famous of these is perhaps the organized/disorganized classification of serial killers developed originally by FBI special agents at Quantico.[2] Other academic examples include Burgess et al.'s (2007) work on sex offenders that delineates offenders according to the spontaneity of their crimes and the level of violence used. Other typologies, however, solely focus upon offender characteristics such as Groth's (1979) psychodynamic classification of lone-offender rapists. Another example is Langman's (2009) typology of rampage school shooters, which focuses on the offender's family history, experience of abuse, mental health, and personality. Others classify both individual-level factors and crime commission characteristics such as Knight and Prentky's (1987) typology of rapists. They used a mixture of family, developmental, educational, occupational, and adulthood variables and combined these with variables related to the meaning of the aggression (instrumental vs. expressive), the meaning of the sexuality in the offence (e.g. compensatory, exploitative, displaced, or sadistic) and the level of impulsivity inherent in the offence. Chambers, Horvath, and Kelly's (2010) multiple perpetrator rape typology and Langstrom, Grann, and Lindblad's (2000) typology of youth sexual offenders both also solely focus upon offender behaviours such as initial contact, the context of the attack, and the level of force used. Given the data utilized in this book, the aim is to use a combination of both individual characteristics and offence-specific behaviours to develop typologies of lone-actor terrorists, characteristics, and behaviours.

Lone-actor terrorist typologies

Qualitatively derived methods

Next I provide a brief outline of a qualitatively derived typology of lone-actor terrorists and how individual characteristics and behaviours differ across this distinction.

Categorizing lone actors by ideology

Terrorist groups are commonly distinguished across motivational and ideological domains (Merari, 1978; Schultz, 1978; Asal & Rethemeyer, 2008). The three most prevalent ideologies held by members in the lone-actor terrorist dataset were right wing, single-issue (animal rights, anti-abortion, environmentalism) and al-Qaeda-related ideologies. Table 7.1 outlines the major significant differences in individual characteristics and antecedent event behaviours associated with lone actors who held these ideologies. Variables without significant differences are not reported in the below tables.

As the results suggest, there are distinctions among lone-actor terrorists with specific types of ideologies. Al-Qaeda-related lone actors were significantly younger than the other cohorts. Members of this subgroup (compared to a combination of right-wing and single-issue lone actors) were also significantly more likely live in larger towns and cities, and to be living away from their hometown when they radicalized. They were also significantly more likely to experience

Table 7.1 Comparing lone actors across ideological domains[1] (%)

	Right-wing (n = 43)	Single-issue (n = 30)	Al-Qaeda-related (n = 38)
Average age	34.3 years	38.9 years***	26.8 years****
University experience	27.9**	43.3	50.0
Has children	16.3	33.3*	21.1
History of mental illness	39.5	53.3*	31.6
Worked in construction	11.6***	0	0*
Lived in town with population > 100,000	27.9*	23.3**	63.2****
Lived in town with population < 2,000	27.9	33.3*	5.3***
Previous military experience	32.6*	13.3	21.1
Living away from home town at time of radicalization	11.6**	20.0	42.1***
Interacted face-to-face with members of a wider network	51.2*	46.7	23.7***
Engaged in fundraising for wider network	14.0*	6.7	6.7
Sought legitimization from epistemic authority figures	9.3	10.0%	23.7**
Spouse/partner part of a wider movement	2.3	13.3***	0*
Experienced being degraded in build-up to attack planning	9.3*	10.0	34.2****
Learnt through virtual sources	41.9	20.0***	60.5***
Possessed bomb-making manuals	55.8**	36.7	31.6*
Received help in procuring weaponry	4.7***	20.0	26.3**
Others aware of individual's attack preparation	37.2	16.7**	47.4*
Command and control links	2.3*	0*	21.1****
Read propaganda of other lone actors	30.2***	13.3	7.9**
Discriminate targeting	74.4	86.7**	60.5**

Notes
1 To identify differences between ideological groups, 2x2 Chi Squared analyses (or Fisher's exact tests where appropriate) were run for each ideological domain against each antecedent and behavioural variable (e.g. Right-wing vs. single-issue/al-Qaeda etc.). Percentages are highlighted if they are significantly different from the percentages associated with individuals espousing the other two types of ideology. A One-Way ANOVA comparison of means test was used for the average age variable.
* $p<0.1$.
** $p<0.05$.
*** $p<0.01$.
**** $p<0.001$.

being degraded by others in the build-up to their attack planning. Given the ideological beliefs of this subgroup, it also not surprising that they were significantly more likely to seek legitimization from religious, political, social, or civic leaders prior to their terrorist event or plot. In terms of preparing for their attack, they were significantly more likely than a combination of the other ideological motivations to learn through virtual sources, receive help in procuring weaponry and have others aware of their attack preparation (sometimes because of command and control links). They were however significantly less likely to interact face-to-face with members of a wider network. In terms of the attack itself, they were significantly more likely to engage in indiscriminate targeting.

Compared to both single-issue and al-Qaeda inspired offenders, right-wing lone-actor terrorists were significantly more likely to work in construction, have previous military experience, interact face-to-face with members of a wider network, and engage in fund-raising for this network. They were significantly more likely to possess bomb-making manuals and significantly less likely to receive help in procuring weaponry or display some form of command and control links. They were also significantly less likely to have experienced any form of university education or live in big towns and cities.

Compared to both al-Qaeda and right-wing offenders, single-issue lone-actor terrorists were significantly older, more likely to have children and a history of mental health issues, live in smaller towns and villages, have a spouse or partner part of a wider movement and engage in discriminate targeting.

There was very little to differentiate among these subgroups of lone-actor terrorists in terms of making verbal statements to a wider audience outside of their immediate friends and family, or other people knowing about the individual's grievance or extremist ideology prior to the event. There were also no differences in their histories of substance abuse, and experiences of hands-on training; engagement with literature and propaganda (of a wider movement and of other lone-actors); or possession of close associates involved in criminal activities.

Quantitatively derived methods

Although the distinctions outlined in the previous section illustrate some key differences between subgroups of lone-actor terrorists based on ideology, they also highlight the limitations of comparing offenders based on these types of distinctions. Although differences can be highlighted on a number of variables, rarely is it the case that behaviour is only present in one subgroup. In other words, there is a lot of overlap across subgroups and often they have much in common. When classifications are dichotomous (e.g. present/absent), the assumption of commonality is even more clear-cut (for a methodological discussion of such problems, see Canter et al., 2004: 299–301). Such concerns therefore may warrant the use of multi-dimensional scaling (MDS) techniques. Such techniques provide geometric representations of the level of association between variables. In other words, MDS outputs represent a matrix wherein variables that regularly co-occur are plotted closer together in a Euclidean space. The utility of such a representation is that the variable configuration is based upon variables' relationships with each other rather than their relationships with pre-determined dimensions (Davis, 2009: 508).

One form of MDS, Smallest Space Analysis (SSA), has been used to examine a wide spectrum of offences including sexual assault (Alison & Stein, 2001;

House, 1997; Canter, Hughes, & Kirby, 1998), homicide (Godwin, 2000; Salfati & Canter, 1999), arson (Canter & Fritzon, 1998), stalking (Canter & Ioannou, 2004) and terrorism events involving hostage taking (Fritzon, Canter, & Wilton, 2001). SSA is

> based upon the assumption that the underlying structure of complex systems is most readily appreciated if the relationship between each and every other variable is examined, but that such examination is much clearer if the relationships are represented visually not only in terms of numbers.
>
> (Canter et al., 2004: 308)

The analysis below depicts an SSA output based on lone-actor characteristic, antecedent behaviour, and network variables that had been treated as dichotomous variables.[3] The Jaccard co-efficient (which represents the level of association between two variables) was calculated for each pair-wise set of variables. The models depicted below are two-dimensional, indicating that the dichotomous nature of the variables means that the relationships should be visible in no more than two dimensions.

The closer two variables appear within the matrix, the higher their co-occurrence across observations. For example in Figure 7.1, whether an individual had military experience (Mil) is depicted at the bottom of the matrix and relatively close to the variables that depict whether an individual had a history of substance abuse (SubAbuse) or provided a pre-attack warning (Warn). This suggests that these behaviours somewhat regularly occur together relative to the other network and antecedent behaviour variables within the analysis. On the other hand, the variables that depict whether the individual had a history of mental illness (Mental), raised money on behalf of a group (Funds) and had previously been rejected from a group (Reject) are the furthest away from the military experience variable suggesting they rarely, if ever, co-occur in this sample.

Figure 7.1 produces four distinct clusters that seem to be thematically related to how an individual, absent of formal membership in a terrorist organization, can engage psychologically, and/or operationally in a terrorist attack. As the study of terrorism has become more empirically focused, terrorism has often been described a group phenomenon because groups provide the operational capabilities necessary to perform a terrorist attack while also providing individuals with a mechanism for moral disengagement. Military psychology suggests that there are many factors that inhibit individuals from engaging in fatal violence against others. For example, Marshall concludes that

> the average and healthy individual ... has such an inner and usually unrealized resistance towards killing a fellow man that he will not of his own volition take life if it is possible to turn away from that responsibility ... at the vital point.
>
> (Cited in Grossman, 1995: 29)

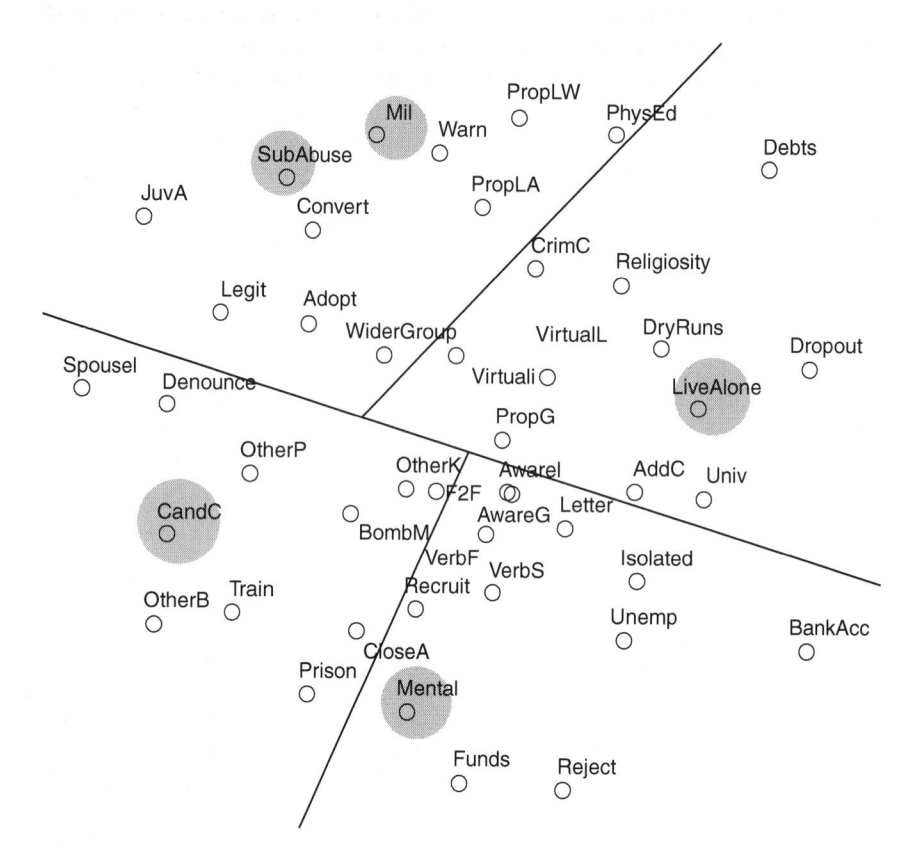

Figure 7.1 Smallest space analysis of 45 lone-actor terrorist characteristics and behaviours.

Absent of a group setting, terrorist violence may be difficult to commit for practical and psychological reasons. The four clusters of variables below may help explain how these inhibitions against violence are overcome or how the practical skills needed to conduct a terrorist attacked are developed.

Theme 1 – Relying on Others' Support. The bottom left quadrant of Figure 7.1 represents a distinct cluster of behaviours related to the plotting and execution of a terrorist attack by an individual with clear command and control links (CandC). This theme includes behaviours that are similar to those involved in the development of a terrorist attack by an organization. Together, these behaviours and experiences provide the individual with the necessary logistical, technical and social support for a terrorist attack. The thematically related factors include whether the individual had help in procuring weaponry (OtherP) or building IEDs (OtherB), received training from a terrorist organization or network (Train), and used bomb-making manuals (BombM). This theme also includes whether others had knowledge of the individual's attack plans (OtherK), whether the individual interacted with members of a wider network face to face

(F2F) and whether the individual had family or close associates involved in criminality or political violence (CloseA) including their spouse (SpouseI).

The other three clusters of characteristics and behaviours are associated with individual terrorists without command and control links.

Theme 2 – Struggling in Isolation. The bottom right quadrant of Figure 7.1 revolves around a cluster of characteristics and behaviours that may be linked to problematic personality disorders (Mental). While numerous studies have demonstrated that individuals who engage in terrorism tend not to be mentally ill, these studies typically focus upon terrorist *groups* and not lone actors. It may be the case that some lone actors possess personality characteristics and motivations quite different from – and which perhaps prevent them from becoming – terrorist group members. The fact that this theme is linked with rejection (Reject) from wider groups of activists strengthens this argument. As terrorist group members may need to cross fewer psychological barriers to commit violence against others (due to factors such as de-individuation, diffusion of responsibility, conformity to group elders, etc.) than lone-actor terrorists, it is in fact likely that a group terrorist offender has on average a less problematic personality structure (see the discussion in Chapter 2). This theme also includes variables related to whether the individual had been recently rejected from a wider group or movement, was unemployed at the time of the terrorist event/plot (Unemp), and was characterized as being socially isolated by neighbours, family, or co-workers (Isolated). This theme is also more strongly linked to behaviours related to money including raising funds on behalf of a wider movement (Funds) and clearing out one's bank accounts prior to the terrorist plot (BankAcc).

Theme 3 – Functioning in a Virtual Network. The top right quadrant of Figure 7.1 involves a series of characteristics and behaviours related to being free from personal constraints such as living with other people (LiveAlone). For this sample, living alone may be either an individual choice related to the terrorist plot, due to a recent address change (AddC) or going to or dropping out of university (Univ and DropOut). At the same time, this theme includes having links through virtual interactions with members of wider networks (Virtuali), learning through virtual sources (VirtualL), reading the propaganda of wider groups or movements (PropG), increasing in religiosity (Religiosity), and engaging in dry-runs (DryRuns). This theme is also more closely associated with having previous criminal convictions (CrimC) and paying off one's debts prior to the planned terrorist event (Debts).

Theme 4 – Preparing for the Attack. The top left quadrant of Figure 7.1 involves a number of characteristics and behaviours that may help condition the individual to engage in violence against others. Primarily, this conditioning comes through previous military service (Mil) but may also be aided by substance abuse (SubAbuse). This theme is also more heavily associated with being arrested as a juvenile (JuvA) and/or being a religious convert (Convert). In terms of antecedent behaviours, the theme is more closely associated with providing pre-attack warnings, increasing levels of physical activity pre-event, and reading the propaganda of and about other lone-actor terrorists (PropLW and PropLA).

Conclusion

The findings suggest that we cannot treat lone-actor terrorists in a homogenous fashion, and that clear distinctions can be made between types of lone-actor terrorists as well as lone-actor characteristics and behaviours using a mixture of qualitative and quantitative analysis techniques. While the SSA output indicates that a preliminary classification system of lone-actor terrorist characteristics and behaviours is possible, it does not classify the lone-actor terrorists themselves. Further work is needed in this regard. However, the big takeaway point here is that we can no longer treat the 'terrorist' in an aggregated homogenous manner if we are to get a more clear understanding of their behaviour. The results here (and elsewhere in this book) suggest that a disaggregated view of these offenders produces interesting, statistically significant results that themselves can feed into assessments of risk of future offenders. The fact that predicting who will become a generic 'terrorist' is problematic should not be surprising. In fact, there is a large body of criminology research that demonstrates the legal, ethical, and methodological difficulties in predicting future criminal offending (Auerhahn, 1999, 2006; Bernard & Ritti, 1991; Gottfredson, 1987; Gottfredson & Moriarty, 2006; Harcourt, 2006). However, the increasing number of studies focusing on criminal careers and offender typologies has produced further interest into predictive studies that seek to understand whether particular types of offenders can be forecasted from a sample of general offenders based on some combination of variables (for example see Laub & Sampson, 2003, Bersani, Laub, & Nieuwbeerta, 2009). Only through disaggregated approaches to understanding types of terrorists, can such the scientific study of terrorist behaviour progress.

Notes

1 An exception being Pantucci's (2011) typology.
2 According to Canter et al. (2004: 295) this dichotomy, however, 'remains a proposal in need of careful definition and systematic testing'.
3 The variables included in the analysis are all dichotomous variables, which are coded as 'present', 'absent', or 'unknown'. For the purposes of SSA, missing data and the absence of a characteristic or behaviour are usually treated in the same manner (i.e. unknown = absent).

References

Alison, L., Snook, B., & Stein, K. (2001). Unobtrusive Measurement: Using Police Information for Forensic Research. *Qualitative Research* 1: 241–254.

Asal, V., & Rethemeyer, K. (2008). The Nature of the Beast: The Organizational and Network Characteristics of Organizational Lethality. *Journal of Politics* 70: 437–449.

Auerhahn, K. (1999). Selective incapacitation and the problem of prediction. *Criminology*, 37(4), 703–734.

Bernard, T. J., & Ritti, R. R. (1991). The Philadelphia birth cohort and selective incapacitation. *Journal of Research in Crime and Delinquency*, 28(1), 33–54.

Bersani, B. E., Laub, J. H., & Nieuwbeerta, P. (2009). Marriage and desistance from crime in the Netherlands: Do gender and socio-historical context matter? *Journal of Quantitative Criminology*, 25, 3–24.

Brennan, T. (1987). Classification: An overview of selected methodological issues. *Crime and Justice*, 201–248.

Burgess, A. W., Commons, M. L, Safarik, M. E., Looper, R. R., & and Ross, S. N. (2007). Sex Offenders of the Elderly: Classification by Motive, Typology and Predictors of Severity of Crime. *Aggression and Violent Behavior* 12: 582–597.

Canter, D., & Heritage, R. (1990). A Multivariate Model of Sexual Offence Behavior: Developments in 'Offender Profiling'. *The Journal of Forensic Psychiatry* 1: 185–212.

Canter, D., & Fritzon, K. (1998). Differentiating Arsonists: A Model of Firesetting Actions and Characteristics. *Legal and Criminological Psychology* 3: 73–96.

Canter, D., Hughes, D., & Kirby, S. (1998). Paedophilia: Pathology, Criminality, or Both? The Development of a Multivariate Model of Offence Behavior in Child Sexual Abuse. *The Journal of Forensic Psychiatry* 9: 532–555.

Canter, D., Alison, L. J., Alison, E., & Wentink, N. (2004). The Organized/Disorganized Typology of Serial Murder: Myth or Model?. *Psychology, Public Policy and Law*, *10*(3): 293–320.

Canter, D. M., & Ioannou, M. (2004). A Multivariate Model of Stalking Behaviours. *Behaviormetrika* 31: 113–130.

Chambers, J., Horvath, M., & Kelly, L. (2010). A Typology of Multiple-Perpetrator Rape. *Criminal Justice and Behavior*, *37*(10): 1114–1139.

Fritzon, K., Canter, D., & Wilton, Z. (2001). The Application of an Action System Model to Destructive Behaviour: The Examples of Arson and Terrorism. *Behavioral Sciences and the Law* 19: 657–690.

Godwin, G. M. (2000). *Hunting Serial Predators: A Multivariate Classification Approach to Profiling Violent Behavior*. Florida: CRC Press.

Gottfredson, D. M. (1987). Prediction and classification in criminal justice decision making. *Crime and Justice*, 1–20.

Gottfredson, S. D., & Moriarty, L. J. (2006). Statistical risk assessment: Old problems and new applications. *Crime & Delinquency*, *52*(1), 178–200.

Groth, A. N. (1979). *Men Who Rape*. New York: Plenum.

Harcourt, B. E. (2008). *Against prediction: Profiling, policing, and punishing in an actuarial age*. Chicago: University of Chicago Press.

Hood, R., & Sparks, R. (1970). *Key Issues in Criminology*. New York: McGraw-Hill.

House, J. C. (1997). Towards a Practical Application of Offender Profiling: The RNC's Criminal Suspect Prioritization System. In J. L. Jackson and D. A. Bekerian (eds.). *Offender Profiling: Theory, Research and Practice* (pp. 177–190). Chichester: Wiley.

Knight, R. A., & Prentky, R. A. (1987). The Developmental Antecedents and Adult Adaptations of Rapist Subtypes. *Criminal Justice and Behavior* 14: 403–426.

Langman, P. (2009). Rampage School Shooters: A Typology. *Aggression and Violent Behavior* 14: 79–86.

Langstrom, N., Grann, M., & Lindblad, F. (2000). A Preliminary Typology of Young Sex Offenders. *Journal of Adolescence* 23: 319–329.

Laub, J. H., & Sampson, R. J. (2003). *Shared beginnings, divergent lives: Delinquent boys to age 70*. Cambridge, MA: Harvard University Press.

Merari, A. (1978). A Classification of Terrorist Groups. *Terrorism*, *1*(3–4): 331–346.

Pantucci, R. (2011). *A Typology of Lone Wolves: Preliminary Analysis of Lone Islamist Terrorists*. Report for the International Centre for the Study of Radicalisation and Political Violence.

Salfati, C., & Canter, D. (1999). Differentiating Stranger Murders: Profiling Offender Characteristics from Behavioral Styles. *Behavioral Sciences and the Law* 17: 391–406.

Schultz, R. (1978). Conceptualizing Political Terrorism: A Typology. *Journal of International Affairs, 31*(1): 7–15.

Taylor, P., Donald, I., Jacques, K., & Conchie, S. (2011). Jaccard's Heel: Radex Models of Criminal Behaviour are Rarely Falsifiable When Derived Using Jaccard Coefficient. *Legal and Criminological Psychology, 17*(1): 41–58.

8 A situational crime prevention approach

Much of the anxiety concerning the threat of lone-actor terrorism stems from concerns regarding the ability to detect and intercept lone-actor terrorist events before they occur. Traditional methods employed against formal terrorist organizations and loosely connected terrorist networks (such as counter-intelligence, HUMINT, interception of communications, surveillance of persons, targeted killing etc.) may not be as readily applicable against the threat of lone-actor terrorists. Strategies aimed at countering radicalization in the community may have no reference point in identifying lone at-risk individuals. Deterrence measures also may prove problematic for countering lone-actor terrorism. As the discussion in Chapter 2 notes, profiling strategies are also fraught with difficulties and the base-line behaviours noted in Chapter 3 illustrate that any tool that promised predictive power may prove useless.

Because prediction and identification are difficult, it might be better to instead guard against future lone-actor terrorists by making the actual undertaking of a terrorist attack more difficult. For example, it might be easier and more cost-efficient to deter a budding lone-actor terrorist by making it more difficult to acquire the necessary bomb-making materials than by convincing him/her of counter-narratives.

This chapter draws heavily from established conceptual frameworks such as Situational Crime Prevention and Routine Activity Theory, in order to understand the behaviours that have underpinned previous successfully executed lone-actor terrorist events. As noted by Horgan (2005: 109), it is useful to view each terrorist offence as comprising of a series of stages 'almost with a natural history from inception to completion'. Through such a process, it may be possible to formulate phase-specific intervention strategies that seek to deter and disrupt future lone-actor terrorist plots. In order to illustrate the applicability of routine activity theory to understanding terrorist events, this chapter provides five routine activity analyses of lone-actor terrorist events.

Situational crime prevention (SCP) focuses upon crime events rather than criminality (for a full exploration of SCP in relation to terrorism see Clarke & Newman, 2006 and Freilich & Newman, 2009). Rather than focusing on individual characteristics of the criminal, situational crime prevention attempts to understand the *how* and *what* of crime: from an analysis of the offender to a greater consideration of the social and behavioural qualities of the offence. Though later analyses reduced the more overt emphasis on rational choice theory, such perspectives view offenders as a rational decision-maker who evaluates the costs and benefit of committing or disregarding the crime (Carroll & Weaver, 1986; Cornish & Clarke, 1986). It has a specific focus upon the 'near causes' of crime, the situational aspects that make a crime more likely to occur or a potential victim more likely to be victimized. Opportunity therefore is seen to be an important cause of crimes and a focus for prevention. The beauty of SCP is that opportunity is often more malleable than an offender's internal disposition. We see SCP everyday in relation to counter-terrorism. On my commute to work in London, I take the Underground with its lack of bins (which were taken away to prevent Provisional Irish Republican Army attacks), I hear the P.A. at Euston Station regularly makes announcements warning passengers to be vigilant and on the look out for strange behaviours, and I notice the bollards and parking restrictions that prevent car bombs from being parked close to high-profile buildings. There are other famous examples of SCP approaches to countering terrorism such as target hardening of key buildings, the West Bank barrier, making fertilizer inert and therefore no use in the development of HME and airport security. All of these measures are in place to reduce the likelihood of a terrorist attack, not to prevent or disrupt the adoption of extremist ideologies or to alleviate perceived grievances. It is about the controlling the process of how terrorist attacks may be executed, rather than ameliorating the drivers behind why the attack is being planned in the first place.

To take a more pertinent example, on 22 May 2013 Michael Adebolajo and Michael Adebowale murdered the British Army soldier Lee Rigby. Adebolajo and Adebowale ran Rigby over with a car and then proceeded to stab him numerous times with a collection of knives and a meat cleaver. Although both men were known to British security services, there was very little in the attack planning that triggered the need for an intervention or increased perceptions of how likely the offenders were to engage in a terrorist attack. For example, the knives used in the attack were bought in a high-street chain and are typical household items that most homeowners possess. While the radical views of Adebolajo and Adebowale were known beforehand, they are just two individuals amongst a much larger cohort who express similar views but are unlikely to act violently upon them. Even if an Armed Response Unit happened to be behind Adebolajo and Adebowale's vehicle at the time, Rigby was still likely to have died before the Unit could have understood what was happening. Rather than focusing upon identifiers of the individual's radicalization or general intelligence capabilities or potential to engage in terrorist activity, SCP approaches are much more interested in factors such as the routine decisions that underpin the actual act of violence. The Woolwich attack was discriminate. They specifically targeted and killed a member of the British Army and did not take the opportunity to kill bystanders (of which there were many) before the first responders arrived at the scene. An SCP approach would be interested in (a) how they identified Rigby as a British soldier (he was off duty at the time) and (b) whether there was anything that could have been done to make the attack less likely. We return to these points in the conclusion.

Using the framework outlined in Horgan (2005), each of five case studies below are disaggregated into four specific stages; (a) decision and search activity, (b) preparation, (c) event execution, and (d) post-event activity and strategic analysis. The decision and search activity phase includes endeavours such as target selection. Targeting is not a random exercise, but rather is usually the result of careful deliberation and can be affected by contemporary political and security climates as well as individual capabilities (Horgan, 2005: 111).

The preparation phase addresses the operational, logistical, and organizational issues affecting the violent event. Whereas the decision phase sets a broad strategic agenda, the preparation phase covers tactical concerns. Choosing the correct tactic for particular operations may be influenced by a number of issues, including technological feasibility, cost-effectiveness, deterrent value, the post-event image of the individual and his/her motives to wider constituents and supporters, the dangers of unwanted results (e.g. extreme repression by counter-terrorists or the possibility of the wrong people being killed), and the ability to overcome security measures (Dolnik & Bhattacharjee, 2002). The direct manifestation of violence may be a function of the individual's ability to procure or develop different types of weaponry or explosives. From a logistics standpoint, this phase usually sees organizational decision-makers choosing individual(s) with the specific skill sets and experience to engage in the event and equipping the individual(s) with the weaponry to do so. With lone-actor terrorists, however, the preparation phase may look different because they cannot rely upon routine activities that may be perfected by groups over time or a terrorist group's network of specialized talent. Surveillance of targets, building a bomb, testing the device, procuring weaponry, and concealing or hiding physical evidence also fall within this phase. If present, these activities illustrate not only premeditation, but also other facets that concern the temporal and sequential flow of the preparation of a terrorist attack.

The event execution stage is the sole phase that the terrorist plays out in public. It may involve a number of discrete events, such as maintaining security pre-event (e.g. priming an IED in secrecy). Other events include the transport of the individual and/or IED to the location of the planned attack, or in the case of a shooting attack, storage of the offending weapon post-attack. It also includes aspects of decision-making that concern the time of day to commit the offence and considerations of risk and opportunity in the commissioning of a terrorist offence.

The final phase of post-event activity and strategic analysis includes ensuring that the lone actor can escape after the event without being arrested or killed as well as conducting a review of the whole attack. The adaptations present in follow-up attacks may reflect aspects of the offender's strategic analysis.

The case studies elaborated upon below include the attacks attributed to David Copeland, Roshonara Choudhry, Timothy McVeigh, Mohammed Reza Taheri-Azar, and Anders Breivik. The chapter concludes with an outline of

David Copeland[1]

David Copeland's nail bombing campaign occurred between 17 and 30 April, 1999. In total, three bombs targeted minority communities across London. The bombings occurred over three successive weekends, killed three (including a pregnant woman), and injured a further 129. The following routine activity analysis is largely concerned with Copeland's first bombing, which targeted an area in London with a large black population. Copeland's subsequent bombings are dealt with in the 'post-event activity and strategic analysis' phase, as they included many adaptations reflecting Copeland's strategic analysis of the original attack.

Decision and search activity stage

Copeland told police that he first came up with the idea of using violence when a bomb went off at the Olympic Games in Atlanta in 1996. The Notting Hill carnival[2] occurred around the same time as that bombing; according to Copeland he 'thought why, why, why can't someone blow that place up? That'd be a good one, you know, that would piss everyone off' (p. 9). Copeland noted that this initial thought 'kept going round, floating round my head, day after day after day. And then after a while I became that thought, you know, I was going to do it. I was going to get it out of my head, and the only way to get rid of it was to do it' (p. 3).

During the two years previous to Copeland's terrorist attacks, he was involved with far-right political groups in the United Kingdom. Originally a member of the British National Party from May 1997, he left within four months insisting that the group was not extreme enough due to its unwillingness to engage in a 'paramilitary struggle'. He then joined the National Socialist Movement and went on to become its regional leader for Hampshire weeks before the bombing campaign began.

Unpacking Copeland's motives is a difficult task, and necessarily limited in the absence of direct contact to enable the collection of first-hand data. However, we can explore some relevant themes. In his confession statement to police, Copeland highlighted his motive of 'Murder, mayhem, chaos, damage, to get on the news. It's a top story really. My main intent was to spread fear, resentment and hatred throughout this country' (p. 2). Copeland denied that he fanaticized about killing people, but he did confess that he fantasized about 'the chaos and disruption' caused by his IED attacks (p. 18). At his subsequent trial, however, Copeland's political motives came to the forefront. There, Copeland stated that his motives were 'Terrorism, fear, to terrorize people. It was my destiny. Political reasons, I am a Nazi'. The intention of the first two bombings was to stir up a race war. Copeland's confession statement admitted to disliking ethnic minorities and he further cites his belief in the 'master race' (p. 13). Copeland, inspired by the *Turner Diaries*, thought his actions would lead to a racial war.

> If you've read the *Turner Diaries*, you know the year 2000 there'll be the uprising and all that, racial violence on the streets. My aim was political. It was to cause a racial war in this country. There'd be a backlash from the ethnic minorities, then all the white people will go out and vote British National Party.
>
> (p. 9)

Copeland planned to be 'just be the spark. That's all I will plan to be, the spark that would set fire to this country' (p. 23). Also, Copeland's third bombing was aimed at an entirely different minority group than the previous bombings. Whereas the first two bombings carried a racial element, the third bombing targeted homosexuals. Some framed this last bombing as personal, rather than political. In Copeland's own words: 'I'm just very homophobic. I've got a thing about homosexuals. You know, I just hate them' (p. 14). Finally, Copeland was also interested in infamy. He reported that he 'wanted to be famous in some sort of way. If no one remembers who you are, you never existed.' Following his initial two bombings, Copeland admitted to keeping 'press cuttings on my wall to get off on it, to see my handiwork being noticed' (Cheston, 2000).

Preparation stage

During the two years between joining the British National Party (BNP) and starting his bombing campaign, Copeland read *The Turner Diaries*, and downloaded bomb-making manuals from the internet. Copeland originally tried to use a recipe from *The Terrorist's Handbook*, a manual that he downloaded in April 1997. He purchased ammonium nitrate and the required detonators; he also managed to steal a large canister of nitric acid. However, the manual failed to provide an exhaustive list of all of the necessary explosive compounds, and Copeland found it 'too complex' to manufacture and procure the missing chemical compounds by himself. Frustrated, Copeland temporarily gave up. In June 1998 he downloaded a second manual, *How to Make Bombs Part 2*. At first he tried to build a fertilizer bomb; he purchased liquid ammonium from a local medical supply store and ordered rocket fuses, but again he failed to manufacture a fully functioning device. Copeland then turned to smaller devices and again used the second manual to learn how to make a pipe bomb. The necessary ingredients were easy to find. For the flash powder, he bought 1,500 sterling pounds worth of fireworks in two shops in Farnborough. Alarm clocks for timing devices, Tupperware boxes, sports bags (for concealment purposes), and thousands of six-inch nails were obtained from various hardware stores. Approximately six weeks before the initial bombing attack, Copeland experimented with three smaller devices, detonating them late at night at a local park called Rushmoor Common. The device itself involved a plastic pipe filled with flash powder and sealed with glue. The pipe was then placed in a box and surrounded by approximately 1,500 nails. The addition of the nails was to supplement the smaller explosive power of the pipe bomb compared with Copeland's earlier aspirational IEDs. All of Copeland's subsequent devices were identical and their main immediate goal, according to Copeland, was to 'smash into windows, stick into people, maim people and kill people' (p. 10).

In the two weeks prior to the initial bombing, Copeland stopped reporting for work.

Event execution stage

On the evening of 16 April, Copeland constructed the IED. The next morning he set the timer for 5:30 p.m. and primed the device. Next, Copeland left his studio apartment on bike and took a train from Farnborough to Clapham Junction, which arrived at 3 p.m. Because of the two and a half hour lag between his arrival and the bomb's intended detonation time, Copeland decided to stall for some time and went to a nearby café for 20 minutes. Copeland then transported the IED, which was primed and taped to the inside of a sports bag, to Brixton by taxi. It was his first time in the area, and he walked the length of the High Street for an hour as he scouted for an appropriate spot, store, or marketplace to leave the bag. In later interviews, Copeland mentioned that he was surprised so many white people frequented the area:

> I always thought Brixton was ... I mean I'd stand out like a sore thumb. I didn't. It's quite multi-cultural now. That surprised me. I thought about it and then I thought.... Well ... I'm here now. I'd say one in ten people could have been white. But I didn't care about hurting them anyway. If they want to live there, it's up to them.
>
> (p. 3)

While he walked High Street, Copeland decided on a location, but again stalled for more time by going into a library for a short moment, and a nearby bar to use the restroom. Copeland left the bag on the corner of Electric Avenue at 5 p.m., at the entrance to a store called Iceland and in close proximity to a bus shelter. This spot was chosen for two reasons. First, Copeland felt it was 'a good place to get away from' (when Copeland was arrested, he insisted to a psychiatric nurse that he had 'logically and rationally' planted the devices). Second, he felt it would maximize the likelihood of casualties: 'I put it there to get the people walking by, and the people at the bus stop.' After he dropped off the device, Copeland walked south down Brixton Road. He then took a taxi back to Clapham Junction and caught a train back to Farnborough station before cycling home. Street traders spotted the bag, looked inside, and guessed the contents were a bomb. One street trader took the IED out of the bag and placed it on a stack of wooden pallets. They contacted police, who arrived at 5:25 p.m. By chance, as the police arrived, the IED detonated and injured 50 people.

At the trial that followed, Copeland stated that he took no effort to avoid CCTV cameras and did not worry about being caught because he 'had no life anyway' and wanted to be famous.

Post-event activity and strategic analysis

A full seven days later, Copeland's second bombing occurred in an area of East London that was home to a large Bangladeshi community. Prior to the attack, Copeland again cycled to Farnborough station, travelled into London by train (this time to Waterloo station) and took a taxi to Brick Lane at 3:10 p.m.[3] He had planned the detonation to occur at the exact time as the week previous, 5:30 p.m., but had to delay it due to forgetting his train ticket and having to return home.

Repeating an error of the first attack, Copeland targeted an area he had never been to before. Hoping to strike the usually busy market at Brick Lane, Copeland had not realized that the market was not open on Saturdays but instead was only open on Sundays: 'I presumed there was going to be a market of some sort up there, but it wasn't' (p. 11). Copeland was undecided about whether to go ahead with the attack or not.

> So then I was in two minds whether to disassemble the device and go, you know, come back Sunday. Then I just ... you know, decided. I walked up Brick Lane looking for somewhere to plant it. It was about an hour to go before detonation. I didn't want to be seen planting the device, so I went down Hanbury Street. There was [sic] two big vans and I slipped in between them and walked out, they masked my escape. It was like an aborted mission you could call it.
>
> (p. 11)

By leaving it between two vans, Copeland also thought it 'would blow up a few cars – cause a bit of smoke, a bit of fire.'

Again, Copeland used a sports bag to conceal the IED. A member of the public spotted the bag, placed it in the trunk of his car, and attempted to contact the police. As the individual dialled 999, the IED detonated. A *Guardian* newspaper source stated, 'putting the bomb in the car meant the damage from flying nails was reduced considerably'. In total, 13 were injured. Immediately after the explosion, Copeland dialled 999 and keyed in C18, a reference to Combat 18.

Perhaps realizing that reconnaissance was a problem in his first two attacks, he went to Soho, the eventual location for his third attack, twice: once straight after the Brick Lane bombing and again on Thursday 29 April. The first time in Soho, his mission was to locate a bar used by homosexuals. He decided that the Admiral Duncan was the bar to attack because it was 'a queer pub full of men hugging each other.' At his trial, Copeland also stated that he targeted a homosexual bar because he not only hated homosexuals but also because he wanted to irritate Britain's political elite. 'I knew it would piss everyone off, especially like Blair and Mandelson[4] and them lot' (p. 14). While in Soho, those investigating the attacks on Brick Lane/Hanbury Street released the CCTV stills of their suspect (who had yet to be identified). Copeland heard about the CCTV stills on a radio broadcast in a Soho sex shop. Knowing he may soon be caught, Copeland changed plans and brought his next bombing forward by a day (from the 1 May to 30 April). He immediately returned to his rented studio, collected the necessary bombing materials and took a train back into London. There, he booked into an Airways bed and breakfast in London using a pseudonym.

On the morning of the 30 April, Copeland left the bed and breakfast at 11 a.m. and checked into a different one that was nearby, The Vegas. There, he constructed the IED. He left for the bar on foot but as before had left himself too much time. He stopped off at a different bar along his route to Soho. When he entered the target bar at 5:50 p.m., it was full. Aware that the previous two IEDs had been moved by members of the public, Copeland decided to wait with the concealed device as long as possible. Copeland stated that he 'watched it [the device] and made sure no-one saw it' (p. 16). Witnesses report that Copeland appeared uneasy and frequently checked his watch. He ordered a soft drink at the bar and spoke with another man who had approached him asking if he was waiting for someone. Copeland replied, 'I'm just waiting for my boyfriend.' He left at 6:05 p.m., leaving the sports bag behind. He told the man that he was leaving in order to get some money and that he would return shortly. The IED detonated at 6:25 p.m. Copeland watched the breaking news from his hotel bedroom before returning home that evening. This bombing killed three and injured a further 79. That night, co-workers identified Copeland through the CCTV images and alerted the police. Copeland was subsequently arrested at his apartment at 1am on the morning after the third bombing.

Within days of the first bombing, anonymous calls to the police separately claimed the bombings on behalf of Combat 18, the White Wolves, the English National Party, and the English Liberation Army. Copeland later complained of the 'thugs who were trying to steal [his] glory'.

Were it not for the arrest, Copeland had further plans. In subsequent debriefs, he mentioned that he planned to bomb Southall, an area in West London with a large Asian community.

Mohammed Reza Taheri-Azar

On 3 March 2006, Taheri-Azar attempted to 'run over' students attending University of North Carolina (UNC) – Chapel Hill with a vehicle. In total, he injured nine. There were no fatalities.

Decision and search activity stage

Taheri-Azar's decision to turn to violence seems largely a response to U.S. foreign policy and developed over the course of two years. His letter of responsibility[5] claimed that

Situational crime prevention 139

> due to the killing of believing men and women under the direction of the United States government, I have decided to take advantage of my presence on United States soil ... to take the lives of as many Americans and American sympathizers as I can in order to punish the United States for their immoral actions around the world.

He cited religious justification for his actions:

> In the Qur'an, Allah states that the believing men and women have permission to murder anyone responsible for the killing of other believing men and women. I know that the Qur'an is a legitimate and authoritative holy scripture since it is completely validated by modern science and also mathematically encoded with the number 19 beyond human ability. After extensive contemplation and reflection, I have made the decision to exercise the right of violent retaliation that Allah has given me to the fullest extent to which I am capable at present.

Although Taheri-Azar did not manage to cause any fatalities through his attack, according to his letter of responsibility his intention was to 'murder citizens and residents of the United States of America ... by running them over with my automobile and stabbing them with a knife if the opportunities are presented to me by Allah'.

Preparation stage

Taheri-Azar began his preparations for the eventual attack two months prior to the attack. He initially wanted to join the U.S. military in order to use their weapons against a U.S. target. In a letter to a local media outlet following his arrest he stated, 'ideally ... I wanted to fly an airplane over Washington, D.C. and drop a nuclear bomb on the city'. As a part of this plan, he allegedly twice met Army recruiters at his office and applied to a number of clinical psychology graduate schools to prepare for a position as a fighter pilot. Within a month, this plan was abandoned.

By February of 2006, his second plan involved a shooting attack inside the Lenoir Dining Hall at the UNC – Chapel Hill campus. Taheri-Azar provides two different accounts of why this plan was abandoned. In his letter of responsibility he states that he applied for a permit for a handgun but 'the process of receiving a permit for a handgun in this city is highly restricted and out of my reach at the present, most likely due to my foreign nationality'. In a letter to local media after his arrest, however, Taheri-Azar states that although he visited a gun store in Raleigh, North Carolina, and obtained the necessary application documents for a gun permit from the Orange County Sheriff's Department in Hillsborough, he changed his mind 'about attacking with a gun because they seem to jam very easily', or 'malfunction and acquiring one would have attracted attention to me from the FBI in all likelihood'.

Taheri-Azar finally decided to engage in a vehicular assault 'by running over several people in a concentrated target zone'. He also acquired two cans of pepper spray, a five-inch knife, and viewed Navy Seals training videos. All of these actions were geared towards aiding Taheri-Azar in the case of a physical confrontation immediately following the vehicular assault.

Taheri-Azar decided to attack students at the University of North Carolina because it was close to his home. He was also familiar with the location – he graduated from UNC the previous December. Taheri-Azar also chose to time his attack to coincide with lunch in order to maximize the number of potential fatalities and injuries. His letter of responsibility claimed that,

> I have chosen the particular location on the University campus as my target since I know there is a high likelihood that I will kill several people before being killed myself or jailed and sent to prison if Allah wills.

Shortly before the attack, Taheri-Azar penned a letter claiming responsibility for the attacks. The day before the attack itself, Taheri-Azar rented a Jeep Cherokee for the specific purpose of using it in the attack. He chose this vehicle because it 'runs things over and keeps going'.

Event execution stage

Between 11:30 a.m. and 11:53 a.m., Taheri-Azar left his apartment and drove towards campus. At 11:53 a.m. Taheri-Azar drove the rented Jeep Cherokee onto UNC Chapel Hill's campus. He drove towards 'The Pit', a student hub, and accelerated aiming to hit nearby students. After his first attempt, he made a 90-degree turn around the dining hall and proceeded to try to assault more students. Taheri-Azar drove two more miles, near the University Mall, and then phoned a police dispatcher and turned himself in. Later, Taheri-Azar stated that he turned himself in 'to assure the world that I wasn't some insane person who went on a killing rampage suddenly'.

Post-event activity and strategic analysis

Overall, Taheri-Azar was disappointed in the attack's outcome. He stated disappointment that 'there weren't more people in the area'. There is little other publicly available information on how Taheri-Azar analysed his event after the fact.

Timothy McVeigh

Executed by Timothy James McVeigh, on 19 April 1995, the Oklahoma City Bombing killed 168 people and injured over 500. This remained the deadliest terrorist act on American soil until the events of September 11, 2001.

Decision and search activity stage

McVeigh had a long-standing interest in firearms. Trained to shoot by his grandfather from an early age, McVeigh would later consume many gun-related publications, and frequented military stores and gun shows talking to others about weaponry and gun rights. Over time, he became gradually more immersed in the survivalist movement and radical right-wing literature. He read *The Turner Diaries*[6] dozens of times, cajoled others into reading it and began to adopt its message.

In May 1988, McVeigh decided to join the army and participated in U.S. Army basic training at Fort Benning, Georgia. There, McVeigh formed a close bond with two of his later co-conspirators in the attack at Oklahoma City: Terry Nichols and Michael J. Fortier. McVeigh and Nichols, in particular, withdrew from others in their unit. McVeigh's interest in survivalism continued during his time in the army. After being transferred (alongside Nichols and Fortier) to Fort Riley, Kansas, McVeigh rented a storage unit that he stocked with 100 gallons of fresh water, weaponry, ammunition, rations, and other supplies.

McVeigh was deployed during Operation Desert Storm. In battle he killed two Iraqi soldiers. In later interviews, McVeigh suggested these killings contributed to his suffering from post-traumatic stress. The underlying reasons behind the war and the depth of power asymmetry in the battle itself bothered him. He also became convinced the United Nations was planning to take over the world. Upon returning from Operation Desert Storm, McVeigh became a decorated soldier (Bronze Star, the Army Achievement Medal, the Southwest Asia Service Medal, and the Kuwait Liberation Medal). He discharged from the Army in 1991, disillusioned by his failure to join the Army's Special Forces. This in turn led to a growing dislike of the U.S. government. After being discharged, McVeigh became increasingly paranoid that the government intended to take away his rights, especially the right to bear arms. McVeigh's anger toward the government increased following the FBI siege at Ruby Ridge during the summer of 1992, and grew further during the stand-off between the U.S. Bureau of Alcohol, Tobacco, Firearms and Explosives (ATF) and the Branch Davidians in Waco, Texas (an event McVeigh drove to and witnessed first-hand). One month after witnessing the fatal raid and fire at Waco (alongside Nichols), McVeigh told Fortier and his wife it was time to act violently against the government.

Prior to the bombing, McVeigh corresponded with a Michigan woman who made the letters available to the FBI after the bombing. One letter reads:

> The people of this nation should have flocked to Waco with their guns and opened fire on the bastards! The streets of Waco should have run red with the blood of the tyrants, oppressors and traitors that have slaughtered our people. Every person responsible for this massacre deserves nothing less than to die. If we want to live in peace, then sometimes we must go to war.... If this is too extreme for you, then bow down, lick the hand of your master like a willing, complacent whore and shut your mouth. Take whatever is dealt to you and your children and do not dare to complain to me about your fate. I do not have the patience to listen to the whining of cowards. There will be future massacres because we allow them to occur.
>
> (cited in Kaplan, 1997: 93)

At McVeigh's trial, the prosecution's opening statement outlined that

> Waco really sparked his anger; and as time passed, he became more and more and more outraged at the government, which he held responsible for the deaths.... And he told people that the federal government had intentionally murdered people at Waco.... He described the incident as the government's declaration of war against the American people. He wrote letters declaring that the government had drawn ... 'first blood' ... at Waco; and he predicted there would be a violent revolution against the American government. As he put it, blood would flow in the streets.

While on death row, McVeigh confirmed the prosecution's arguments. In a letter to Fox News Correspondent Rita Cosby, McVeigh explains that

> foremost, the bombing was a retaliatory strike, a counter attack, for the cumulative raids (and subsequent violence and damage) that federal agents had participated in over the preceding years (including, but not limited to Waco).... This bombing was also meant as a pre-emptive (or proactive) strike against these forces and their command and control centers within the federal building.

In a separate letter shown to the *Observer* newspaper, McVeigh stated further that when the

> branches of government concluded that the federal government had done nothing fundamentally wrong during the raid ... the system not only failed the victims who died during the siege but also failed the citizens of this country. This failure in effect left the door open for more Wacos.

He then

> reached the decision to go on the offensive – to put a check on government abuse of power, where others had failed in stopping the federal juggernaut running amok.... Borrowing a page from U.S. foreign policy, I decided to send a message to a government that was becoming increasingly hostile, by bombing a government building and the government employees within that building who represent that government.

Preparation stage

McVeigh's plan required more than 5,000 pounds of ammonium nitrate fertilizer, approximately 1,200 pounds of nitro methane racing fuel, 350 pounds of Tovex, and 16 55-gallon drums; this contributed to a total of 7,000 pounds. McVeigh realized this was far too much to assemble on his own, so he persuaded Fortier and Nichols to help him. At some point, McVeigh and Nichols experimented with smaller explosives on Nichols' farm in Michigan. Much of McVeigh's knowledge came from a mail order bomb-making manual entitled *Home Made C4*, which he purchased in the Spring of 1993. According to the prosecution, 'This book provides essentially a step-by-step recipe as to how to put together your own fertilizer fuel-based bomb. And the book even provides helpful hints as to where to acquire the various ingredients, the components.' The locations where McVeigh eventually purchased ammonium nitrate fertilizer and nitro methane were both suggested in this book.

On 30 September 1994, McVeigh and Nichols purchased a ton of ammonium nitrate from the McPherson branch of the Mid-Kansas Co-op using the names 'Mike Havens' and 'Terry Havens'. They needed two tons but feared such a large purchase would create suspicion. On 2 October, McVeigh and Nichols stole explosives from the Martin Marietta Aggregates Rock Quarry in Kansas, near Nichols' home. In total, they stole more than 500 electric blasting caps, seven cases of Tovex explosives (which would later serve as a booster to help ignite the IED's main charge), and 80 spools of shock tube, or ignition cord.[7] Using his real name, McVeigh rented a storage locker in Kingman, Arizona on 4 October 1994 for the stolen explosives. This was largely funded through McVeigh's actions on the gun show circuit, where he sold anti-government T-shirts, hats, bumper stickers, and guns (often illegally). On 18 October, Nichols bought the second ton of ammonium nitrate using the same pseudonym at the same store as the 30 September purchase. The ammonium nitrate was then kept at a rented storage unit in Herington, Kansas.

Originally, McVeigh wanted to use anhydrous hydrazine, a potent rocket fuel, to mix with the ammonium nitrate fertilizer. After making several calls to chemical companies using a phone card under the alias Daryl Bridges, McVeigh was unable to find a sufficient supply of anhydrous hydrazine at an affordable price. Realizing he could use a different chemical, McVeigh changed his plan to nitro methane, a motor-racing fuel. On 21 October, McVeigh attended a drag race in Dallas, Texas. There he met with Racing Fuels employee Tim Chambers, and asked for fuel so that he and his friends could ride motorcycles back home. McVeigh purchased three 55-gallon drums of nitro methane for between $925 and $2,775 (dependent upon which source is used).

On 5 November 1994, McVeigh convinced Terry Nichols to rob a gun dealer in Arkansas who had once been a friend of McVeigh. Nichols stole an estimated $60,000 in valuables and weapons from Roger Moore, justified by McVeigh as capital for the bomb expenses. Nichols stored the stolen guns in a locker in Council Grove, Kansas. Heavily influenced by the attack on the J. Edgar Hoover FBI building in Earl Turner's *The Turner Diaries*, McVeigh decided to bomb a government building. Unlike Turner's location in Washington D.C., McVeigh wanted to hit the heartland of America. His initial list included possible targets in Arkansas, Missouri, Oklahoma, Arizona, and Texas. Ultimately, he decided on the Alfred P. Murrah Federal Building in Oklahoma City because he understood that it held offices for the ATF, Drug Enforcement Administration, and Secret Service, thereby providing maximum federal government causalities.

Additionally he believed the U-shaped glass building would be easily damaged with a bomb placed inside the 'U'. On 15 December, McVeigh and Fortier set out to Kansas to pick up the stolen guns from the locker in Council Grove. On the way there, they drove through Oklahoma City to scope out the Murrah building and surrounding area for suitable locations for the getaway car.

Now that McVeigh had chosen a location, he needed to choose a day. The date of 19 April was chosen for two reasons. First and foremost, it was exactly two years to the day after the tragic incident at Waco. Second, it was exactly 220 years after the 'shot heard round the world' at the Battle of Lexington and Concord, the first military battle between the Patriots and the Loyalists in the American Revolutionary War.

McVeigh needed a fake drivers' license to rent the Ryder truck, which Michael Fortier's wife, Lori Fortier, helped him laminate. The alias on the license was Robert D. Kling, born 19 April 1972. On 14 April 1995 around 4 p.m., McVeigh checked into the Dreamland Motel in Junction City, Kansas; he used his real name but gave the Nichols' farm as his address. Since McVeigh was having problems with his current Pontiac station wagon, he decided to purchase a new getaway car. McVeigh purchased a 1977 Mercury Marquis from Tom Manning at the Firestone Service Center for $250 in Junction City, Kansas. McVeigh left Nichols' home address and telephone number on the bill. McVeigh then used his phone card to reserve a 20-foot Ryder truck from Elliot's Truck Agency. During the phone call, McVeigh stated that he needed a vehicle capable of carrying 5,000 pounds. He used the alias 'Bob Kling' for the one-way rental to Omaha, Nebraska. On 15 April, McVeigh completed the requisite paperwork for his truck rental and paid $280.32 in cash. He did not buy insurance. On 16 April, Nichols drove to Oklahoma City to meet McVeigh and help him with the getaway car. McVeigh parked the car in an alley very close to the Murrah Building and placed a sign that said, 'Not abandoned. Please do not tow. Will move by April 23 (needs battery and cable)'. Then McVeigh rode with Nichols back to Kansas. On 17 April, McVeigh picked up the Ryder truck at 4:20 p.m., and returned to the motel in Junction City.

On 18 April at 9am, McVeigh drove the truck to the storage unit at Geary Lake, Kansas, where he met Nichols. There the two men set to work creating the bomb. They mixed the nitro methane with each of the 50-pound bags of ammonium nitrate fertilizer in the 55-gallon drums, using a bathroom scales for measuring. McVeigh placed the barrels in a 'T' configuration so that he would not break an axle or flip the truck over. Once everything was mixed, McVeigh began working on the dual-fuse system. He drilled two sets of holes through the cab and the cargo box. Then he ran plastic fish-plank tubing through the holes, creating a two-minute fuse, and a five-minute fuse as backup. At the end of each fuse, he placed non-electric blasting caps. He also placed blasting caps onto two lines of shock tube so that when the caps exploded they would instantly spark the Tovex, which was placed in the centre drum at the intersection of the T. The bomb took over three hours to construct. At one point, work had to stop because there were passers-by. McVeigh then made his way to Oklahoma City, disposing of the clothes he wore while mixing the explosives along the way. He stayed overnight in a roadside motel.

Event execution stage

The bombing occurred the following morning, 19 April. The original plan was for the bomb to detonate at 11 a.m. On the morning of the bombing, McVeigh decided that waiting that long was too risky, so he moved the time forward to 9 a.m. McVeigh felt that by 9 a.m., there would be a requisite number of bystanders who could be killed in the bombing. McVeigh's intention to maximize the number of killings came through in his alleged statement to his defence attorneys that he 'would not have gotten the point across to the government' without a heavy casualty toll. At 7 a.m., he left the motel where he had stayed overnight. He entered Oklahoma City at approximately 8:50 a.m. Shortly after, he pulled his truck to the side to ignite the five-minute fuse. A block from the Murrah building, he stopped at a traffic light and lit the two-minute fuse. He accelerated slowly, fearing that sudden movement would prematurely detonate the bomb. The front parking area of the Murrah building was empty so he parked in front of the building, checked the fuses, locked the truck, and walked away.

McVeigh walked about 150 yards before he felt the explosion. The explosion created a crater 20 feet wide and eight feet deep. The bombing killed a total of 168 people: 163 were inside the building during the explosion. At least 500 people were injured.

Post-event activity and strategic analysis

McVeigh made it to the Mercury Marquis and was on the road by 9:10 a.m., eight minutes after the bombing. At approximately 10:20 a.m., McVeigh was pulled over 80 miles north of the bombing by trooper Charles Hanger for driving without a licence plate. Hanger searched the car and arrested McVeigh for carrying an unregistered gun. McVeigh was held at the Noble County Jail in Perry, Oklahoma. Meanwhile, the police had found the vehicle ID number from the Ryder truck's axle and traced it back to Robert Kling. Two days later, McVeigh was transferred to federal custody on federal bombing charges.

There is very little evidence of McVeigh's post-event strategic analysis. McVeigh's published letters, to a large extent, do not go into much detail about this issue. Operationally, he viewed the bombing as successful. Strategically, he was unsure of the long-lasting impact of the bombing. McVeigh felt that he left his fellow Americans with 'the choice to try to learn from me or … choose to remain ignorant, and suffer the consequences.'

Roshonara Choudhry

On 14 May 2010, Roshonara Choudhry stabbed Stephen Timms, a Labour Party Member of Parliament, causing him serious bodily injury.[8]

Decision and search activity stage

In the subsequent trial, the court heard a draft letter of Choudhry's addressed to her mother that was found on Choudhry's computer. The letter stated that she hated living in Britain and did not want to spend the rest of her life in a non-Muslim country. She said that she could not live under the British Government, which she described as an 'enemy of Islam', and that she could not pay taxes to it or work as a teacher in its education system.

Investigators established that Choudhry began downloading Anwar al-Awlaki's videos and sermons in the autumn and winter of 2009. She began spending an abundance of time in her bedroom; her parents believed that she was studying, but in reality she was downloading extremist material, including more than 100 hours of al-Awlaki's sermons. It was supposedly during this time that Choudhry decided to engage in a violent attack. During her police interview, Choudhry responded to a question concerning the transition from immersing herself in religion to committing violence. Choudhry's response stated:

> Because as Muslims we're all brothers and sisters and we should all look out for each other and we shouldn't sit back and do nothing while others suffer. We shouldn't allow the people who oppress us to get away with it and to think that they can do whatever they want to us and we're just gonna [*sic*] lie down and take it.

Choudhry referred to a specific YouTube video of Sheikh Abdullah Azzam that made her understand that 'even women are supposed to fight' and that she had an obligation to turn toward violence. According to the police interviews, Choudhry made this realization at some point in April and soon after began her preparations for the attack.

Preparation stage

As part of her preparations, Choudhry devised a list of Members of Parliament who voted for the 2003 invasion of Iraq. She researched the backgrounds of London-based Members of Parliament using the website 'They Work For You', which includes information on voting records. She appears to have concentrated her research on Labour ministers Jim Fitzpatrick, Margaret Hodge, Nick Raynsford, and Stephen Timms. Detectives later declared that Timms was her 'sole and easiest target'. The decision to attack Timms was made three to four weeks prior to the attack itself. Timms was Choudhry's local Member of Parliament. Her online research showed that Timms regularly voted with his political party (which held power at that time). Choudhry later told detectives that,

> he just voted strongly for everything, as though he had no mercy. As though he felt no doubts that what he was doing was right even though it was such

an arrogant thing to do and I just felt like if he could treat the Iraqi people so mercilessly, then why should I show him any mercy?

Choudhry had met Timms twice previously. The first occasion occurred three years prior to the attack on a trip organized by her secondary school; she was 17. On the second occasion, Choudhry met Timms at his offices and sought a grant to continue her £3,290 a year English degree at King's College London. She felt entitled to a grant because her father was unemployed and her family was relying on social welfare. Timms rejected her request, and according to Newham Councillor Lucky Mish, Choudhry got 'very angry'.

Weeks before the attack, Choudhry bought two new knives: a three-inch blade, which was eventually used in the stabbing, and a five-inch blade, which was kept in her handbag as back-up in case the first broke during the attack. Before the attack, Choudhry stored both knives in a shoebox underneath her bed.

Event execution stage

Choudhry made an appointment to see Timms at his office at the Beckton Globe community centre at 2:45p.m. on 14 May 2010. On the day of the attack, Choudhry left her home in East Ham at 1:45p.m. She took the 101 bus to a NatWest bank, where she set straight her financial affairs. Choudhry used her academic prize money and savings to pay off her student loan because she was afraid that her family would become liable once she was arrested for the attack. She also emptied her bank accounts fearing the British state would take the money upon her conviction.

She then took a second bus to Timms' constituency office at the Globe community centre in Beckton, East London. Choudhry asked to see Timms himself, rather than his assistant. She then waited for her appointment. At the beginning of the appointment, she approached the desk where Timms sat. In Choudhry's words she 'purposefully walked round the side of the desk so I could get close to him. He pointed for me to sit down on the chair but instead I walked towards him'. Timms noticed that Choudhry's left hand was outstretched; presuming it was because she wanted to shake hands, he moved to reciprocate. In her words, she then 'pulled the knife out of my bag and I hit him in the stomach with it. I put it in the top part of his stomach like when you punch someone'. Choudhry explained that she aimed for this area because it was soft and she feared being too weak to force the knife into another area. She then managed to stab Timms a second time before she was pulled from him and overpowered by his staff. When asked why she stabbed him twice, Choudhry told detectives 'I was not going to stop until someone made me. I wanted to kill him ... I was going to get revenge for the people of Iraq'.

Post-event activity and strategic analysis

In her interview with police on the day of the attack, Choudhry was asked how she felt about what she had done that day. She replied;

> I feel like I did what I'd planned to do ... I feel like I've ruined the rest of my life. I feel like it's worth it because millions of Iraqis are suffering and I should do what I can to help them and not just be inactive and do nothing while they suffer.

Because of the attack, Choudhry felt that she had 'fulfilled my obligation, my Islamic duty to stand up for the people of Iraq and to punish someone who wanted to make war with them'.

Anders Breivik

Anders Breivik's coordinated attacks occurred on 22 July 2011 in Oslo and Utøya Island, Norway. In total, 77 were killed and approximately 320 were injured.[9]

Decision and search activity stage

Breivik described himself as a member of the Knights Templar of Europe. In the initial interview on the evening of his terrorist attacks, Breivik emphasized that the Knights Templar were not Nazis, supported the Israeli state, and only wanted political Islam out of Europe. Breivik's intention was for the Knights Templar to take power in Europe within 60 years through conservative revolution.

Breivik was alleged to have been involved in this ideological movement for 10 years. Initially, he only wanted to contribute financially to the Norwegian Defence League, an anti-Islamic group. According to the psychiatric report, his

> goal was to raise 30 million kroners before he was 30 years old. When he was 26 years old, he had saved 6 million and he realized that he would not be able to reach the goal. He then decided to write a compendium consisting of three books.
>
> (Husby & Sorheim, 2011: 28)

Breivik alleges that violence would not have been necessary, but the mainstream media censored his beliefs and did not publish his statements. He mentioned two newspapers, *Dagbladet* and *Aftenposten*, as being primarily culpable (Husby & Sorheim, 2011: 24). The psychiatric report states 'he thought he could win in a democratic manner, but the day he lost faith in this, he considered violence as the only option' (Husby & Sorheim, 2011: 26).[10] Breivik saw his violent actions as being 'just the beginning [of the] civil war ... between Communists and nationalists'. His actions, according to the psychiatric report, were viewed as the 'fireworks for something that will happen' (Husby & Sorheim, 2011: 14–15).

His manifesto projects 73 years of conflict and situates his violence as a component of phase one which was due to continue until 2030. During this phase, 'our only objective ... is to create awareness about the truth and contribute consolidation/recruitment' (Breivik, 2011: 1351). The goal of repeated small-scale attacks is to 'sap the will of the current E.U. regimes to continue the fight or at least will force them to open their eyes ... and identify the Islamization of Europe as a threat to all Europeans' (Breivik, 2011: 1352).

On a strategic level, there were many motives for engaging in violence according to Breivik.

> The operation was necessary for revenge, and it was a preemptive attack to prevent more activity from those individuals who betray Norway. The operation also functions as a warning. Most importantly, the operation expresses my love for my own people and country, and is my contribution to getting rid of the evil in the country.
> (Husby & Sorheim, 2011: 121)

During the trial, Breivik called the attacks an act of 'self-defence on behalf of my people, my culture, my religion, my city, and my country'. According to Breivik, these actions would precede European nationalists successfully seizing power between 2030 and 2070 and later safeguarding European economic interests and engaging in a mass deportation of all Muslims from Europe before 2090.

Preparation stage

In total, Breivik claims that he planned the operation for two years, but that many aspects went wrong.

Evidence suggests that Breivik considered appropriate targets at great length. Broadly, he drew up four categories of individuals, all of whom he labelled as 'traitors'. In Breivik's terminology, Category A traitors encompassed 12 individuals, most of whom were members of government. They included Jonas Gahr Store (Norway's Minister of Foreign Affairs), and Jens Stoltenberg (Norway's Prime Minister) as well as other key high-profile Labour party ideologues. Category B traitors consisted of 4,500 people. They included cultural Marxist/multicultural politicians, E.U. parliamentarians, journalists, editors, teachers, lecturers, university professors, school or university board members, publicists, radio commentators, fiction writers, cartoonists, artists, celebrities, technicians, scientists, doctors, and Church leaders. 'Stereotypical socialists, collectivists, feminists, gay and disability activists, animal rights activists, environmentalists etc. are to be considered on an individual basis only' (Breivik, 2011: 930). Category C consisted of 85,000 individuals in Norway, and the criteria for inclusion were that they facilitated Category A and B traitors in their actions and also possessed some political influence. Category D appears more exclusive and included 'union leaders, chief of police, fire chiefs and industry leaders' (Husby & Sorheim, 2011: 145). They had 'little or no political influence but are facilitating category B and C traitors ... through various means' (Breivik, 2011: 931). Those attacked on Utøya Island were Category C traitors in Breivik's eyes. In his words, 'we have a mandate to execute category A and B traitors. We do not really have the mandate to execute category C traitors' (Husby & Sorheim, 2011: 22).

Breivik provided two contradictory reasons as to why he did not focus on assassinating a Category A individual. First, he thought that it would be too difficult because Category A individuals are often well protected; Breivik stated that it was necessary to go further down the list of acceptable targets for this attack. Second, he estimated that killing the Prime Minister would take one month of preparation, including surveillance. Although the Prime Minister was a Category A target, Breivik felt that the value of killing one person would be too small, and according to the psychiatric report, 'that for someone with his intellect and intelligence, it would be a waste of resources to spend time planning the murder of just one person' (Husby & Sorheim, 2011: 25).

Breivik consistently referred to the bombing in Oslo and the shootings at Utøya Island as 'Plan B'. Plan A involved placing car bombs at a government building, Gunerius (a major shopping mall in Oslo), the Labour Party headquarters and the royal castle. If he survived these bombings, the plan was then to shoot as many people as possible at the Blitz anarchist community, the offices of the *Dagsavisen* newspaper and finally the Socialist Left Party (*Sosialistisk Venstreparti*) headquarters. Plan A, which was his main plan from December 2010 until December 2011, could not be implemented due to time and effort constraints related to making the requisite amount of explosives.

Breivik had considered other attacks such as taking over the Norwegian Broadcasting Corporation in order to broadcast propaganda, detonating the Halden nuclear reactor and blowing up the royal castle by itself. These plans were abandoned due to the need for extra personnel and doubt about whether the royal family was a legitimate target (Husby & Sorheim, 2011: 119).

Ultimately, Breivik decided to engage in Plan B, a coordinated attack against government buildings and a political party conference. The goal of the government building attack was to 'kill as many as possible' (Husby & Sorheim, 2011: 120). Breivik claimed that the intent of the original bombing was to kill between 200 and 500 people, and that he would consider anything less than 12 killings to be a failure. He also claimed that if he heard on the radio that several hundred were dead he would 'have driven to Gronland (police station) to surrender' (Husby & Sorheim, 2011: 119). He claimed, 'in order to get international press, there must be a large impact ... one must exceed a certain limit.'

As mentioned previously, Breivik's second target in the coordinated attacks was a political party conference. The time of the year necessitated it to be at Utøya because once Breivik dropped his plan for four car bombings, the conferences of the major political parties had already taken place. Theoretically, he could have waited for the conferences to take place in 2012, but he was having liquidity problems.

> There were bills for fertilizer, rent, lease, and I would have to buy food, and then the PC broke down. I could not afford a bad credit rating, because then I would not be able to lease a car. I could not wait any longer.
> (Husby & Sorheim, 2011: 122)

Breivik saw the students at Utøya Island as legitimate targets because he viewed them as 'extreme Marxists.... These are not innocent people. This is the Labor Party's ... youth organization. They have been in power in Norway. They have arranged the Islamization of Norway' (Husby & Sorheim, 2011: 14). During his trial, Breivik spoke about the victims on Utøya.

> These were not innocent civilians or children, but political activists who actively promoted multiculturalism and cultural Marxism. As many as 44 of 65 AUF-ers had leading positions in the AUF, and many took part in other political boards, and are nominated for county boards for the Labour Party. AUF is very similar to the Hitler Jugend. Utøya is an indoctrination camp for political activists, and on July 20th they had been indoctrinated for several hours by one of the most extreme communists in Norway: Marte Michelet, daughter of the arch-communist Jon Michelet. She had been invited by the AUF's leadership as a speaker.

Breivik stated that choosing Utøya Island was 'ingenious ... since it was like stabbing the Labour Party in its heart' (Husby & Sorheim, 2011: 26). He continued that

> the operation was not to kill as many as possible, but to give a strong signal that cannot be misunderstood ... as long as Labour follows its ideological line, continuing to deconstruct Norwegian culture and mass import Muslims, they must take responsibility for this treachery.
> (Husby & Sorheim, 2011: 29)

From an operational perspective, Utøya Island was also ideal because it was 'isolated', 'police would have problems' accessing the site, there would be access to '730 activists at one time' and there would be 'no civilians present' (Husby & Sorheim, 2011: 120). Breivik also recognized that targeting Utøya Island was problematic because 'some of the people there were only potential traitors and it's not ideal with people under 18' years of age (Husby & Sorheim, 2011: 120).

In preparing for the attacks, Breivik mentions that a main strength of his was the fact that he had no contact with extreme right-wing circles in Norway; this allowed him to stay clear of police attention (Husby & Sorheim, 2011: 24). Breivik also became socially withdrawn from significant others, becoming 'completely absorbed' by the game *World of Warcraft*, (Husby & Sorheim, 2011: 34) according to a former friend.[11] Breivik states that this social withdrawal was a 'natural' and 'pragmatic' decision to ensure 'secrecy' (Husby & Sorheim, 2011: 108). He was also careful in his internet usage, as he avoided 'websites that use very strong symbols' and hid his IP address (Husby & Sorheim, 2011: 114).

Between February 2007 and November 2009, Breivik wrote his manifesto, which he viewed as a radicalizing tool.

> All it takes is access to the compendium. If you read it from the first word to the end, you will be radicalized. The [compendium] is both a tool and an application. The entire standard difficult recruitment process is being replaced. This is much more effective because the compendium is structured so that you are automatically radicalized.
>
> (Husby & Sorheim, 2011: 101)

Further, Breivik alleged, 'the work is the first step, a ground-breaking start. It cannot be read without the reader being radicalized' (Husby & Sorheim, 2011: 109). In the manifesto, he refers to the attacks as the 'marketing operation' (Breivik, 2011: 8). The manifesto itself covers the following topics: the rise of cultural Marxism/multiculturalism in Western Europe, why the Islamic colonization and Islamization of Western Europe began, the current state of the Western European Resistance Movements (anti-Marxists/anti-jihad movements), and finally solutions for Western Europe and how the resistance should move forward in the coming decades. The opening pages of the manifesto outline that it 'presents advanced ideological, practical, tactical, organizational and rhetorical solutions and strategies for all patriotic-minded individuals/movements. The book will be of great interest to you whether you are a moderate or a more dedicated cultural conservative/nationalist' (Breivik, 2011: 4). In total, approximately half of the manifesto is written in Breivik's words while the rest encompass a compilation of works by others.

Between February 2010 and July 2010, Breivik made a prototype of body armour, and stored 'four bulletproof vest inserts, a pair of self-made bulletproof pants, a bulletproof vest, and bulletproof shoes' as well as smoke grenades in a box near the Swedish border (Husby & Sorheim, 2011: 115). He referred to this period of time as his 'armor acquisition phase' (Breivik, 2011: 1420). In August 2010, Breivik began to acquire weapons and ammunition. Originally he travelled to Prague but failed to find any contacts and 'lost the motivation' to acquire weapons on the trip; he returned home within ten days (Husby & Sorheim, 2011: 118) and cancelled his plans to travel to Berlin and/or Copenhagen to acquire weaponry (2011: 1422). Because he was a member of the Oslo pistol club, he was allowed to buy a Ruger Mini 14. All of the guns eventually used in the attack were purchased between late 2010 and early 2011 (Husby & Sorheim, 2011: 77) apart from the shotgun that he had legally owned for seven years previous (2011: 1422). He opted for guns that were 'light, mobile, and rich in content' (Husby & Sorheim, 2011: 118).

By October 2010 and until the beginning of 2011, Breivik entered what he referred to as the 'explosion acquisition phase'. During this time, he studied bombs and acquired the ingredients needed to make them. During his trial, Breivik stated that he:

> did research and got access to more than 600 guides on how to produce explosives. And there were more, up to 100, different types of explosives. And then I considered really the explosives that were realistic to make the

basis of the difficulty in acquiring the components. And they had been very popular with al-Qaida, they are difficult. So.... The ones I chose, it was really.... It was known that it was extremely difficult to make them. But the components was very easy to get hold of [as opposed to] the ones that were difficult to make. So there ... I chose to make one.... Or, I would try with one that was very difficult.

Between October and January 2011, he acquired items such as sulphur powder, sodium nitrate, aspirin, aluminium powder, and fertilizer sensitizers from Polish, Norwegian, and Chinese suppliers he found online as well as eBay and local drug stores. In December 2010, he bought a fuse and various chemical substances (Husby & Sorheim, 2011: 118). Breivik's manifesto reckoned this phase was 'the most vulnerable phase of them all' because of security concerns regarding the purchase of all of these bomb-making materials (2011: 1423).

In January and February 2011, Breivik claims to have done 'a lot of shooting and a lot of training' (Husby & Sorheim, 2011: 118). During this time, he used the pistol club's facilities for target practice twice weekly. He also began 'training like Rambo' in the gym and started using anabolic steroids. During this period he also bought other ingredients for the IED including caustic soda and acetone (Husby & Sorheim, 2011: 119). Between 15 and 26 February, Breivik created a 12-minute movie trailer promoting the manifesto. That month Breivik also became aware of the need for 'an operational base' (Husby & Sorheim, 2011: 120). On 10 April, Breivik rented a 23-acre farm in Hedmark for 10,000 kroner a month. He took out a one-year rental contract. The farm was big enough to allow for a 3,000-kilogram delivery of fertilizer and not raise suspicion. He used the cover of using the farm for 'test production of sugar beet' (Breivik, 2011: 1437). On 27 April, he ordered the fertilizer, which was to be delivered the following week. On 2 May, he left all of the equipment and clothing he needed at the farm. On 7 May, he moved full-time onto the farm. He would have moved in sooner to start the production process but was delayed because of illness and the incumbent tenants being slow to move out (Breivik, 2011: 1453).

Breivik refers to May and June of 2011 as the 'chemistry phase'. On 3 May, he installed a ventilation hood and fan on the farm. On 4 May, he 'finished creating the metal skeletons for the blast devices' (Breivik, 2011: 1455). On 5 May, Breivik ground aspirin tablets at first with a mortar and pestle and later with a dumb-bell. On 6 May, Breivik began to synthesize acetylsalicylic acid from the ground down aspirin. This proved problematic because the instructions he followed did not work. He 'began to somewhat panic ... and began to lose heart' (Breivik, 2011: 1455). This delayed him for three days until a YouTube video provided a viable alternative solution that he tested successfully on 9 May. Because of this delay, Breivik became concerned that the owners of the farm might catch him creating the IED. He then spent 10 and 11 May formulating an evacuation plan and packed an evacuation kit. Further acetylsalicylic acid production and the purchase of extra materials to speed up the process occurred from 12 to 16 May. The main instrument (hot plate stirrer) used in this process broke down however, so Breivik was forced to work on other components of the IED. From 16 to 20 May, Breivik boiled the sulphuric acid outside. At one point, a neighbour interacted with Breivik as he boiled the sulphuric acid. Breivik remarked in his manifesto: 'I'm going to stick to nighttime boiling from now on to reduce my exposure to any unwanted surprises. I was very lucky today, something I cannot take for granted in the future'. At this time, the plan was to engage in four car-bombings, but it proved too time-consuming. Breivik began grinding the fertilizer on 23 May using newly purchased dumb-bells. This process failed and delayed Breivik by a further four days until 27 May when he began to test 12 newly purchased blenders. By 31 May, Breivik decided to settle on grinding 60% of the weight he originally intended. On 6 June, he completed crushing the fertilizer. On 7 June, he purchased a new hot plate stirrer and returned to synthesizing the acid until 10 June, when he tested the acid and found it to be either inert or of low purity. He spent 11 June researching alternative procedures online but was disrupted by a power outage that lasted through the evening. The following day he decided to produce the much more complex material diazodinitrophenol (DDNP) from a different batch of acid. This device was successfully tested on 13 June at a 'very isolated site' (2011: 1459). Breivik immediately left the area but returned hours later to check which compounds had detonated. Around 15 June, he adapted his plan to involve a one-ton car bombing of a government building, when he realized that he could not make multiple one-ton bombs. His actions were nearly uncovered again between 19 and 21 June when the farm owner's wife made a trip to the location and ended up staying overnight. After she left, Breivik continued to develop his DDNP batch until 25 June when another important piece of equipment broke. This slowed down progress and he did not complete the task until 30 June.

In total, in the four weeks prior to the attacks, Breivik spent seven to eight hours a day in the final production of the bomb. The primary and secondary boosters took one week, and the chemical mixture took over two weeks to complete. Breivik loaded the explosives into the car a week before the attacks.

On 2 July, Breivik began reconnaissance of his attack plans. Between 5 and 19 July, Breivik put together the final components of the IED. These newer explosive mixtures were tested in a location that was an 11-hour drive away from the farm on 22 July.

Breivik claims that the whole operation cost 130,000 Euro (Breivik, 2011: 9). Much of this funding came through Breivik's personal wealth. He had previously earned several million kroner from outsourcing electronic services. He also sold fake diplomas online (Husby & Sorheim, 2011: 36), advertising space on various apartment buildings (Husby & Sorheim, 2011: 37), and mobile phone covers (Husby & Sorheim, 2011: 43).

There is evidence to suggest that Breivik took drugs before the event. Upon being apprehended, he announced that he had taken a combination of ephedrine, caffeine, and aspirin (Breivik referred to this combination as an 'ECA-Stack') in order to enhance performance. His manifesto outlines that the ECA-Stack will significantly increase your strength, agility and focus ... up to 30–50% for 1 to 2 hours after taking one capsule. This enhancer, in combination with a steroid cycle, will increase your physical and mental abilities by up to 100%, transforming you into an unstoppable one-man army when used in combination with proper training and a full range of body armor and weapons.

(Breivik, 2011: 898)

In the words of the psychiatric report, 'he had taken the substance in order to achieve as much as possible during the operation' (Husby & Sorheim, 2011: 13). Breivik was tested for a higher than normal concentration of ephedrine. According to the psychiatric report, 'higher doses and higher blood concentrations may give intoxication symptoms where increased confidence, increased risk-taking and loss of critical skills may occur' (Husby and Sorheim, 2011: 63). The doctors who examined Breivik stated further that he 'may have been under the influence of caffeine to such an extent that a moderate intoxication effect cannot be ruled out' (Husby & Sorheim, 2011: 65). Breivik also claims to have taken two forms of anabolic steroids from the spring of 2011 until the day of the attacks, and a mixture of ephedrine, caffeine, and aspirin for nine weeks prior. Breivik refers to the use of these drugs as a 'military strategy' (Husby & Sorheim, 2011: 113) and they were largely purchased online (Breivik, 2011: 899).

Event execution stage

Breivik left his rented farm the night before the attacks and stayed at his mother's house.

Breivik's initial plan was to distribute his manifesto at 3 a.m., conduct the bombing at 10 a.m., and be on Utøya Island at 11 a.m. in order to execute Gro Harlem Brundtland, a Norwegian politician who was due to give a talk to the young people at Utøya. The plan was delayed, however. According to Breivik, 'This delay was disastrous for the whole thing' (Husby & Sorheim, 2011: 28). The original delay occurred because his installation of a high-speed modem and the configuration of Microsoft Outlook on his PC took longer than expected.

After these installations were complete, he drove his car into Oslo and parked it at Hammserborg Square. He left his equipment in the vehicle and did some reconnaissance at Grubbegaten Street. He walked to Domkirkeplassen and took a taxi back to his mother's house. Breivik then 'realized that I did not have much time. I started to realize that most people had left the government building already'. The delay ultimately reduced the number of possible victims in Oslo. The independent parliamentary report on the attacks acknowledges that on a normal working day, approximately 3,100 people work in these government offices. On that particular summer Friday, this number was down to just over 600, half of which had left by the time the IED detonated at 3.25 p.m. The delay also stopped Breivik from getting to Utøya in time in order to assassinate

Brundtland. At his mother's house, he uploaded a film he had made to YouTube and wrote the last message in his manifesto at 2:45 p.m. At 3:05 p.m., Breivik distributed his more than 1,500-page manifesto to approximately 8,000 people via email. Breivik largely cultivated these email addresses through Facebook between October 2009 and March 2010. According to Breivik, 'Utøya Island and the government building was all about publishing the manifesto, to reach the 350,000 militant nationalists who are the audience' (Husby & Sorheim, 2011: 100).

At 2:30 p.m., Breivik consumed the mixture of ephedrine, caffeine, and aspirin for the purpose of raising performance, left his mother's apartment and walked to the rented car that held the bomb and which he had parked nearby. In the car, he changed 'from civilian to military clothing' (Husby & Sorheim, 2011: 123). In order to prevent premature detonation of the IED, Breivik wrapped the detonators in foam rubber containers. He drove the car to the government building.

At 3:13 p.m., he was 200 metres from the target. At that point, he parked the car and attached blue lights to the roof of the car. He sat in it for two minutes and put on his bulletproof vest and a helmet with a visor. At 3:15 p.m. he drove the remaining 200 metres and parked again. He then lit the fuse, left the car, and carried a Glock pistol in his hand and walked quickly away. By 3:20 p.m., he reached Hammersborg Square where he had previously parked another rented car and began to drive toward the ferry. At 3:25 p.m., the bomb exploded, killing eight people and injuring 209.

At 4:55 p.m., Breivik arrived at Utoykaia in Tyrifjorden, 40 kilometres north-west of Oslo. From there he was transported to Utøya by ferry. He arrived at 5:18 p.m. and began shooting at 5:22 p.m. Breivik was heavily armed for the shooting attack. He took a Benelli Super Nova, a Ruger Mini 14 calibre 5.56 (with 10 pieces of 30-shot magazines), and a Glock 34 (with six cartridge clips – four of which had 30-shot magazines). He left his shotgun behind in the car because all of the equipment was too heavy to carry. He also wore an Israeli protective vest to protect himself if he was shot at. Breivik fortified the vest with additional protective panels to negate armour-piercing ammunition.

Breivik stated that he had intended to set fire to all of the buildings on Utøya Island. For this task, he brought eight litres of diesel fuel. This plan was foiled, however, when he lost his lighter during the shootings.

At 6:01 p.m., Breivik made the first of nine calls to police looking to surrender. On six occasions, he failed to make a connection. He alleges that he failed to make his message clear in the three connected calls because of 'incompetent persons' on the other end of the line. For these calls, he used a mobile phone without a SIM card. He initially decided to make the call because he thought, 'the operation was completed' and because he could not 'find more targets and had ... been searching a long time' (Husby and Sorheim, 2011: 138). Despite making these calls, Breivik continued to shoot people. In total, 69 were shot and killed at Utøya, and a further 110 were injured.

Post-event activity and strategic analysis

Over the course of his debriefing interviews, Breivik distinguished between the combat success and the media success of the attacks. In the early interviews, Breivik was doubtful about his media success. He conceded that few of his co-ideologues would defend his 'bestial actions' (Husby & Sorheim, 2011: 16), and that the day of the actions was 'the worst day of his life' (Husby & Sorheim, 2011: 17). He acknowledged further that the events were 'completely awful' and that he was 'not proud' of what he 'was forced to do' in response to Labour Party policies (Husby & Sorheim, 2011: 20). Much of this early antipathy towards his own actions was due to the fact that he defined these victims as 'Category C traitors' (Husby & Sorheim, 2011: 22).

On the other hand, however, he saw the attacks as a combat success, and stated that the fight will continue via 'the pen from jail' (Husby & Sorheim, 2011: 23). On the whole, Breivik stated that the success of the violent actions could only be 'measured by the spreading of the compendium' (Husby & Sorheim, 2011: 131).

On a practical level, Breivik's manifesto concludes with the statement, that 'if I had known then, what I know today … I would have managed to complete the operation [building the IEDs] within 30 days instead of using almost 80 days'.

Conclusion and implications

This chapter has provided a sequential breakdown of five successfully executed lone-actor terrorist events. Some aspects of these cases mirror each other, while others involved noticeably different behaviours. These differences are perhaps unsurprising; together they illustrate that lone-actor terrorist events are complex, develop over a long period of time, and involve a high level of planning and organization.

Similarities and differences were noticeable across the first three phases. For example, during the decision and search activity phase, Copeland, Breivik, and McVeigh all operated within a broader political movement, became exasperated with the movement's means, and later viewed themselves as the progenitors for wider movements of violent co-ideologues. Choudhry, on the other hand, downloaded, consumed, and planned her attack in isolation from co-ideologues.

There were also similarities and differences in how the perpetrators viewed themselves and their actions. Copeland saw himself as the 'spark' of future attacks, and Breivik saw himself as 'just the beginning' of a civil war between communists and nationalists. Taheri-Azar and Choudhry, however, saw themselves as one piece of a historical number of actors who turned to violence for the sake of their ideology. Breivik and McVeigh framed their violence as 'pre-emptive' of future hostile government actions against their beliefs and co-ideologues. McVeigh also framed his actions as revenge for contemporary government policies; both Taheri-Azar and Choudhry also largely shared this view. McVeigh considered violence to be a 'retaliatory strike, a counter attack' that would 'put a check on government', whereas Choudhry's violent action was to show her fellow Muslims that she would not 'allow the people who oppress us to get away with it'. Taheri-Azar framed his violence as a response to the 'killing of believing men and women under the direction of the United States government'. In terms of inspiring and justifying their acts, both Copeland and McVeigh cited *The Turner Diaries*, while Taheri-Azar and Choudhry cited religious texts. Breivik, on the other hand, developed his own manifesto, which cited a broad range of historical and contemporary thinkers.

Finally, the timeframe between the beginning of the decision and search activity phase and the eventual event execution varied between less than six months (Choudhry), two years (Taheri-Azar and Breivik), and three years (Copeland and McVeigh). This suggests that in many cases the development of a lone-actor terrorist attack occurs over a long period of time, but that this time can be lessened dramatically when individuals choose to conduct more technically primitive attacks.

During the preparation phase, each of the five lone actors adapted ordinary household or personal items that were purchased at regular shopping outlets into either a weapon or a component of a weapon. Copeland purchased components from medical supply stores, hardware stores, and fireworks distributors. McVeigh purchased his components from co-ops and a motor-racing company employee; he also stole a number of other materials from a rock quarry. Breivik purchased many materials for both his bomb and gun attacks online.

There is also evidence to suggest that each individual considered the optimal targets to attack. McVeigh's initial list included possible targets in Arkansas, Missouri, Oklahoma, Arizona, and Texas. Choudhry devised a list of Members of Parliament who voted for the 2003 invasion of Iraq. Taheri-Azar first considered attacking Washington D.C., and Breivik considered attacking many people and locations, including members of Norway's political elite, government buildings, shopping malls, political party conferences, newspaper offices, the Norwegian Broadcasting Corporation, a nuclear reactor, and the royal castle.

Copeland, Breivik, and McVeigh all relied upon bomb-making manuals and tested their IEDs prior to the attack. Both Breivik and Copeland's testing occurred between five and six weeks prior to their initial attacks. While four of the individuals acted alone in all stages of their plots, McVeigh solicited help from others in the manufacturing of homemade explosives. Taheri-Azar and Choudhry planned more primitive attacks (vehicular assault, knife attack) that did not require much, if any, expertise, training, testing or technical skill. In terms of transportation, Taheri-Azar, Breivik, and McVeigh rented vehicles used in their attacks, whereas Choudhry and Copeland used public transportation in travelling to their attacks.

In terms of attack timing, McVeigh planned his event to coincide with the two-year anniversary of the Waco stand-off, the other events appeared to occur either through necessity (e.g. Breivik experiencing liquidity problems) or because all of the aspects of the plot happened to crystallize at that time (e.g. Copeland). Finally, most of the perpetrators chose attack locations that they had previous knowledge of, either through having conducted previous business there (Taheri-Azar, Choudhry), or through prior surveillance (Breivik, McVeigh). This appears to be important for a successful attack, as Copeland's problems during his first two bombings were largely a result of ill-considered targets and poor surveillance. While the intent of Breivik, McVeigh, Taheri-Azar, and Copeland was to kill as many people as possible, Choudhry's preparations were quite different as they involved plotting against one high-profile figure.

The event execution phase highlights consistent differences between the five cases. The technical sophistication varies markedly between quite unsophisticated attacks (Taheri-Azar, Choudhry) to repeated attacks using basic IEDs (Copeland), to sophisticated large-scale bombings (McVeigh) and multi-method attacks (Breivik). The offenders also differed in their intention to get away from the scene of the attack. McVeigh chose the Murrah Federal building specifically because of its proximity to various possible getaway routes. Copeland's first attack location was chosen on the day of the attack because he felt that it was 'a good place to get away from'. Breivik and Taheri-Azar both expected to be killed in the commissioning of their attacks, and Choudhry anticipated being arrested following hers.

To a large extent, the case studies also reflect the large number of roadblocks and hurdles that a lone-actor terrorist encounters and must overcome in the successful commission of an attack. Often, this requires abandoning a more ambitious original plan for something less complicated. Copeland struggled in his original attempts at bomb making because the manuals he relied upon did not provide exhaustive lists of the necessary ingredients and he found it 'too complex' to manufacture and procure the missing chemical compounds by himself. After originally giving up on his intent to commit violence, he subsequently downscaled the size of the IED he wanted to use and began constructing far smaller devices. Taheri-Azar initially wanted to join the U.S. military, 'fly an airplane over Washington, D.C. and drop a nuclear bomb on the city'. He abandoned this plan, however, within a month after meeting with Army recruiters and applying to clinical psychology graduate schools in preparation for a position as a fighter pilot. He also abandoned plans to engage in a shooting attack when he felt that he could not obtain the necessary permits and worried that the purchase of weapons would attract the attention of the FBI. The quantity of explosives needed by McVeigh necessitated stealing from a rock quarry; even with stealing some of the ingredients, his initial explosive mix needed to be abandoned because of cost and the unavailability of anhydrous hydrazine. Breivik abandoned his original plan of placing car bombs at a government building, Gunerius (a major shopping mall in Oslo), the Labour Party headquarters, and the royal castle due to time and effort constraints related to making the requisite amount of explosives. Breivik's other plans including attacking the Norwegian Broadcasting Corporation or detonating the Halden nuclear reactor were abandoned due to the need for extra personnel. Breivik also failed to procure weaponry on his trip to Prague. Further, faulty bomb-making recipes and equipment failure hampered Breivik's preparation of explosive materials, and ultimately forced him to downscale the number and size of the IEDs he had planned to develop.

A final problem, shared by Copeland and Breivik, concerned the issue of the timing and execution of the event. For Copeland's first bombing, he arrived two and a half hours ahead of the intended detonation time. Although this allowed him time to scout the area for an appropriate target, once he placed the IED it left a considerable amount of time for members of the public to notice it and move it (which also occurred during Copeland's second attack). Copeland's next attack, a week later, was due to occur at the same time as his first attack (5:30 p.m.) but was delayed due to difficulties with his train ticket. The attack was also intended to target a busy market but Copeland showed up on a day when the market was closed, reducing the number of casualties he could cause. Breivik's bombing was originally planned for 10 a.m. but was delayed by over five hours because of a problem with the installation of a high-speed modem and the configuration of Microsoft Outlook on his PC (the purpose of which was to distribute his manifesto). In Breivik's words, 'this delay was disastrous for the whole thing' because it lessened the number of those the bomb would ultimately wound and kill.

These hurdles and problems are also evident in a number of other cases. Eric Rudolph gave up on producing enough explosives for the main charge of his later IED attacks, stating that the effort was 'not worth the cost in time, money and brain cells' (Rudolph, 2013: 22). Instead, he turned to trying to steal commercial explosives from quarries and a explosives manufacturer. His landlady who searched his trailer on a number of occasions could also have rumbled Rudolph's preparations. Rudolph also pushed back the date of his initial IED attack on the Atlanta Olympics when his truck was broken into and a window was smashed in the process. Rudolph feared police pulling him over for the broken window so had to get it fixed before he could use the truck to transport his pipe bombs to the target site (Rudolph, 2013: 11). On the night of the bombing itself, a third-party took a picture of a water fountain at the Olympic Park. Rudolph was convinced he also was in the picture and in his autobiography admits that this was enough to engender 'several tense moments of indecision' and the 'strong urge to flee' without priming and detonating the IED (Rudolph, 2013: 13–14). In his third bombing (this time on a lesbian bar in Atlanta), Rudolph almost abandoned the bombing because of the presence of a police car that unfortunately drove off just moments after Rudolph flipped the kill-switch to make the device inert. Once he noticed that the police car had moved on, the kill-switch was turned back off and the bomb detonated four minutes later (Rudolph, 2013: 31). Naser Abdo unsuccessfully attempted to purchase firearms on at least one occasion before police interrupted his plot. Floyd Lee Corkins originally planned to conduct a bombing attack but told police he 'didn't have the patience for it'.[12]

These hurdles may reflect why terrorism has historically been largely a group-based phenomenon – the pooling of talent, resources, expertise, and experience in a group setting likely helps mitigate the difficulties in successfully committing a terrorist attack. Such resources are absent for many lone-actor terrorists, which may help explain why lone-actor terrorism has an even lower base rate than group-based terrorism. With the exception of Choudhry, the lengthy nature of each of the cases' preparation phases (in terms of the number of steps and the time it took to complete them), may also mean that many more lone-actor terrorist plots are conceived of but are subsequently abandoned due to difficulties in financing, acquiring weaponry, or developing reliable IEDs. Developing an understanding of these potential roadblocks, as well as how they function, may aid future investigations that seek to disrupt future potential lone-actor terrorist plots.

The operational usefulness of routine activity analysis is in the implication that there is a need for different counterstrategies dependent upon the stage of the lone-actor terrorist event. In other words, through sequentially breaking down these events, we may be able to get a better sense of what may be needed to manage, control, and alter the situations and contexts in which terrorist events emerge. Prevention strategies with a long-term focus should therefore be broad and wide-ranging in order to increase the perceived costs involved for lone-actor terrorists in engaging in potentially lethal forms of violence and thereby lessen their incentives to do so.

Though exploratory, and certainly an area for far greater future consideration, the function of Table 8.1 is to provide a list of measures (based on the routine activity analyses above) that could help in detecting, disrupting, and deterring the development and/or execution of lone-actor terrorist events. It is not an exhaustive list, nor is it a list that will provide solutions to all problems. Rather, the intention is to facilitate rigorous thinking about how aspects of situations and contexts can be designed or managed to hinder a potential lone-actor terrorist. We categorize this summary of recommendations using Clarke and Eck's (2005) problem triangle (Figure 8.1). As depicted, the triangle is composed of an inner triangle that consists of an offender, a place, and a target or victim. Each of these must converge for the crime or event to occur (i.e. there must be an offender to commit the crime, a target of the crime itself, and a place for it to occur).

The outer triangle consists of the actors responsible for regulating each of the components in the inner triangle. Handlers supervise the offender, guardians supervise the target, and managers supervise the crime location. Handlers are individuals that are influential in the lives of potential offenders (e.g. friends, family, and peers), but can also include police investigators, among others. Guardians include police, security, counter-terrorism operators, as well as those tasked with protecting people and property from harm and crime. Guardians can also include those present at the location of the target. Without guardians, targets become more easily attacked. Managers constitute those individuals who either own a location or who regulate access to a site. By attributing intervention points across a spectrum of actors who can counter lone-actor terrorists, this problem triangle aims to show who has jurisdiction over each offensive action taken by the terrorist. Further, if a jurisdiction is shared, Table 8.1 illustrates how responsibilities could be coordinated among the actors.

Table 8.1 Lone-actor terrorist event script and intervention points

Phase	Offender actions	Handler-offender actions	Guardian-target actions	Manager-place actions
Decision and search activity	Deciding to engage in violence as a strategy		Conduct risk assessment of current vulnerabilities	
	Deciding to replicate previous offenders		(a) Counter with narratives of previous lone-actor terrorist offenders	Increase vigilance after other lone-actor terrorist events
			(b) Increase vigilance after other lone-actor terrorist events	
	Leaving other political means behind	Encourage other activists to report individuals who espouse violent intentions	Assess 'risk' of reported individuals	
	Stating intention to act violently to significant others (e.g. friends, family)	Encourage significant others to report individuals	Assess the 'risk' of reported individuals	
	Stating extremist ideology to third-parties (e.g. media)	Encourage outlets to report letters espousing extremist propaganda or agendas	Assess the 'risk' of reported individuals	
	Grievance formation		(a) Counter underlying grievance with accurate information	
			(b) Address underlying grievance	
Preparation	Deciding location of attack		Harden targets	Increase vigilance
	Choosing between violent tactics		(a) Harden targets	Increase vigilance
			(b) Increase difficulty in procuring weapon components	
	Choosing a specific target		Harden targets	(a) Conduct video surveillance of prestigious locations
				(b) Increase policing

Attempting to recruit co-offenders	(a) Provide adequate resources and avenues to facilitate disengagement (b) Encourage significant others and unsuccessfully recruited co-offenders to report suspicious activity	
Collecting weapon components	Encourage significant others and third parties to report suspicious activity	(a) In the case of IEDs, strengthen regulations that limit the purchase of particular chemicals (b) Educate sales clerks to detect and report suspicious purchases (c) In the case of IEDs, mark commercial explosives/detonators/casings/timer components etc. with unique codes so that supplies can be traced back to supplier	(a) Encourage public reports to police. (b) Create retail controls, such as improved record keeping and customer identification practices (c) Reduce available stock of possible weapons (d) Prevent state/business supply of commercial explosive materials
Manufacturing explosives		(a) Promote fake recipes to frustrate efforts of inexperienced bomb-makers and increase costs (b) Educate hospital staff and encourage them to report suspicious chemical burns and related injuries (c) Develop forensic capabilities to trace manufacturing of explosives to supply evidence (d) Limit access to bomb-making manuals	

continued

Table 8.1 Continued

Phase	Offender actions	Handler-offender actions	Guardian-target actions	Manager-place actions
	Storing weapon components	Encourage significant others to report suspicious activity		Increase security and monitoring at public locations (e.g. storage units)
	Constructing IEDs	Provide channels for significant others to report suspicious activities		Conduct surveillance of former/suspected bomb-making sites
	Testing IEDs			(a) Educate the public regarding suspicious activity (b) Encourage public reports to police (c) Conduct surveillance
	Acquiring vehicles			(a) For purchased vehicles, use retail controls such as improved record keeping and customer identification practices (b) For rented vehicles, increase monitoring of identification papers
	Loading explosives into vehicle			Educate the public regarding suspicious-looking vehicles (vehicles that appear laden down with explosives)
	Conducting dry-runs	Conduct surveillance	Conduct surveillance	Conduct surveillance
	Purchasing additional weaponry (including protective vests/clothing)		Conduct surveillance of online purchasing	
Event execution	Travelling to attack location		Increase video surveillance	Increase video surveillance

	Parking and abandoning car bomb/getaway vehicle	Educate public workers to facilitate the reporting of suspicious vehicles	(a) Train and educate the public and special personnel to increase vigilance
			(b) Create/enforce parking restrictions and control zones
	Priming of device	Conduct EOD Render Safe Procedures	Encourage public reports to police
	Conducting getaway	Provide video surveillance	
	Publishing a manifesto/making a public statement of motive	(a) Counter the narratives put forth by the lone actor	
		(b) Increase vigilance for similar offenders	
Post-event activity and strategic analysis			
	In the case of avoiding capture, conducting repeat attacks	Triage reports from the public	Increase surveillance
	Encourage significant others to report strange behaviours/suspicions		

166 *Situational crime prevention*

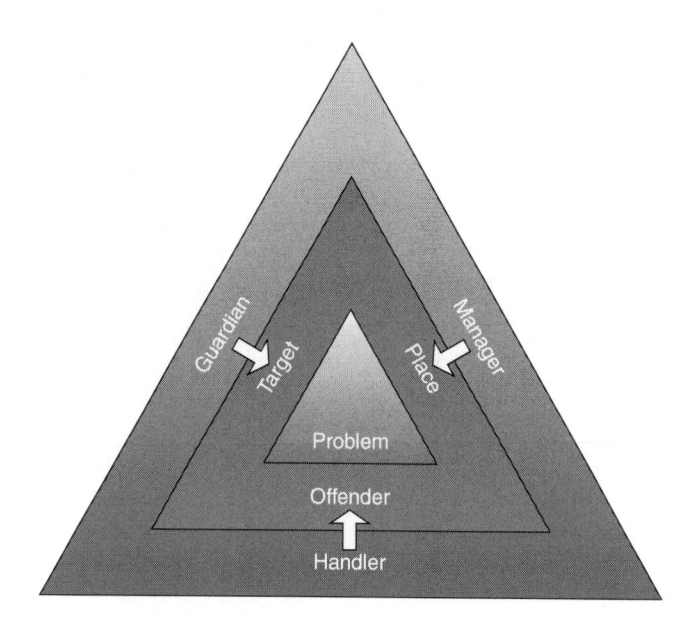

Figure 8.1 Problem triangle.

Finally, as depicted in Table 8.1, perhaps the most effective intervention points may occur within the preparation phase of the terrorist event, as opposed to the execution phase. This is due to: (a) there being more individual activities occurring within this phase, (b) it being a temporally longer phase, and (c) there potentially being more people exposed to what is developing. It also shows that countering lone-actor terrorist threats may entail intelligence work, military, or law enforcement activities, forensic analysis, neighbourhood and community policing, as well as regulatory legislative action.

In the absence of a group's cumulative human, financial, political, and logistical capital, know-how and capability, lone-actor terrorist events are difficult to conduct in all but the most basic means. SCP approaches look to squeeze the opportunities of potential offenders even further. Issues concerning the access to, for example, either precursor chemicals or the individually chosen targets could have helped prevent these attacks from occurring.

Returning to the case of the Woolwich attack outlined in this chapter's introduction, the perpetrators discriminately targeted a British soldier. It was not an act of luck or happenstance that Rigby happened to be a soldier. It was intentional and directed. After the attack, Adebolajo provided justification for the attack to a bystander who recorded him on a mobile phone:

> The only reason we have killed this man today is because Muslims are dying daily by British soldiers. And this British soldier is one.... Remove your governments, they don't care about you. You think David Cameron is

gonna get caught in the street when we start busting our guns? Do you think politicians are going to die? No, it's going to be the average guy, like you and your children. So get rid of them. Tell them to bring our troops back ... leave our lands and you will live in peace.

Rigby was off-duty at the time, returning from Woolwich Arsenal train station on his way back to the Royal Artillery Barracks where he was stationed. The attack took place close to the perimeter of the barracks. As Rigby crossed the road, Adebolajo and Adebowale drove into him at a speed of approximately 30–40 mph. During the trial, evidence emerged that Rigby was identified as a potential soldier because of the military-style rucksack that he carried on his back. The Woolwich attack was preventable, not in the sense of identifying the perpetrators beforehand, or in the sense of convincing them of the illegitimacy of the attack beforehand but in the sense of making the deliberate identification and targeting of a British soldier harder to commit. Such measures also have a diffusion of benefits in the fight to prevent other terrorist perpetrators, such as dissident Irish Republican groups who have experienced a resurgence in the past couple of years (Horgan & Morrison, 2011).

Notes

1 In this section, direct quotes are taken from Copeland's confession statement that was made to police after his arrest. Large segments of the statement were made publicly available by a BBC documentary entitled 'The Nailbomber' which aired 30 June 2000. The page numbers refer to the transcript of the documentary acquired by the research team.
2 This carnival celebrates London's multicultural diversity.
3 After the fact, the taxi driver on that day remembers that Copeland appeared overdressed for what was a very hot day: 'He had a shirt buttoned up right to the neck and a baseball cap covering his head'. For the duration of the journey, Copeland held his money in his hand. Upon payment, the taxi driver noticed that the cash was 'saturated with sweat'.
4 Mandelson was a member of Prime Minister Blair's Cabinet and was 'outed' as homosexual in 1998.
5 Taheri-Azar left this letter in his apartment for police to find. The contents of which are widely available online.
6 The day of the bombing, McVeigh was arrested. Inside his getaway vehicle, officers found an envelope with slips of paper McVeigh had clipped from books and newspapers. One such slip of paper contained a paragraph from the *Turner Diaries* that read 'The real value of our attacks today lies in the psychological impact, not in the immediate casualties'.
7 McVeigh later cut the electric blasting caps from the plan because he felt the risk of static electricity accidentally setting off the bomb was too high.
8 This case study largely relies upon both court reporting from both the BBC and the *Guardian* and *Telegraph* newspapers.
9 For the purposes of this case study, we primarily used both an English transcript of Breivik's original psychiatric assessment and Breivik's manifesto. Where the psychiatric assessment is used, we cite the report's authors, Husby and Sorheim. Where the manifesto is cited, it is in format of (Breivik, 2011: page number).

10 In 2003, Breivik also attempted to gain nominations for the city council elections but failed, coming twentieth or twenty-third in the ballot. He later left the Progress Party. The Progress Party is currently the second-largest political party in Norway and considers itself ideologically libertarian. Breivik claims in his manifesto that he gradually 'lost faith in the democratic struggle to save Europe from Islamification' (2011: 1414).
11 Breivik's manifesto encourages future offenders to tell close friends and family that the offender has become focused on playing online games such as *World of Warcraft* because it can partly justify your patterns of activity (isolation/travel) while planning for an attack (2011: 841).
12 Cited in the Government's Sentencing Memorandum.

References

Carroll, J., & Weaver, F. (1986). Shoplifters' perceptions of crime opportunities: A process-tracing study. In D. B. Cornish, & R. V. G. Clarke (eds.). *The reasoning criminal* (pp. 19–38). New York: Springer.

Cheston, P. (2000, 9 June). Nail bomber: Killers should be executed. *The Evening Standard*.

Clarke, R. V. G., & Newman, G. R. (2006). *Outsmarting the terrorists*. Portsmouth, N.H.: Greenwood Publishing Group.

Clarke, R. V., & Eck, J. E. (2005). *Crime analysis for problem solvers*. Washington D.C.: Center for Problem Oriented Policing.

Cornish, D., & Clarke, R. (1986). Situational prevention, displacement of crime and rational choice theory. *Situational Crime Prevention: From Theory into Practice*, London: HMSO, 1–16.

Dolnik, A., & Bhattacharjee, A. (2002). Hamas: Suicide Bombings, Rockets, or WMD?. *Terrorism and Political Violence*, *14*(3): 109–128.

Finn, P., & Fordham, A. (2011, 30 June). Ft. Hood Bomb Plot Suspect Recalled as 'Anti-American'. *The Washington Post*.

Freilich, J. D. (2009). *Reducing terrorism through situational crime prevention*. G. R. Newman (ed.). Monsey, NY: Criminal Justice Press.

Horgan, J. (2005). *The psychology of terrorism*. London: Routledge.

Horgan, J., & Morrison, J. F. (2011). Here to stay? The rising threat of violent dissident republicanism in Northern Ireland. *Terrorism and Political Violence*, *23*(4): 642–669.

Husby, T., & Sorheim, S. (2011). *Anders Breivik Psychiatric Report 2011–11–29*. Case no.: 11–120995EN E-OTI R/o8. Retrieved from: http://issuu.com/js-ror/docs/111129_hs-psych-rep/1. Accessed 1 June 2014.

Kaplan, J. (1997). Leaderless resistance. *Terrorism and Political Violence*, *9*(3), 80–95.

McFadden, T. D. (1993, 12 December). A Tormented Life: A Long Slide from Privilege Ends in Slaughter on a Train. *The New York Times*.

Rudolph, E. (2013). Between the Lines of Drift: The Memoirs of a Militant. Retrieved from: www.armyofgod.com/EricRudolphHomepage.html. Accessed 1 June 2014.

9 Lone-actor terrorist dilemmas

Existing research often focuses upon the security dilemmas that lone-actor terrorists pose to counter-terrorism systems set up to detect, investigate, prevent, and disrupt group based activities. Very little emphasis is given to dilemmas faced by the lone actors themselves. In trying to mobilize, individuals with a malevolent intent face a number of crucial decisions. First, they need to decide whether to act alone or in combination with others. As different sections of this book demonstrated, the strategic call for lone actors is often driven by the need to evade the typical state intelligence gathering procedures. Acting alone increases security but at the cost of (in most circumstances) downgrading capability. Co-offending depends upon trust, credible commitments, and mutual transactions. An apparent co-ideologue may also be a government agent. This is especially apparent within the United States.

Once the individual decides to act alone, they face the second dilemma of achieving technical attack capability. This appears to be a major problem. Many cases illustrate that lone actors typically tend to originally plot large-scale attacks. Eric Rudolph initially wanted to bomb Atlanta's power grid during the Olympics rather than place a bomb at the Olympics itself. He dropped this plan because 'making enough charges to disable Atlanta's power grid would take too much time and money. I had neither. The Olympics was fast approaching, and I needed to come up with a new plan' (Rudolph, 2013: 7). Abdulhakim Mujahid Muhammad represents another example. His shooting at the U.S. Army Recruitment Office at Little Rock killed one person. In his words:

> It wasn't part of Plan A. Plan A was aborted because of failed attacks in Tennessee and Kentucky, so the Crusader Center in Little Rock was Plan B. And compared to what I had planned originally, it was like a grain of sand. One crusader dead, one wounded, 15 terrorized, big deal. Nidal Malik is the real Islamic Warrior, and my plan A was on that scale. It included Little Rock, Memphis, Nashville, Florence KY, Philadelphia, Baltimore, and was supposed to end in DC.

The third dilemma is related to gaining the psychological ability to engage in a violent attack. Consider this passage from Paul Hill's account of murdering an abortion clinic doctor and his bodyguard.

> In spite, of my careful plans, the morning of the shooting was not easy. Although I had gone to bed late, I forced myself to rise about 4 a.m. to spend time in prayer and Bible reading, and to prepare myself for the day. I was fully determined to act, but my usual zest, and the zeal I expected to feel were missing. The lower half of my body was gripped with a gnawing emptiness. This was not an easy task. While driving to the clinic, I decided to drive past it first, to see if everything looked normal (I was concerned that someone may have become suspicious and called the police). Just as I approached the clinic, a police cruiser drove by me in the opposite direction. I forced my fears under control as I continued down the road. After driving about a quarter of a mile, it was time to head back, but the truck did not want to turn around; it had to be forced. I could hear the undercarriage groan as I did a tight turn around in an open parking lot. As hard as it was to turn around, I knew I could not continue down the road. Obedience was the only option.

James Kopp's recollection of his actions evokes similar sentiments: 'To pick up a gun and aim it at another human being, and to fire, it's not a human thing to do. It's not nice. It's not pleasant. It's gory, it's bloody. It overcomes every human instinct'.

Military psychology shows that developing psychological capability to kill within a group setting (given the right conditions) is easier than going it alone (Grossman, 2005; Gill, 2012). Within a cell of like-minded individuals, cognitive, evaluative, and affective components of the group can impact and shape behaviour. Group identity may override individual identity upon the acquisition of group norms. If a group maintains strong cohesiveness, insulates itself from external information/influence, develops an unquestioned belief in the group's inherent morality and develops stereotyped (over-dehumanized) images of the enemy, it can make killing psychologically easier. In other words, given the right settings a shared group identity can condition the individual group members towards a state of mind that they may not reach independent of a group setting. Without group pressures, the possibility of defecting from the violence is greater. This lengthy piece of Breivik's court testimony shows how he overcame these barriers absent of a group setting:

> And you can say that I was reasonably normal until 2006 when I started training, and started my desensitation through meditation. And thus, all the people I know will attest, they will describe me as a very likeable person who is genuinely caring towards near and friends, and generally to all. But when it comes to building up for an enemy, you choose the tactics and strategies to try to dehumanise.... So, to be able to attack anyone, no matter in what way you attack one, you can almost justify it to yourself.... These are basic principles that are used in warfare. One has to dehumanise the enemy. If not, when you meet the enemy face to

face, you will not be able to attack him. And the same goes for me. I've driven a dehumanisation strategy against them which I consider as legitimate targets to be in a situation where I am able to kill someone. If I had not done it in a very thorough manner, I would not have been able to do it [kill]... You do not really have any choice, that is, if one is to kill someone, you can not do that unless you prepare yourself mentally, very thorough. And it takes at least two years of training, and it is extremely difficult even if you have the training. But it is a choice, yes... And that, the minute that is lasted [prior to the first fatal shooting], it was, it seemed like it was a year. Or somehow, that it was, indeed, my body was trying to fight back when I took the gun in my hand. It was like if one hundred voices in my head said 'do not do it'. And I noticed that my body fought it.... It was extremely difficult... it goes against human nature... But I got in sight or flight mode which made it much easier.... It's called a first person shooter game, it is simply a war simulator. I do not really have very much sense for those games, but it is very good if one is to simulate for practice sake... It is a war simulator used by the armed forces in the world... So what was the purpose of spending some time on it.... The only thing, that you can never prepare you for a so-called suicide operation, but you can, you can, you can, hammering away your fears through various exercises. For my part, I have used something called *bushidomeditasjon* to displace fear, and a side effect of the meditation is that it affects the whole *emosjonsspekteret*, so you will *avemosjonarisert*. It is a technique, if you practice it over a year or two, so you *avemosjinarisert*, and you accrue one *dødsforakt*, and for me, it's something that I'm depending on, for example, be able to conduct this trial. So I meditate daily.... Well for starters, you normalize your spectrum of emotions, meaning that all emotions are normal. And as you become more fearful, you become more emotional.... So I've experimented with it, what works and what does not. What kind of music works and what kind of music does not. And I've tried everything from trance music to everything else. There are some specific songs that you can use for that purpose... It is a type of meditation that makes you suppress your fears... It affects the whole range of emotions. You desensitize yourself.

The fourth dilemma relates to targeting. Most lone actors act on behalf of an established ideology. It appears a disparity exists between the types of tactics the wider movement promotes and the types of tactics that will draw the level of infamy and social status that lone actors might seek. Metzger's *Laws for the Lone Wolf* implores lone actors to

> always start off small. Many small victories are better than one huge blunder (which may be the end of your career as a Lone Wolf). Every little bit counts in a resistance.... Remember, even the smallest things make a difference. You will see that what you are doing is making an impact. If you

never get caught, you are better than any army. Others will notice your activities, but never try to take any credit for them, your success should be all the recognition you need.

(Metzger)

Metzger later lamented Ted Kaczynski's change of tack toward public recognition of his goals. Metzger's other famous essay *Begin With Lone Wolves* elaborates further:

No matter what the ideology many modern lone wolves most likely have been involved with, in most successful cases their ideology is kept secret, some even taking it to the grave.... So when the membership groups bug you and ask what Lone Wolves have done recently, simply say just keep watching the news and reading the newspapers, especially between the lines. Give it time. Everything is moving along very well if you know what to look for and how to interpret it. Read the signs. Watch the market. Watch the world food and water supply along with many other clues. Your time is coming. You will know when it arrives. Keep Smiling. THIS IS WAR!

(Metzger)

The al-Qaeda movement offers similar advice to would-be lone actors. *Inspire* magazine issue number two provides a couple of potential attack strategies for engaging in individual jihad including vehicular assaults and other relatively small-scale ventures. These suggestions do not fit the vast majority of lone-actor plots captured in the dataset. Instead these actors typically plotted to attack publicly using high-profile attack methods.

A fifth dilemma relates to falling in line with the wider movement's goals and strategies. Some analysts argue that the deployment of lone-actor terrorists greatly enhances a movement's ability to have terrorist attacks perpetrated in its name. This is true of course. However, there is always the threat that a lone actor's operation can be hugely detrimental to the wider movement because their planning, preparations, and attack were not informed by the movement's strategists. For example, Timothy McVeigh's bombing in Oklahoma is widely acclaimed with damaging and setting back the extreme right-wing movement in the United States. Dissent within the anti-abortion movement on the shift towards violence by lone-actors was also very apparent in the early 1990s. Take the example of Shelley Shannon. Her first violent action involved burning down an abortion clinic in Oregon. One prominent anti-abortion picketer, Vicki Plankenhorn, expressed her dismay at the turn toward violence. 'I'm kind of stunned – I still can't believe this.... You don't do things like this. It's negative. If anything it only hurts our cause. Somebody who would do something like that definitely has emotional problems and needs help' (cited in Bray & Bray, 2009: 17). Another famous case is that of Paul Hill's murder of an abortion clinic doctor and his bodyguard. Michael North, a well-known advocate of non-violent resistance against abortion clinics, sent a letter to Hill in the aftermath of the attack. The letter expressed dismay at the turn towards violence because once one violent action is committed, subsequent actions by supposed co-ideologues may spiral out of control.

> If I have the right to gun down a local abortionist, I have the right to gun down his accomplice. If I can lawfully fire a shotgun and wound the accomplice's wife because she, too, is basically an accomplice, then I have a right to gun down the ministers who excommunicated me for publicly advising violence against abortionists. If I have the right to gun down a practitioner, don't I have a right to gun down the judge who has authorized the practice? Don't I have the right to gun down the politician? Don't I have the right to gun down the voter who has voted for the politician, who in fact is in favor of abortion? Don't I have the right to gun down everybody who is pro-abortion? Aren't they all responsible, and if they are, am I responsible for stopping them in any way I can?

North's warning proved prescient. Hill's action clearly inspired Eric Rudolph. The opening paragraphs of Rudolph's autobiography praise Hill's actions. Within the autobiography, Rudolph outlines a list of justified targets:

> The judge who upholds *Roe* v. *Wade*, the FBI agent who enforces the FACE Act, the receptionist who schedules the abortion, the nurse who assists in the abortion – they are as guilty as the doctor who performs the actual procedure. All are active participants in mass murder ... I wanted to send a lethal message to the entire abortion industry and their protectors in Washington: If you work in an abortion mill or provide aid and protection for abortionists, you may end up looking like one of the 5,000 unborn babies who are mangled by abortionists every single day in this country.
>
> (Rudolph, 2013: 28)

Al-Qaeda in the Arabian Peninsula's *Inspire* magazine issue nine, offers a number of ways to overcome the potential divergence between a lone actor's intended actions and the overriding goals of the wider movement. One article encourages potential lone actors to send basic information about themselves to AQAP's 'military committee', which in turn will help prospective candidates plan for the execution of their attack, and advertise these actions post-event. One issue of *Inspire* provides a laundry list of legitimate targets including the usual military and political targets and also 'non-combatants'. Other articles stress that although individual actions are necessary, they acknowledge a need for operational leadership. This strategy is explicit in al-Suri's 'Global Islamic Resistance Call'. Al-Suri makes the case for individual jihad to be guided by a central authority that guides the movement. 'Thus operations can be coordinated in order to give meaning to the various acts of terrorism so that they serve broader strategic ends' (Michael, 2012: 145).

The final dilemma is that of avoiding the pitfall of 'messageless resistance'. Terrorism, by its very nature, is a form of political communication. The violence targets not those directly involved in the incident but instead the wider unharmed public. The 'violence is mainly perpetrated for its effects on others than the immediate victims' (Schmid, 1987: 2). For this to be successful, accessing the mass media with a political message is crucial. Violent acts open access to communication structures and the surrounding publicity provides a social meaning to the acts (Crelinsten, 1987; McNair, 2003). Politically violent acts intend to demonstrate the vulnerability of the state, to communicate to organizational sympathizers, to provoke repressive counter-measures and to highlight the heroism of the perpetrators (Wilkinson, 1990). Without the corresponding political message or justification for the violence, it is not terrorism. It is messageless and easily framed as the actions of a mad man. This dilemma may go some way to explain why such a large proportion of lone-actor terrorists leak information about their ideology, grievance, and specific plot despite the security risks associated with such behaviour. This leaking of information, if relayed to the media, helps frame the individual as a rationally-oriented actor propelled to action by an overriding ideology rather than a desperate individual acting as a response to a personal grievance. During day two of his trial, Anders Breivik argued the necessity of outlining his ideology during the trial proceedings. The main purpose was to counter the messages proffered in the media as to his motivation. Without it, he felt that the 'massive sickening demonization of my character is going to continue'. To quote him at length:

> Norwegian media and prosecutors have argued and will continue to argue that the reasons that I executed the 22/7 attack were inconsequential, and because I was a pathetic and spiteful loser who lacks integrity, does not have dignity or trust, that I am a notorious liar, that I lack morals, that I'm crazy and that I therefore should be immediately ignored and forgotten by others Cultural conservatives and nationalists in Norway and Europe.
>
> They will say that I lost my job and social standing, that I am a cruel and insane person who is only looking for attention to my own person. All of this, they claimed. They also claimed that I am narcissistic, antisocial, psychopathic, that I have a phobia for germs and put on a face mask daily for many years, that I only like red sweaters and that I've had an incestuous relationship with my own mother.
>
> They also claimed that I am a miserable, pathetic child and baby killer despite the fact that I have not killed anyone under the age of 14. That I'm a coward, inbred, homosexual, pedophile, necrophile, racist, sociopath, fascist, Nazi, Zionist and anarchist. All this has been claimed. They also claimed that I am physically and mentally retarded with an IQ around 80.

Using the example of Joseph Paul Franklin, Kaplan and Costa (2014: 30) note that successful 'leaderless resistance' may lead to 'messageless resistance' if the offender tries to keep so secure, he/she does not get his/her message out to the masses. Franklin engaged in a 'coast to coast shooting rampage … [targeting] … interracial couples jogging in Seattle, Vernon Jordan, a civil rights leader and later presidential advisor to Bill Clinton, and most famously the publisher of Hustler magazine Larry Flynt'. This shooting rampage spanned decades. While he was a successful shooter, he was not a successful terrorist because his message was not disseminated. 'The public was unaware than an active terrorist was attempting to terrorize them and likeminded would-be terrorists were equally unaware of Franklin's message'. However, in Metzger's *Begin With Lone Wolves*, Franklin is lauded. This illustrates some of the complexities at the heart of lone-actor terrorism. In a single case we have an individual celebrated by a noted ideologue for his actions yet at the same time these actions remained unconnected to one another and to a wider cause within the public domain.

Examples of 'messageless resistance' are numerous. Paul Ross Evans' first attempted mail bombing targeted the First Church of Satan in San Francisco. Because he intended to engage in a series of follow-up bombings on other targets, Evans took care not to give his identity away. Some of his actions really constrained his ability to get his message out though. For example, on the initial bombing's envelope, Evans wrote 'The Temple of Set' as the return address. The Temple of Set is another rival Satanist organization to the First Church of Satan. In a follow-up action, Evans intentionally sent an inactive IED to the attorney Michael Newdow who stood for a range of atheist positions with relation to the separation of church and state. For this 'bomb', the return address on the envelope was that of a pornographic distributor in California.

At times, 'messageless resistance' occurs not because of a lack of trying to broadcast a message. Take Eric Rudolph's bombing of the Atlanta Olympics as an example. Rudolph planned to disrupt the event by phoning in an advanced warning. After priming the device, he sought to leave a warning with police from a pay phone. Rudolph notes:

> Quickly, I stuffed each nostril with wet toilet tissue and slipped on my pair of gloves and pulled a little plastic funnel from my pocket. The tissue and funnel should help distort my voice. 'Atlanta – nine – one – one' said the woman operator. 'Do you understand me?' I asked. 'Yah'. 'We defy your…' suddenly the line went dead". Rudolph's attempt to provide a justification alongside the warning failed.

Rudolph then left that scene and found another set of payphones close by

> but the street was packed with people. Groups of tourists shuffled past me. I waited. Agonizing minutes were wasted. A break in the crowd developed. I faced the other way and found a phone. 'Make it quick; just a flat warning; no statement' I told myself.
>
> (Rudolph, 2013: 14)

Without leaving the justificatory message, Rudolph acknowledges that the bombing 'sent the wrong message. Aimed at Washington and the corporate sponsors, the bombing came off as an indiscriminate attack on innocent civilians. I would see to it that never happened again. From now on I'd choose specific targets' (Rudolph, 2013: 21).

On other occasions, external forces may try to steer the attack toward 'messageless resistance'. For example, in the immediate aftermath of Ali Hassan Abu Kamal's shooting attack atop the Empire State Building, his family back in Palestine insisted that Kamal was driven to this after losing $300,000 of his lifetime savings in the couple of months he spent in the United States. Kamal killed himself at the scene of the crime and on his body police found a two-page statement of justification that had salient political connotations. Much later, Kamal's family admitted that the loss of lifetime savings story was falsified and provided to them by the Palestinian Authority who feared the backlash the attack may have had on a nascent peace deal with Israel.

The possibility of 'messageless resistance' can often be the downfall of the lone-actor terrorist. We have already mentioned the case of James Kenneth Gluck who plotted to develop ricin and attack Colorado's Jefferson County judiciary system in 1999. Gluck sent a 10-page letter to a judge where he threatened to wage biological warfare. He refers to Ricin as 'a quintessential American weapon for 'making a killing' (literally) without any responsibility because it cannot be determined who used it and cannot be determined where it came from'. While most of the letter provides an ideological reason behind the threat (for example 'to prevent future depredation by any predator, including government forces'), the violent means he lauds would, in his mind at least, lead to the offender not being identified. But what if the offender sought some recognition for these deeds? Well, you write a letter, and sign it off with the words 'James Kenneth Gluck'.

Learning from past cases

Returning to the issue of detecting, preventing, interdicting, and disrupting lone-actor terrorists, this section outlines how previous cases were caught. Some offenders were caught through an examination of the crime scene and/or weapon utilized. For example, police caught Roy Moody (who committed a series of mail bombs) through an examination of some of his earlier IEDs that failed to detonate. The same occurred in the Paul Ross Evans case. Evans packed the contents of his pipe bomb into a soft-sided cooler. Police contacted the manufacturer and found that this particular cooler was only sold at Wal-Mart. A scan of nearby Wal-Mart stores highlighted that one individual used a debit card to purchase the cooler alongside nails, sugar, electrical tap, and a timer – each of which were individual components in the IED. A day prior to these purchases, the same debit card purchased nine-volt batteries and a copper pipe – both of which also were utilized in the IED. Terence Gavan, similarly, was arrested after police identified that he purchased two manuals on how to make explosive device, homemade firearms, and ammunition.

Others were caught through either eyewitness or statements from the individual's social network. Eyewitnesses spotted Eric Rudolph leaving the scene of his third IED attack, followed him and took down the licence plate number. Ted Kaczynski's brother provided the police a tip-off once he read the Unabomber's manifesto printed in the *Washington Post* and the *New York Times*. Luke Helder's adoptive father tipped off police after a letter Helder wrote to him convinced him Luke was the perpetrator of the widely publicized bombing campaign. Later that evening, Helder's roommate reported finding suspicious objects that could be related to IED manufacturing under Helder's bed. Similarly, Mir Aimal Kasi's roommate reported him missing. When police investigated Kasi's room they found an AK-47 that ballistics tests matched to the fatal shootings outside of the CIA headquarters. The week before Kasi's shooting attack, he told the same roommate of his need to make a 'big statement' by conducting a shooting at the CIA, White House, or Israeli Embassy. The roommate was also aware of Kasi's grievance against U.S. foreign policy and his purchases of a firearm and bulletproof vest. Members of Andrew Ibrahim's mosque grew concerned about his radical views and the injuries on his hands and informed police. Sean Gillespie showed the video of his firebomb attack to co-ideologues, one of which ultimately informed on him to the authorities. Dennis Mahon leaked information of his previously committed bombing in Phoenix to a government informant. Soon after their marriage ended, Matthew Fairfield's ex-wife informed authorities of the IEDs he developed. Ian Forman's work colleagues at a glass recycling firm alerted police when they found he had been researching how to obtain dangerous chemicals on the internet at work.

A few were caught because they raised suspicion while making purchases associated with their attack. A chemical supplier alerted the FBI to Khalid Aldawsari's purchase of concentrated phenol. Police interrupted Naser Abdo's plot after receiving a tip-off from a gun store employee who was suspicious of Abdo's purchases. According to court documents, Abdo

> purchased six one-pound containers of different types of smokeless gunpowder despite an apparent lack of knowledge about the substance, as well as three boxes of shotgun shells and an extended magazine for a handgun. Abdo's purchases were suspicious because smokeless gunpowder, which is normally used to re-load ammunition, is typically purchased in one to two pound quantities of the same type along with other supplies, such as bullets or primers. Adbo purchased six pounds of different types of powder and no bullets or primers. He paid cash, left in a hurry, and did not take his change or receipt.

This is highly interesting but of course begs the question whether this particular gun store worker was highly vigilant because the same store had sold Nidal Malik Hasan firearms that he utilized in his mass shooting event a year and a half beforehand. Police also learnt that Abdo also purchased an army uniform and Fort Hood patches from army/navy surplus stores the next day.

A small number were caught through the alertness of individuals who had no prior contact with the offender. For example, cleaners discovered bomb-making manuals and materials on a foreclosed house formerly belonging to Mark Krause. The FBI linked this discovery to a bombing that had recently occurred in the area.

Associated with the concept of 'self-selection' outlined in a previous chapter, many were caught (either pre- or post-event) after engaging in other criminal or illicit activities. Police stopped Franz Fuchs in response to a call that Fuchs was driving dangerously close to his neighbour's car on a dark country road with his full beams on. Fuchs detonated a letter-IED, survived, and was arrested. Police interrupted Martyn Gilleard's plot when they searched his property in relation to child pornography possession. In addition to 39,000 indecent images of children, police also found explosive materials, camouflage clothing, balaclavas, bomb-making manuals, gun powder, ready made fuses, and a notebook containing extreme anti-Semitic views. Police arrested Neil Lewington as he travelled by train to a date with a woman he met online. En route to the date, Lewington smoked and conducted a number of public order offences on the train including urinating on the platform. Upon his arrest, police discovered that in his rucksack, Lewington carried enough components to assemble two IEDs, detailed handwritten notes on how to assemble electronics and produce chemical mixtures for bombs and also a list of possible places to target.

Others were overpowered at the scene of their crime including Floyd Lee Corkins, Jim David Adkisson, and Roshonara Choudhry. Many died in the commission of their attack such as Larry Shoemake and Andrew Joseph Stack. Others, such as Michael Griffin, voluntarily handed themselves over to authorities. On 12 October 2004, Ivan Duane Braden, a discharged National Guard soldier, filled a backpack full of large knives and IED components. He planned to travel to the local National Guard Armory, take a number of hostages and murder them by detonating the IED. En route, he changed his mind and instead checked himself into an outpatient mental health facility.

The existing literature also offers a number of other potential counter-terrorism strategies. Van Buuren and de Graaf (2014) outline some interesting approaches taken in the Netherlands. First, increased surveillance of the internet seeks to proactively detect 'fixated persons'. Second, those with mental health issues and possible fixations on targets are steered toward the mental health care route with the help of front-line services such as police, community workers, teachers, youth groups, and those working in the health care sector. Third, increased monitoring of suspects occurs on the days of important events. This can often involve ensuring that the individual does not attend. Cohen, Johansson, Kaati, and Mork (2014) suggest using linguistic markers for detecting when a potential lone-actor terrorist virtually leaks plans of the upcoming plot, starts to become more fixated on a target and starts to become more heavily identified with a threat group ideology.

There are no examples of community-based approaches preventing a lone-actor terrorist plot. However, these types of approaches tend to be aimed at a much earlier stage of an individual's radicalization. These approaches are not too applicable once the individual decides upon acting out violently. It is also problematic because there is the issue about who should be realistically tasked with policing extremism at the individual level. As mentioned in a previous chapter, Taimour Abdulwahab al-Abdaly blew himself up on a crowded Stockholm street in December 2010. Prior to this attack, al-Abdaly resided in England and attended a mosque in Luton in late 2006 and early 2007. During this time, he made statements focused on 'suicide bombings, pronouncing Muslim leaders to be disbelievers, denouncing Muslim governments' and was confronted by mosque elders and eventually left the mosque altogether (Lawless & Rising, 2010). In newspaper accounts after the event, the chairman of the mosque relayed the thrust of the philosophical argument he had with al-Abdaly. 'We were challenging his philosophical attitude to jihad. He got so angry that he left. He was just supporting and propagating these incorrect foundations [of Islam] so I stepped in'. The chairman also noted that he felt these philosophical discussions constituted the limits to which he would be justified in acting against al-Abdaly's extremist position. It was not his position to report al-Abdaly to the police, or intelligence services. 'You can't just inform on any Muslim having extreme views. In the past many Muslims have had extreme views but have become good balanced Muslims' (Jones & Haroon, 2010). A secretary of the same mosque stated:

> His preaching was a precursor to violence, but not a violent act. Many Muslims share similar views but would never act violently. If we rang up the police and reported him on his views at the time, they would have laughed at us and done nothing.
>
> (Sears & Kisiel, 2010)

The future

This book encompassed empirically grounded analysis of lone-actor terrorist behaviours in terms of who they are, what they do, the roles of the internet and mental health, how lone actors differ, and potential strategies to deal with the threat. It provided an empirical foundation from which much future research can develop. Current efforts to analyse the violent extremist behaviour tend to be limited by conceptual errors and severely hampered by lack of empirical support. Many attempts to understand radicalization and/or terrorist motivation have largely tended towards generalist explanations. Such explanations, be they psychopathological, psychoanalytical, theoretical models, or descriptive analyses of large-n datasets tend to treat each individual group member equally. Other analyses tend to treat different offender types (e.g. lone wolf vs. AQ-member) separately. Where comparisons exist, they tend to be conducted on an anecdotal basis devoid of crime prevention paradigms (for example McCauley, Moskalenko, & Van Son, 2013).

The lack of emphasis upon empirically-based comparative approaches to different offender types largely account for the lack of progress in identifying any trace of a behavioural analysis that may help distinguish violent actors from one another. In the absence of useful comparison or control groups, even empirical analyses can only offer a descriptive or partial account of how radicalization occurs. Empirically, while the study of who joins and leaves terrorist groups has grown through the use of first-hand interviews (see Horgan, 2005, 2009), there has been relatively little emphasis within the current literature upon comparative approaches to different offenders. Some recent analyses (e.g. Hegghammer, 2013) have drawn attention to the heterogeneity of subgroups of violent offenders (e.g. foreign fighters), but these distinctions have been proposed as a reflection of different motivational types, rather than being based on an attempt to distinguish offenders through their behaviours. There are offender types such as mass casualty offenders who conduct similar types of violent acts alone but we know little about how similar their 'radicalization pathways' are to lone-actor terrorists. Is attitudinal affinity with a wider ideological cause the sole difference? At this moment in time, we cannot answer for sure. By providing such empirically informed and practitioner-oriented research, these analyses can pinpoint where practice should be crime-specific and where it can be crime-general with a diffusion of benefits across criminal offender-types.

We also know very little about the temporal trajectories of violent radicalization. While radicalization is regularly depicted as a 'process', we have no knowledge of what this process looks like over time. How long does it take? What types of events, experiences, and behaviours speed up or slow down the process?

Finally, this study remains largely exploratory, delivering statistical descriptions rather than explanations. It does not explain why different ideological subgroups have different 'profiles' or involvement patterns for example; it only documents that they do. A step-change requires that research move from exploration to hypothesis-driven designs, going beyond statistical descriptions or the qualitative study of individual pathways. Only then can issues such as the false positive problem (i.e. the fact that statistical markers, like the ones described previously, will often be found among a much larger population than the one of interest, making detection difficult) and the problem of prevention (which requires intervention against causal factors, not markers) be addressed.

However, the analyses in this book offer a number of novel insights on the nature of lone-actor terrorism. While there is no profile, there are distinguishable differences across ideologies. Clusters of behaviours are identifiable, many of which are suitable to ongoing counter-terrorism procedures originally set up to counter the threat of group-based activities. Issues related to mental health and terrorism are far more complex than originally thought. Lone-actor terrorists are not free from constraints but are constrained by a number of factors related to opportunity and capability. The internet helps overcome some of these hurdles. Finally, the analyses show that lone-actor terrorism is a detectable and preventable phenomenon.

In the weeks prior to submitting the final proofs for this book (November 2014), lone-actor terrorism returned to the headlines. In the space of four days, three separate lone actors managed to kill two and injure three in Canada and the United States. Two of the attacks utilized primitive weaponry (vehicular assault, hatchet) and each attack targeted either soldiers, policemen, or politicians. Each individual was said to be an Islamic extremist inspired by the ISIS-movement's call for 'lone wolf' operations a month earlier.

At face value at least, there appears to be little difference between ISIS's strategic call for action from earlier calls by al-Qaeda, right-wing extremists, and anti-abortion activists. ISIS also promotes low-tech, difficult to detect operations. What does appear to be different is that this message has produced an almost-immediate response by rank-and-file followers. Many credit ISIS's communication strategy including its 'sophisticated' use of social media. However, I think a different dynamic is at play and the credit should not go to ISIS. As the analyses in this book have repeatedly shown, there is a clear disjuncture between the types of attacks that strategists ask lone actors to commit and the types of attacks that lone actors seek to commit. The killing of Lee Rigby in Woolwich managed to effectively bridge this gap. By using such a simple attack method in such a public setting in a discriminate way, the Woolwich attackers managed to effectively overcome one of the critical dilemmas lone-actor terrorists face. How can I bypass effective counter-terrorism protocols, engage in a successful attack, and still claim the infamy, social status, and public renown that goes with it? Others had tried unsophisticated attacks before but either failed to kill (see Taheri-Azar in Chapter 8) or engaged in an attack in a private setting and missed the opportunity to scare the masses (see Choudhry in Chapter 8). The Woolwich attackers knew the area, efficiently carried out the attack, and relayed a (most definitely rehearsed) speech to a passerby who recorded it. Television stations couldn't beam the images quick enough. Michael Adebolajo's blood-stained hands were an evocative image that will unfortunately live long in infamy. On that day in London, two attackers showed a multitude of budding lone actors how to fall in line with the strategist's calls and still be remembered and eulogized by co-ideologues. The scary thought shouldn't be about ISIS's communication strategies, it should be about how to contain the problem of lone-actor terrorism now that one of the most difficult dilemmas to overcome has been made redundant.

References

Bray, M., & Bray, J. (2009). Tiller's Unheeded Warning: The Shelley Shannon Story. Retrieved from: www.armyofgod.com/POCShelleyShannonBookMikeBray.html. Accessed 1 June 2014.
Cohen, K., Johansson, F., Kaati, L., & Mork, J. C. (2014). Detecting Linguistic Markers for Radical Violence in Social Media. *Terrorism and Political Violence*, *26*(1): 246–256.
Crelinsten, R. D. (1987). Power and meaning: Terrorism as a struggle over access to the communication structure, pp. 419–450 in P. Wilkinson & A. Stewart (eds.). *Contemporary research on terrorism*. Aberdeen: Aberdeen University Press.
Gill, P. (2012). Terrorist Violence and the Contextual, Facilitative and Causal Qualities of Group-Based Behaviors: A Case Study of Suicide Bombing Plots in the United Kingdom. *Aggression and Violent Behavior* 17(6): 565–574.
Grossman, D. (1995). *On killing: The psychological cost of learning to kill in war and society*. London: Bay Back Books.

Hegghammer, T. (2013). Should I Stay or Should I Go? Explaining Variation in Western Jihadists' Choice between Domestic and Foreign Fighting. *American Political Science Review*, *107*(01): 1–15.

Horgan, J. (2005). *The psychology of terrorism*. Oxon: Routledge.

Horgan, J. (2009). *Walking away from terrorism: Accounts of disengagement from radical and extremist movements*. London: Routledge.

Jones, S., & Haroon, S. (2010, 14 December). Swedish Suicide Bomber in Fight at Luton Mosque. *The Irish Times*.

Kaplan, J., & Costa, C. P. (2014). On Tribalism: Auxiliaries, Affiliates, and Lone Wolf Political Violence. *Terrorism and Political Violence*, *26*(1): 13–44.

McCauley, C., & Moskalenko, S. (2014). Toward a Profile of Lone Wolf Terrorists: What Moves an Individual From Radical Opinion to Radical Action. *Terrorism and Political Violence*, *26*(1): 69–85.

McCauley, C., Moskalenko, S., & Van Son, B. (2013). Characteristics of lone-wolf violent offenders: A comparison of assassins and school attackers. *Perspectives on Terrorism*, *7*(1).

McNair, B. (2003). *An introduction to political communication*. London: Routledge.

Michael, G. (2012). *Lone Wolf Terror and the Rise of Leaderless Resistance*. Nashville: Vanderbilt University Press.

Rudolph, E. (2013). Between the Lines of Drift: The Memoirs of a Militant. Retrieved from: www.armyofgod.com/EricRudolphHomepage.html. Accessed 1 June 2014.

Schmid, A. P. (1987). *Political terrorism: A new guide to actors, authors, concepts, databases, theories and literature*. Oxford: North Holland Publishing Company.

Sears, N., & Kisiel, R. (2010, 14 December). Too Fanatical For the Mosque So Why Did No One Tell The Police? *The Daily Mail*.

van Buuren, J., & de Graaf, B. (2014). Hatred of the System: Menacing Loners and Autonomous Cells in the Netherlands. *Terrorism and Political Violence*, *26*(1), 156–184.

Wilkinson, P. (1990). Terrorism and propaganda (pp. 26–32), in Y. Alexander and R. Latter (eds.). *Terrorism and the media: Dilemmas for government, journalists, and the public*. Washington: Brassey's (US) Inc.

Select bibliography

Ackerman, G. A., & Pinson, L. E. (2014). An Army of One: Assessing CBRN Pursuit and Use by Lone Wolves and Autonomous Cells. *Terrorism and Political Violence*, *26*(1): 226–245.

Alarid, L.F., Buron, V.S, & Hochstetler, A. (2009). Group and solo robberies: Do accomplices shape criminal form? *Journal of Criminal Justice*, *37*(1): 1–9.

Anderson, M. (1997). Mental Illness and Criminal Behaviour: a Literature Review. *Journal of Psychiatric and Mental Health Nursing*, *4*(4): 243–250.

Andre, V., & Harris-Hogan, S. (2013). Mohamed Merah: From Petty Criminal to Neojihadist. *Politics, Religion & Ideology*, *14*(2): 307–319.

Bakker, E., & de Graaf, B. (2011). Preventing lone wolf terrorism: some CT approaches addressed. *Perspectives on Terrorism*, *5*(5–6).

Barnes, B. D. (2012). Confronting the one-man wolf pack: Adapting law enforcement and prosecution responses to the threat of lone wolf terrorism. *BUL Rev.*, *92*: 1613.

Bates, R. A. (2012). Dancing with wolves: Today's lone wolf terrorists. *The Journal of Public and Professional Sociology*, *4*(1): 1.

Berntzen, L. E., & Sandberg, S. (2014). The Collective Nature of Lone Wolf Terrorism: Anders Behring Breivik and the Anti-Islamic Social Movement. *Terrorism and Political Violence*, (ahead-of-print), 1–21.

Betley, P. (2013). The Continuum of Aloneness, Direction, Ideology and Motivation: Identifying the Behaviours in the Dimensions of Islamic Lone Actor Terrorism. Unpublished Dissertation.

Bloom, M., Gill, P., & Horgan, J. (2012). Tiocfaidh ar mna: Women in the Provisional Irish Republican Army. *Behavioral Sciences of Terrorism and Political Aggression*, *4*(1): 60–76.

Borum, R. (2013). Informing Lone – Offender Investigations. *Criminology & Public Policy*, *12*(1): 103–112.

Borum, R., Fein, R., & Vossekuil, B. (2012). A dimensional approach to analyzing lone offender terrorism. *Aggression and Violent Behavior*, *17*(5): 389–396.

Bouhana, N., & Wikstrom, P. O. (2011). Al Qai'da-Influenced Radicalisation: A Rapid Evidence Assessment Guided by Situational Action Theory. Retrieved from: www.gov.uk/government/uploads/system/uploads/attachment_data/file/116724/occ97.pdf. Accessed 1 June 2014.

Bray, M. & Bray, J. (2009). Tiller's Unheeded Warning: The Shelley Shannon Story. Retrieved from: www.armyofgod.com/POCShelleyShannonBookMikeBray.html. Accessed 1 June 2014.

Brynielsson, J., Horndahl, A., Johansson, F., Kaati, L., Mårtenson, C., & Svenson, P. (2013).

Harvesting and analysis of weak signals for detecting lone wolf terrorists. *Security Informatics*, *2*(11): 1–15.

Chermak, S. M., Freilich, J. D., & Simone Jr, J. (2010). Surveying American State Police Agencies About Lone Wolves, Far-Right Criminality and Far-Right and Islamic Jihadist Criminal Collaboration. *Studies in Conflict & Terrorism*, *33*(11): 1019–1041.

Clark, R. D. (1995). Lone versus multiple offending in homicide: Differences in situational context. *Journal of Criminal Justice*, *23*(5), 451–460.

Clarke, R. V. G., & Newman, G. R. (2006). *Outsmarting the terrorists*. Portsmouth, N.H.: Greenwood Publishing Group.

Corner, E. & Gill, P. (2014). A False Dichotomy? Lone Actor Terrorism and Mental Illness. *Law and Human Behavior*.

da Silva, T., Woodhams, J., & Harkins, L. (2013). Heterogeneity within multiple perpetrator rapes: A national comparison of lone, duo, and 3+ perpetrator rapes. *Sexual abuse: a journal of research and treatment*, 1079063213497805.

De Mesquita, E. B. (2005). The quality of terror. *American Journal of Political Science*, *49*(3): 515–530.

Delisi, M., Hochstetler, A., Scherer, A. M., Purhmann, A., & Berg, M. T. (2008). The Starkweather Syndrome: exploring criminal history antecedents of homicidal crime sprees 1. *Criminal Justice Studies*, *21*(1): 37–47.

Drysdale, D., Modzeleski, W., & Simons, A. (2010). *Campus Attacks: Targeted Violence Affecting Institutions of Higher Education*. Washington D.C.: United States Secret Service, United States Department of Education and Federal Bureau of Investigation.

Ellis, P. D. (2014). Lone Wolf Terrorism and Weapons of Mass Destruction: An Examination of Capabilities and Countermeasures. *Terrorism and Political Violence*, *26*(1): 211–225.

Fein, R. A., & Vossekuil, B. (1999). Assassination in the United States: an operational study of recent assassins, attackers, and near-lethal approachers. *Journal of Forensic Sciences*, *44*(2): 321–333.

Feldman, M. (2013). Comparative Lone Wolf Terrorism: Toward a Heuristic Definition. *Democracy and Security*, *9*(3), 270–286.

Felson, M. (2003). The process of co-offending. *Crime prevention studies*, *16*: 149–168.

Freedman, D., & Hemenway, D. (2000). Precursors of lethal violence: A death row sample. *Social Science and Medicine*, *50*: 1757–1770.

Gardell, M. (2014). Crusader Dreams: Oslo 22/7, Islamophobia, and the Quest for a Monocultural Europe. *Terrorism and Political Violence*, *26*(1): 129–155.

Gartenstein-Ross, D. (2014). Lone Wolf Islamic Terrorism: Abdulhakim Mujahid Muhammad (Carlos Bledsoe) Case Study. *Terrorism and Political Violence*, *26*(1), 110–128.

Gill, P. (2012). Terrorist Violence and the Contextual, Facilitative and Causal Qualities of Group-Based Behaviors: A Case Study of Suicide Bombing Plots in the United Kingdom. *Aggression and Violent Behaviour* *17*(6): 565–574.

Gill, P., & Young, J. (2011). Comparing role specific terrorist profile, paper presented at the International Studies Association annual conference, March 2011.

Gill, P., & Horgan, J. (2013). Who Were the Volunteers? The Shifting Sociological and Operational Profile of 1240 Provisional Irish Republican Army Members. *Terrorism and Political Violence*, *25*(3): 435–456.

Gill, P., Horgan, J., & Deckert, P. (2014). Bombing Alone: Tracing the Motivations and Antecedent Behaviors of Lone – Actor Terrorists. *Journal of forensic sciences*, *59*(2): 425–435.

Gottfredson, S. D., & Moriarty, L. J. (2006). Statistical risk assessment: Old problems and new applications. *Crime & Delinquency*, *52*(1), 178–200.

Grossman, D. (1995). *On killing: The psychological cost of learning to kill in war and society*. Boston, MA: Little, Brown.

Gruenewald, J., Chermak, S., & Freilich, J. D. (2013a). Distinguishing 'loner' attacks from other domestic extremist violence. *Criminology & Public Policy*, *12*(1), 65–91.

Gruenewald, J., Chermak, S., & Freilich, J. D. (2013b). Far-Right Lone Wolf Homicides in the United States. *Studies in Conflict & Terrorism*, *36*(12), 1005–1024.

Hauffe, S. & Porter, L. (2009). An interpersonal comparison of lone and group rape offenses. *Psychology, Crime and Law*, *15*, 469–491.

Hewitt, C. (2003). *Understanding terrorism in America: from the Klan to al Qaeda*. Hove: Psychology Press.

Hickle, K. E., & Roe-Sepowitz, D. E. (2010). Female juvenile arsonists: An exploratory look at characteristics and solo and group arson offenses. *Legal and Criminological Psychology*, *15*, 385–399.

Hirschi, T., & Gottfredson, M. (1983). Age and the explanation of crime. *American journal of sociology*, 552–584.

Horgan, J. (2005). *The psychology of terrorism*. London: Routledge.

Horgan, J. (2008). From profiles to pathways and roots to routes: Perspectives from psychology on radicalization into terrorism. *The ANNALS of the American Academy of Political and Social Science*, *618*(1), 80–94.

Horgan, J., & Morrison, J. F. (2011). Here to stay? The rising threat of violent dissident republicanism in Northern Ireland. *Terrorism and Political Violence*, *23*(4), 642–669.

Jenkins, B. M. (2011). *Stray dogs and virtual armies*. Santa Monica: RAND Corporation.

Jensen, R. B. (2014). The Pre-1914 Anarchist 'Lone Wolf' Terrorist and Governmental Responses. *Terrorism and Political Violence*, *26*(1), 86–94.

Juergensmeyer, M. (2000). *Terror in the Mind of God*. California: University of California Press.

Kaplan, J. (1997). Leaderless resistance. *Terrorism and Political Violence*, *9*(3), 80–95.

Kaplan, J., Lööw, H., & Malkki, L. (2014). Introduction to the Special Issue on Lone Wolf and Autonomous Cell Terrorism. *Terrorism and Political Violence*, *26*(1), 1–12.

LaFree, G. (2013). Lone-Offender Terrorists. *Criminology and Public Policy*, *12*(1): 59–62.

Kenney, M. (2010). Beyond the Internet: Mētis, Techne, and the Limitations of Online Artifacts for Islamist Terrorists. *Terrorism and Political Violence*, *22*(2), 177–197.

Langman, P. (2009). Rampage School Shooters: A Typology. *Aggression and Violent Behavior* 14: 79–86.

Laqueur, W. (1999). *The new terrorism*. New York: Oxford University Press.

Malkki, L. (2014). Political elements in post-Columbine school shootings in Europe and North America. *Terrorism and political violence*, *26*(1), 185–210.

McCauley, C., & Moskalenko, S. (2014). Toward a Profile of Lone Wolf Terrorists: What Moves an Individual From Radical Opinion to Radical Action. *Terrorism and Political Violence*, *26*(1), 69–85.

McGloin, J. M., & Nguyen, H. (2012). It was my idea: Considering the Instigation of Co-Offending. *Criminology*, *50*(2), 463–494.

McGloin, J. M., & Nguyen, H. (2013). The importance of studying co-offending networks for criminological theory and policy. *Crime and Networks*, 13.

McGloin, J. M., & Stickle, W. P. (2011). Influence or convenience? Disentangling peer influence and co-offending for chronic offenders. *Journal of Research in Crime and Delinquency*, *48*(3), 419–447.

Meloy, J. R., & O'Toole, M. E. (2011). The concept of leakage in threat assessment. *Behavioral sciences & the law*, *29*(4), 513–527.

Meloy, J. R., & Yakeley, J. (2014). The Violent True Believer as a 'Lone Wolf' –Psychoanalytic Perspectives on Terrorism. *Behavioral sciences & the law*, *32*(3), 347–365.

Michael, G. (2012). *Lone Wolf Terror and the Rise of Leaderless Resistance*. Nashville: Vanderbilt University Press.

Moskalenko, S., & McCauley, C. (2011). The psychology of lone-wolf terrorism. *Counselling Psychology Quarterly*, *24*(2), 115–126.

Nesser, P. (2012). Research Note: Single Actor Terrorism: Scope, Characteristics and Explanations. *Perspectives on Terrorism*, *6*(6).

Osgood, D. W., Wilson, J. K., O'Malley, P. M., Bachman, J. G., & Johnston, L. D. (1996). Routine activities and individual deviant behavior. *American Sociological Review*, 635–655.

Pantucci, R. (2011). *A typology of lone wolves: preliminary analysis of lone Islamist terrorists*. London: International Centre for the Study of Radicalisation and Political Violence.

PET – Centre for Terror Analysis (CTA) (2011, April 5). The threat from solo terrorism and lone wolf terrorism. Copenhagen: Denmark. Retrieved from: www.pet.dk/upload/the_threat_from_solo_terrorism_and_lone_wolf_terrorism_-_engelsk_version.pdf. Accessed 1 June 2014.

Peterson, J. K., Skeem, J., Kennealy, P., Bray, B., & Zvonkovic, A. (2014). How often and how consistently do symptoms directly precede criminal behavior among offenders with mental illness?. *Law and Human Behavior*.

Phillips, P. J., & Pohl, G. (2012). Economic profiling of the lone wolf terrorist: can economics provide behavioral investigative advice?. *Journal of Applied Security Research*, *7*(2), 151–177.

Reinares, F. (2004). Who are the terrorists? Analyzing changes in sociological profile among members of ETA. *Studies in Conflict and Terrorism*, *27*(6), 465–488.

Roach, J. (2007). Those who do big bad things also usually do little bad things: Identifying active serious offenders using offender self-selection. *International Journal of Police Science & Management*, *9*(1), 66–79.

Rudolph, E. (2013). Between the Lines of Drift: The Memoirs of a Militant. Retrieved from: www.armyofgod.com/EricRudolphHomepage.html. Accessed 1 June 2014.

Sageman, M. (2004). *Understanding terror networks*. Pennsylvania: University of Pennsylvania Press.

Salfati, C., & Canter, D. (1999). Differentiating Stranger Murders: Profiling Offender Characteristics from Behavioral Styles. *Behavioral Sciences and the Law* 17: 391–406.

Seegmiller, B. (2007). Radicalized Margins: Eric Rudolph and Religious Violence 1. *Terrorism and Political Violence*, *19*(4), 511–528.

Silke, A. (2001). The devil you know: Continuing problems with research on terrorism. *Terrorism and Political Violence*, *13*(4), 1–14.

Silke, A. (2004). The road less travelled: recent trends in terrorism research. *Research on terrorism: trends, achievements and failures*, 186–213.

Silke, A. (2013). Research on terrorism: A review of the impact of 9/11 and the global war on terrorism. In Adam Dolnik (ed.). *Conducting Terrorism Field Research: A Guide*. London: Routledge.

Simon, J. D. (2013). *Lone Wolf Terrorism: Understanding the Growing Threat*. New York, NY: Prometheus Books.

Smith, B. L. (2004). Terrorism and empirical testing: Using indictment data to assess changes in terrorist conduct. *Sociology of Crime Law and Deviance*, *5*, 75–90.

Spaaij, R. (2010). The Enigma of Lone Wolf Terrorism: An Assessment. *Studies in Conflict and Terrorism*, *33*, 854–870.

Spaaij, R. (2012). *Understanding Lone Wolf Terrorism*. London: Springer, *98*, 80–95.

Stern, J. (2003, September). *Terror in the name of God: Why religious militants kill*. New York: Ecco.

Stolzenburg, L., & D'Alessio, S. (2008). Co-offending and the age-crime curve. *Journal of Research in Crime and Delinquency*, *45*, 65–86.

Tillyer, M. S., & Tillyer, R. (2014). Maybe I Should Do This Alone: A Comparison of Solo and Co-offending Robbery Outcomes. *Justice Quarterly*, (ahead-of-print), 1–25.

Ullman, S. E. (1999). A comparison of gang and individual rape incidents. *Violence and Victims*, *14*, 123–133.

van Buuren, J., & de Graaf, B. (2014). Hatred of the System: Menacing Loners and Autonomous Cells in the Netherlands. *Terrorism and Political Violence*, *26*(1), 156–184.

van der Heide, E. J. (2011). Individual terrorism: Indicators of lone operators. Masters Thesis, Utrecht University.

Van Mastrigt, S. B., & Farrington, D. P. (2009). Co-offending, age, gender and crime type: Implications for criminal justice policy. *British Journal of Criminology*, azp021.

Van Mastrigt, S. B., & Farrington, D. P. (2011). Prevalence and characteristics of co-offending recruiters. *Justice Quarterly*, *28*(2), 325–359.

von Behr, I., Reding, A., Edwards, C., & Gribbon, L. (2013). *Radicalisation in the digital era: The use of the internet in 15 cases of terrorism and extremism*. Retrieved from: www.rand.org/content/dam/rand/pubs/research_reports/RR400/RR453/RAND_RR453.pdf. Accessed 1 June 2014.

Vossekuil, B., Fein, R. A., Reddy, M., Borum, R., & Modzeleski, W. (2002). 'The final report and findings of the Safe School Initiative'. Washington D.C: US Secret Service and Department of Education.

Weimann, G. (2012). Lone Wolves in Cyberspace. *Journal of Terrorism Research*, *3*(2), 75–90.

Wright, R. & West, D. J. (1981). Rape – A comparison of group offenses and lone assaults. *Medicine, Science and the Law*, *21*, 25–30.

Index

Page numbers in *italics* denote tables, those in **bold** denote figures.

al-Abdaly, Abdulwahab 8, 77, 179
Abdo, Naser 61, 63, 66–7, 160, 177–8
Abdulmutallab, Umar Farouk 8, 70–1, 77
abortion clinics 6–7, 10, 32, 35, 37, 49, 52, 55, 59–62, 65, 78–9, 95, 169, 173
Abu Ghraib prison (Iraq) 54, 95
Adebowale, Michael 132, 167
Adkisson, Jim David 38–40, 83, 178
Aftenposten (newspaper) 148
age at time offence 29–31; effect of 97
Aldawsari, Khalid 53–5, 90, 95, 177
Al-Qaeda 3, 35, 50, 54, 66, 80, 94, 109, 122, 153; advice to would-be lone actors 172–3; bomb-making instructions 8; 'A Call to Arms' video 7; championing of lone-actor attacks 4; propaganda for individual acts of terrorism 10
Al-Qaeda in the Arabian Peninsula (AQAP) 8, 10, 81; military committee 173
Al-Shabaab 81
Amoss, Ulius 4
anti-abortion movement 8, 62, 172
Anti-Defamation League 5
anti-Islamic terrorism 36
antisocial personality disorders 104
Army of God (anti-abortion group) 6–8, 78, 93
arson 32, 48, 59, 79, 82, 125
assassination, of public figures 21, 48, 54, 58
Atlanta Olympic Games, bombing of (1996) 60, 62, 78, 83, 134, 160, 175
attack, by lone-actor terrorists: commissioning of 62–73; crystallization of risk and 65–73; going it alone *see* going it alone, in attack planning/preparation; operational capabilities necessary to perform 125; poor tradecraft 64–5; preparation for 52–3, 95; signaling for 58–9, 92–3; target identification 62–4; usage of virtual learning for 95
avemosjonarisert, idea of 171
al-Awlaki, Anwar 61, 77, 90, 93, 120, 146
Azzam, Abdullah 93, 146

Bajuvarian Liberation Army 83
Baumhammers, Richard 6, 36, 49, 83, 92, 106–7
Baz, Rashid 41, 61
Beam, Louis 4–7, 17
Bedell, John Patrick 36, 91, 112–13
behaviour, of lone-actor terrorists: attack commission 62–73; attack preparation 52–3; attack signaling 58–9; distal factors influencing 47–51; learning from other lone actors 59–61; network related *53*; other distal factors influencing 51; planning process 53–8; prevalence of distal factors *51*; prevalence of proximal factors *51*; previous criminal history and 47–50; proximal factors influencing 51–2; turn to violence 52–61
Bijleveld, C. 27
Bin Laden, Osama 82
biological warfare 39, 176
Bishop, Charles 82, 92, 95
bomb making: *Home Made C4* (bomb-making manual) 143; instructions for 8, 96; manuals 96, 124, 126, 135, 143, 158, 178; materials used for 131, 135, 142, 153; training for 78, 83
Bray, Michael 62, 79

Breivik, Anders, coordinated attacks in Oslo and Utøya Island (2011) 1–3, 9, 35, 36, 83, 96, 170, 174; decision and search activity stage 148–9; event execution stage 155–6; post-event activity and strategic analysis 157; preparation stage 149–55
British National Party (BNP) 82, 134–5
British Royal Family 110
Brockhoeft, John 79
Bulman, Mark 82
Bureau of Alcohol, Tobacco and Firearms (ATF) 4–5, 141, 143
burglary 29, 32, 48
Bush, George W. 54, 95
bushidomeditasjon, idea of 171

'cause of the cause', notion of 48
child abductions 32
child molestation 48
child pornography 48, 50, 63, 67, 178
Choudhry, Roshonara, stabbing of Stephen Timms 93–4; decision and search activity stage 146; event execution stage 147; post-event activity and strategic analysis 147–8; preparation stage 146–7
Christie, Stuart 3, 64
'classic age' of lone-actor terrorism 3
Clinton, Bill 175
Colorado's Jefferson County judiciary system, attack on (1999) 39, 176
command and control links (CandC) 20, 108, 124, 126–7
communication, between co-offenders 59
Copeland, David, nail bombing campaign (1999) 60–1, 95–6, 160; decision and search activity stage 134–5; event execution stage 136–7; post-event activity and strategic analysis 137–8; preparation stage 135–6
Corkins, Floyd Lee 56–7, 160, 178
counter-intelligence practices 58
counter-terrorism community 2
criminal careers 28, 128
criminal history, of lone-actor terrorists 47–50
criminal justice system 121
cultural conservative nationalism 36, 152
Curtis, Alex 5–6; Lone Wolf Point System 6

Dagbladet (newspaper) 148
Dagsavisen (newspaper) 150
Danish Centre for Terror Analysis 4

Danish Security and Intelligence Service 13–14
diazodinitrophenol (DDNP) 154
Discovery Channel 36, 71, 91
Dutch National Counterterrorism Strategy (2011–2015) 13

ECA-Stack 154
education and employment 32–3
emosjonsspekteret, idea of 171
Empire State Building, shooting attack at (1997) 36, 39, 176
'enemy of Islam' 146
Evans, Paul Ross 10, 58, 64–5, 175–6

Facebook 1, 61, 67, 87, 90–1, 156
Family Research Council (FRC) 56
female terrorist: motivational structure and life experience 31; role in terrorist organizations 31
Ferguson, Colin 67–70
First Church of Satan (San Francisco), bombing of 64, 175
fixated persons: definition of 14; detection of 178
Fixated Threat Assessment Centre (FTAC) 110–11
Forsane Alizza (radical Salifist group) 81
The Free Market Party 83, 92
Fuchs, Franz 83, 178

Gavan, Terence 176
Gilleard, Martyn 50, 84, 178
Gillespie, Sean 36, 64, 177
Global Islamic Resistance Call 7, 173
Global Terrorism Database 17, 19–20
Gluck, James Kenneth 39, 176
going it alone, in attack planning/preparation: framing issues 77–84; situational drivers 76–7
Goldstein, Baruch 20, 61
Griffin, Michael 55, 59–60, 79, 178
group-based terrorism 17, 31, 48, 105, 107, 161
group identity, notion of 12, 170
group offenders: attack, preparation for 52–3; average age of 29–31; criminal careers 28; criminal convictions 28; difference with lone offenders 27–9; engaging in homicides 28; gender 31–2; mental illness among 107; personality traits of 27; robbery cases 27; substance abuse, history of 28; turn to violence 52–61

Index

Gulf War (1991) 112

Hadayet, Hesham Mohamed 69
Haq, Naveed 95
Hasan, Nidal Malik 7–8, 61, 66–7, 90, 120, 177
hate crimes 6, 29, 38
Helder, Luke 35–6, 177
Hendriks, J. 27
Hezbollah 105
Hill, Paul 37, 59–60, 169, 172
homegrown terrorism, evolution of 9
homegrown violent extremists (HVEs) 10
Home Made C4 (bomb-making manual) 143
homicide 28, 33, 48, 125
hostage taking 125
human capital, to support lone actor 53
human intelligence (HUMINT) 131

Ibrahim, Isa 70, 94
imprisonment 34, 48, 63
improvised explosive device (IEDs) 58, 65, 96, 126, 133, 136, 176–7; constructed from pressure cookers 8
individual terrorism jihad 8
Industrial Revolution 71
Inspire (English language magazine) 3, 6, 8, 10, 67, 172–3
Internet, relationship with terrorism: behaviour covariates and **99**; demographic correlates and virtual activity 96–7; event outcomes and virtual activity 97–8; ideological differences and radicalization 97; nature of 86; and threat posed by lone-actor terrorists 86–7; virtual interaction, nature of 88–93; virtual learning, nature of 93–6
interpersonal aggression 32
intimate partner violence 32, 33
Irish Republican Army (IRA) 105
Islamic child-rearing practices 104
Islamic Group of Algeria 80
Islamic Salvation Front 80
Islamization of Western society 36, 149, 152
Islamophobia 36

jihad 77; individual terrorism 8; and martyrdom 54, 78, 94; open-source 8
Jordi, Stephen 7

Kaczynski, Ted 16, 35, 62, 120, 172, 177

Kamal, Ali Hassan Abu 36, 39–40, 176
Kasi, Mir Aimal 37–8, 177
Knights Templars of Europe 83, 148
Kopp, James 49, 170

leaderless resistance, idea of 4–5, 11, 17, 92, 175
learning, from other lone actors 59–61
Lewington, Neil 61, 82–3, 178
lone-actor terrorists: age crime curve of **30, 31**; behaviour of *see* behaviour, of lone-actor terrorists; cases of 16; education and employment 32–3; event script and intervention points *162–5*; family factors and relationship status 33–4; features of 9–11; functioning in a virtual network 127; history of mental illness 110; ideological motivation of 35–41, 122–4; learning through virtual sources **88**; per year **87**; pre-attack behaviours of 87; preparing for the attack 127; prior offenders amongst 49; problem triangle **166**; qualitatively derived typologies of 122–4; quantitatively derived typologies of 124–7; relying on others' support 126–7; security dilemmas associated with *see* security dilemmas, associated with lone-actor terrorists; strategic utility of 58; struggling in isolation 127; threat of 131; types of 14; virtual communication **88**; without command and control links 126–7
lone offenders: attack, preparation for 52–3; average age of 29–31; categorizing of 121–2; criminal careers 28; criminal convictions 28; difference with group offenders 27–9; engaging in homicides 28; family dynamics of 33–4; female 31–2; personality traits of 27; substance abuse, history of 28; turn to violence 52–61
loners *see* lone offenders
'The Lone Wolf Pack' 14; definition of 11; members of 121
Lone Wolf Point System 6
'lone wolf' terrorism 2, 80, 121; benefits of 83; definitional issues 11–15; mental illness and personality 105; strategy for 9, 52
Luke, Keith 94

McVeigh, Timothy: Oklahoma City bombing (1995) 61, 172; decision and

search activity stage 140–2; event execution stage 145; post-event activity and strategic analysis 145; preparation stage 142–5
Mahon, Dennis 6, 80, 177
al-Masri, Abu Jihad 7
mass murder 7, 58, 105, 173
mental illness: association with social isolation 109; case studies 111–15; co-morbidity of 108; Corner and Gill study (2014) on 108–11; history of 125; prevalence among terrorist group and lone actors 107; psychopathological mechanisms 107; risk factors of violence and 110; role in terrorism 105; symbiotic relationship with criminal behaviour 108
Merah, Mohamed 34, 50, 80–1
messageless resistance 174–6; pitfall of 174–5
Metzger, Tom 5–6, 8; *Begin With Lone Wolves* 172, 175; *Laws of the Lone Wolf* 8, 52–3, 171–2
military psychology 98, 125, 170
Moody, Roy 176
Moody, Walter Leroy, Jr. 109
motivation, issue of 35–41; political ideology and 35
Muhammad, Adbulhakim Mujahid 49–50, 57–8, 81, 83, 89, 94–5, 169
Multi-Agency Public Protection Arrangements (MAPPA) 110–11
multi-dimensional scaling (MDS) techniques, for examining offences 124
Muslim militants, analyses of 104
MySpace 87

nail bombing campaign (1999) 60, 134
Napolitano, Janet 9–10
narcissism, concept of 104
narcissistic rage 104
'near causes' of crime 132
Neumann, P. R. 86, 89, 97
North, Michael 173
Norwegian Defence League 1, 148

oath of *bayat* 81
Operation Desert Storm 141
organizational aggression 32

Panetta, Leon 9
Pantucci, R. 11, 14, 89, 105, 121
passive resistance, idea of 7
Peters, Pete 5

'phantom cell' strategy 4
pipe bombings 35
Plankenhorn, Vicki 172
planning for attack, process for 53–8
political terrorism 36, 104
pre-attack warning 125, 127
probation sentences, multiple 48
problematic personality disorders *see* mental illness
Project Regulus (U.K.'s North West Counter Terrorism) 110
Provisional Irish Republican Army (PIRA) 22, 33, 132; age crime curve of **29**
public mass shooting attacks 8

racially motivated crime 49
RAND Corporation 99
Reilly, Nicky 113–14
religious extremism 97
ricin, development of 13, 39, 89, 176
right-wing movement 4, 6, 8, 13, 35, 61, 108, 109, 172
Roach, Jason 47
robbery 48, 68
Roeder, Scott 71–3, 92, 109
Routine Activity Theory 131
Ruby Ridge, Idaho 4–5, 141
Rudolph, Eric 58, 60, 62, 78, 83, 169, 175, 177

Sacred Warfare Action Tactics committee 5
Sada al Jihad (2003) 7
Schizophrenia 71, 110, 112
Second Life 87
security dilemmas, associated with lone-actor terrorists: counter-terrorism systems and 169; learning from past cases 176–9
Seegmiller, B. 62, 78
self-esteem 104
self-selection, concept of 48, 178
sexual assault 124
Shahzad, Faisal 83
Shannon, Shelley 32, 59, 61, 72–3, 78–9, 172
sharia law 80
situational crime prevention (SCP) 19, 109, 131–2, 134, 166
smallest space analysis (SSA) 121, 124–5; of lone-actor terrorist characteristics and behaviours **126**
social networking 86, 177
social support networks 84

solo offenders *see* lone offenders
Stack, Andrew Joseph 62–3
Stern, J. 37–8, 104
Stop Islamization of Norway movement 1
strategic utility, of lone-actor terrorism 58
Study of Terrorism and Responses to Terrorism (START) 20
substance abuse 21, 27–8, 32–3, 47, 108, 124–5, 127
suicide bombing 8, 70, 77–8, 93–4, 104, 179
al-Suri, Abu Musab 7–8; Global Islamic Resistance Call 173

Taheri-Azar, Mohammed Reza, attempt to 'run over' students: decision and search activity stage 138–9; event execution stage 140; post-event activity and strategic analysis 140; preparation stage 139–40; religious justification 139
Taliban 81
targeted violence, act of 106
terrorism: definition of 14, 22n3; as group phenomenon 97–8; growth in female involvement in 31
terrorist: attack by *see* attack, by lone-actor terrorists; 'motivation' 26, 105; personality, characteristics of 103; profile 26; psychoanalytical approaches 104; socio-demographic characteristics of 26
Terrorist's Handbook, The 95, 135
Tiller, George 32, 60–1, 71–3, 78, 92

Twitter 87

Van der Graaf, Volkert 40
virtual activity 97–8
virtual communication, evolution of 86
virtual interaction, nature of 88–93, 96; for attack signaling 92–3; for disseminating propaganda 90–2; for recruitment 92; for reinforcement of beliefs 89–90; for seeking legitimization for their actions 90
virtual learning, nature of 93–6, 98; for accessing ideological content 93–4; for attack preparation 95; for choosing a target 94–5; opting for violence 94; for overcoming hurdles 95–6

Waagner, Clayton Lee 93, 95
'Waffen SS UK members' handbook 82
Wal-Mart stores 58, 176
Weaver, Randy 4–5
Western European Resistance Movements 152
White Aryan Resistance 80
word cloud: for Anders Breivik's compendium 36, **37**; of Paul Hill's justification for his killing 37
workplace bullying 32

youth-related crime, social nature of 30
YouTube 1, 87, 91–3, 96, 146, 153, 156